HEAVEN OPENED

Richard Alleine

BAKER BOOK HOUSE
Grand Rapids, Michigan

Reprinted 1979 by Baker Book House
from the edition issued in 1838 by
The Religious Tract Society

ISBN: 0-8010-0136-6

PHOTOLITHOPRINTED BY CUSHING - MALLOY, INC.
ANN ARBOR, MICHIGAN, UNITED STATES OF AMERICA
1979

TO THE READER

Reader,

The providence of God hath led me to the publication of the ensuing treatise, much beyond my first intentions.

There came to my hands a Synopsis of the covenant of grace on God's part, with a Soliloquy annexed, (both penned by the worthy author of that form of man's covenanting with God, inserted in my Vindiciæ Pietatis,*) attended with the author's desires, and of divers other christians, that this also might be incorporated into the same book.

These desires, neither being able to resist, nor willing to deny, I prepared some meditations to be premised, with a purpose to have put forth another edition of that book with this addition; but finding it to grow into too great a bulk to be there inserted, both this on God's part, and the former on man's part, come into thy hands in this distinct treatise, followed with my prayers—that the good land, whereof some clusters are here presented to thee, may be thine inheritance. See and take.

> Thine, because the Lord's
> covenant servant,
>
> R. Alleine

July 8, 1665

* His brother Joseph Alleine, author of the "Alarm."

CONTENTS

HEAVEN OPENED

The Introduction

GOOD news from heaven! the day-spring from on high hath visited this undone world.! After a deluge of sin and misery, behold the bow in the cloud! the Lord God hath made and established a new covenant, and this is it that hath cast the first beam on the dark state of lost and fallen man, and hath brought life and immortality to light. This covenant is the hope of sinners, the riches of saints, the Magna Charta of the city of God. The forfeited lease of eternity renewed; God's deed of gift, wherein he hath, on fair conditions, granted sinners their lives, and settled upon his saints an everlasting inheritance.

Hear, O ye forlorn captives, who have sold yourselves to eternal bondage, spoiled yourselves of all your glory, sealed yourselves up under everlasting misery, you are dead in your sins, guilty before God, under wrath, under a curse, bound over to eternal vengeance. But behold, there is yet hope in Israel concerning this thing; the Lord God hath taken compassion upon you, hath opened a way for you to escape out of all this misery and bondage. Lift up the hands that hang down, comfort the trembling knees; an ark, an ark hath God prepared, in which is salvation from the flood ; a covenant, a new covenant hath he made and established, which, if you lay hold on it, will recover all you have lost, ransom you from death, redeem you from hell, and advance you to a more sure and blessed condition, than your original state from which you have fallen. This is the hope of sinners ; this is the heritage of the servants of the Lord.

Glorious tidings, good news indeed! but what is this covenant ? Or what is there that is given and granted therein ? Why, in sum, there is all that heaven and earth can afford ; all that can be needed or desired ; and this, by a firm and irrevocable deed, made over, and made sure to all that will sincerely embrace it.

Particularly, God hath in his covenant granted and made over,

First.   Himself.
Second.   His Son.
Third.   His Spirit.
Fourth.   The earth.
Fifth.   The angels of light.
Sixth.   The powers of darkness.
Seventh.   Death.
Eighth.   The kingdom.
Ninth.   All the means of salvation.

CHAPTER I —*God in the Covenant*

THE Lord God hath made over himself in this covenant. That is the great and comprehensive promise, " I will be their God," Jer. xxxi. 33. I am God, and what I am, it is all theirs ; myself, my glorious incomprehensible essence, all my glorious attributes, my omnipotence, my omniscience, my wisdom, my righteousness, my holiness, mine all-sufficiency, my faithfulness, &c. I will make over myself to them to be henceforth and for ever theirs.

Their Friend, their Portion, their Sun, their Shield.

I. Their Friend. I was angry, but mine anger is turned away; I was an adversary, I had a controversy with them, but I am reconciled; I have found a ransom, the quarrel is composed, my wrath is appeased, I am friends with them: " I will forgive their iniquity, and their sin will I remember no more," Jer. xxxi. 34. I will take away their iniquity and receive them graciously; " I will heal their backsliding, I will love them freely; for mine anger is turned away from them," Hos. xiv. 4. " Glory be to God on high, on earth peace, goodwill towards men." Fury is not now in me; favour and friendship, love and goodwill, is all they may henceforth expect from me. Sinners, what is there to be feared? what is there dreadful, but an angry provoked God? Thence is sorrow and anguish, thence is famine, and pestilence, and sword; thence is death and hell: he doth not know what the wrath of God means, who does not see in it all the plagues above ground, and all the vengeance of eternal fire. Whatever terrors or torments have seized upon thee; upon thy body, upon thy soul; whatever losses, crosses, vexations, afflictions, plague thee on this earth; whatever horror and anguish, whatever amazing, confounding torments are like to meet thee, and feed upon thee in the lake beneath, thou mayest say of all, This is the wrath of God. That day the Lord says to thee, Fury is not in me, he saith also, Fear shall be no more to thee. That hour the Lord saith, I am thy Friend, death and hell vanish. The day is broken, the shadows fly away. And this is one thing included in that promise, I am their God, I am their Friend.

II. Their Portion. Fury cease; fears vanish; friendship, favour, life granted. But what shall he have to live upon? Man was never intended to be a self-sufficient; he was created under a necessity of dependence on something without him, not only for the continuation of his being, but of the comfort of his being; he cannot live upon the air, though he hath escaped the fire: the soul of man is too big for all the world; like Noah's dove, it can find no rest below, and where shall it find it, or on what shall it subsist? Why, God will not starve his friends; he who hath saved their lives will find them a livelihood; because there is no other to be found, he himself will be a livelihood to them; their portion, their maintenance, and their heritage for ever. As their deliverance is from him, so their dependence shall be on him; he is their substance, and on him is their subsistence; he writes himself, " The portion of Jacob," Jer. x. 16. and as such his saints accept him; " The Lord is the portion of mine inheritance," Psa. xvi. 5. he is their bread and their water, their stock and their store. The Lord gives portions to his enemies; not only the young ravens, but the old lions and tigers; the worst of men do seek their meat from God; they " have their portion in this life, whose bellies thou fillest with thy hid treasure," Psa. xvii. 14. They have their portion: some of them have their portion in the city, others a portion in the field: to some he gives a por-tion of gold, to others a portion of worldly glory, to others a portion of pleasures; by all these he deals as the father of the prodigal, he gives them their portion, and sends them away. But whilst he gives portions to these, he is the portion of his saints: he makes over and settles himself upon them, as their inheritance for ever: they shall never be in want whilst there is in him to supply them; they shall never be in straits whilst there is in him to relieve them: all their wants be upon me.

The Lord is their Portion, and he is a sufficient portion: " With thee is the fountain of life," Psa. xxxvi. " In thy presence is fulness," Psa. xvi. The Lord God is all things to them, enough and to spare: " In my father's house there is bread enough, and to spare." He that hath all things below God, but not God, hath nothing; he that hath nothing besides God, but hath God, hath all things; enough and to spare: filling up, and running over; there is still more to be had, if more could be held: the soul hath never enough, till it hath more than enough; is never full till it runs over: while it can contain and measure and number all that it has; this is its judgment of all.

In God is enough for filling up, and running over; enough there is in him to fill up all their faculties, their understandings; there are infinitely beautiful perfections where we may gaze and fill our eyes with unspeakable delight; but when we have looked the farthest into them, when the most searching eye, the most intense thoughts have searched and run their utmost, they come not near the end; they shall look, and look, and see, and see, and when they can reach no farther, then they shall wonder at those treasures of light and beauty, that are still beyond them. Admiration is the understanding full, and running over: when it is non-plussed, and can reach no further, then it wonders at what it perceives still beyond it. The apostle tells us, Eph. iii. 18. that the gospel, which presents God in flesh, hath in it a height, and depth, and length, and breadth; and I may tell you from him, it is a height without top, a depth without bottom, a length without limits, a breadth without bounds; in one word, immensity, unmeasurable, and therefore unspeakable, unsearchable glory. Whilst the blind world deride and despise the portion of the saints, looking on God, and all the things of God, as shallow things, that have no depth in them, they will be found by those who search into them, to be deep things, that have no bottom in them, " The deep things of God," 1 Cor. ii.10. All the raptures and extasies of glorious joys of the saints in the other world are the running over of their eyes upon their hearts, and do break in upon them from their vision of God.

There is enough to fill up their wills and affections: there is infinite goodness, incomprehensible love, marvellous loving kindness, unspeakable delights, glorious joys. " Oh! how great is thy goodness which thou hast laid up for those that fear thee!" Psa. xxxi. 19. " Oh! how great is thy goodness !" It is the voice of exultation, an admiring word; great beyond expression, great beyond imagination ; " Eye hath not seen, ear hath not heard, neither have entered into the heart of man to conceive, the things which God hath prepared for them that love him :" and it is of a heart leaping for joy, rejoicing in hope of the glory of God, which is laid up for his saints. Laid up! where? Why, laid up in himself; that is the fountain, that is the treasury ; there is love, there is joy, there is satisfaction, our life is hid with Christ in God. O love the Lord all ye his saints. O bless the Lord all ye his saints. He that is mighty hath done for you great things : " Since the beginning of the world men have not heard, nor perceived by the ear, neither hath the eye seen, O God, besides thee, what he hath prepared for him that waiteth for him," Isa. lxiv. 4. Or, as it is in the margin, " There hath not been heard or seen a God besides thee, which doth so for him that waiteth for him."

There is enough to fill up our time ; there is admiring work, and praising work for ever : there is matter for love and joy, to live and feed upon for ever ; endless praises, eternal pleasures, everlasting rejoicings, " Everlasting joy," Isa. xxxv. 10. " Pleasures for evermore," Psa. xvi. 11. There is enough to reward all our labours, and repay all our expenses : there is a full reward. " Fear not, Abraham, I am thy shield, and exceeding great reward," Gen. xv. 1. Christian, thou shalt not serve the Lord for nought, he will reward thee, and it is little in his eyes, that thou shouldest serve him for corn and for wine, for sheep and for oxen ; yea, for the crowns and kingdoms of this world ; these shall not be thine hire ; the everlasting God will be thy reward, thine exceeding great reward ; exceeding not thy work only, but thy very thoughts also. A little is too much for thy earnings, but the whole world is too little for his bounty. Less than nothing might satisfy for thy labours, but less than himself will not satisfy for his love : the eternal God will be thy reward. Oh the unsearchable riches of the poorest of saints ! Poor ! what ! and yet hast a God ! In want ! what ! and yet hast all things ! Is he a God that is thine, and art thou still in straits ! Would a few sheep and oxen, vineyards and olive-yards make thee a rich man, and can a God leave thee a beggar? Is not a pearl more than pebbles? Milk and wine, than mud and water? Men use to say, money is all things: meat, and drink, and clothes, and friends, and land, virtually all things. And is not God more than money? Sure he hath said to his gold, Thou art my god, who cannot say, Let God be mine, and then go thou thy way. Hast thou a God, and yet poor? Nay farther, would the fatness of the earth, and fulness of heaven, if thou hadst both, be enough for thee? Would corn, and wine, and houses, and lands, and pleasures here, and eternal life hereafter suffice thee? And is not God alone as much as all this? Dost thou want star-light when thou hast the sun? Is the ocean more full for the rivers that run into it? Or would there be any want there, if all these were stopped and dry? Can they contribute to it, which have their rise from it? Hath the almighty God a self-sufficiency, and hath he not enough to satisfy a poor worm? Is he blessed in himself, and mayest not thou be blessed in him? He that thinks any thing less than God will suffice, understands not a soul; and he that wants any thing more, understands not God. God alone is as much as God and all the world; and this is the heritage of the servants of the Lord, God is their Portion.

If enough be not yet said, look awhile, and consider whence thou art taken up into this blessedness? What hast thou left? What an exchange hast thou made? Thou wert taken with the prodigal from the trough, with the beggar from the dunghill, yea, as a brand out of the burning; there thy lot had fallen. O where hast thou left the rest of the world? Blessing themselves in vanity, pleasing themselves with shadows and apparitions, feeding on ashes, warming themselves at their painted fire, sporting themselves with the wind, rejoicing in a thing of nought; their crackling thorns, their glozing pleasures, their drinkings, and dancings, and roarings, their horses, and their dogs, and their hawks and their harlots; making a shift awhile to make merry with these whilst they are hastening to the pit, to that fire and brimstone which is the portion of their cup.

Consider man, what is the chaff to the wheat? What is a comet to the sun? What is the night to the day? What are bubbles and children's toys to the durable riches? What are things that are not, to him whose name is, I AM? But oh! what is death, and wrath, and the curse, which was once all thine heritage, to that life, and love, and peace, and joy, and glory, which thou now possessest in that God who is thy portion? What a poor wretch wert thou once, when thou hadst nothing but sin, and shame, and misery, that thou couldst call thine own? these thou mightest call thine, sin was thine, woe was thine, death, and the grave, and the curse, and the pit were thine own; but that was all thou hadst; thy good things thou livedst upon, had they been of ever so great value, were none of thine; thy house and thy lands are none of thine; thy gold, and thy silver, and thy substance are none of thine; they are all but borrowed, or committed to thee as a steward, and all to be given up upon demand; and what thou hast spent of them thou must be brought to a reckoning for; a poor wretch thou wert, and hadst just nothing, all that thou hadst was none of thine.

But now God is thine own, all that he is, all that he has is thine; never couldst thou lay such a claim to anything thou possessedst; to house, or wife, or

child, or body, or soul, as now thou mayest to thy
God.   God is as surely thine as thou art thyself : as
sure as thou art a man, thou hast a God.

Come christian, here is now thy portion, the light
of thine eyes, the lifting up of thy head, the joy of
thy heart, the strength of thy bones, thy stock, thy
treasure, thy life, thy health, thy peace, thy rest, thine
all : " Whom have I in heaven but thee, and there
is none upon earth that I desire beside thee.   My
flesh and my heart faileth : but God is the strength
of my heart, and my portion for ever," Psa. lxxiii.
25, 26.   Here is thy portion, know it for thy good,
take it for thine own ; live upon it, and live up to it.

1. Live upon thy Portion.   Here thou mayest
feed, herein thou mayest rejoice, herein thou mayest
bless thyself for ever.   " Let him that blesseth himself on the earth bless himself in the God of truth."
Let him that rejoiceth in the earth rejoice in the
God of truth.   Let the strong man live upon his
strength, let the wise man live upon his wits, let the
rich man live upon his lands, come thou live upon
thy God ; come enjoy God and thy soul ; enjoy God
in thy soul, enjoy thy soul in God.   Thou hast
possession, what should hinder thy fruition?   In
fruition the schools tell us there are three things
which go to the making it up ; knowledge, delight,
and satisfaction.

(1.) Knowledge : according to the clearness or
cloudiness of our apprehensions of any good, we
more or less take the pleasure or comfort of it ;
and therefore the full fruition of God is not till at
last, when we shall know as we are known.   Here
we see as but in a glass, and darkly ; we know but
in part, and while we know but in part, we love but
in part, and joy but in part; the dimness of our

sight makes an abatement upon our joy. When the vail shall be taken away, when we shall come to see face to face, then we shall fully feel what it is to have a God. Christian, know thou the God of thy fathers ; the more thou knowest the more thou hast.

The carnal world enjoy not God at all : God is not known in their tabernacles : in Judah is God known, his name is great in Israel : at Salem is his tabernacle, and his dwelling in Zion. But what of God in Edom, or Ammon, or Amalek, or Egypt ; those dark regions wherein neither sun nor star appears ? Leave them to their dunghill gods, to the gardens which they have desired, and the oaks which they have chosen. The Lord is before thee, know it for thy good. Study thy God, christian, roll over his sweetness in thy mind, as thou dost the sweet morsel in thy mouth; see what he is, and what thou hast laid up in him. read over daily his glorious names; walk through those chambers of his presence, his glorious attributes. Look into the chamber of his power, and see what thou hast laid up for thee there. Go into the chamber of his wisdom, and see what that will afford thee. Look into the chambers of his goodness, mercy, faithfulness, holiness, and behold what treasures are laid up for thee in each of these. Enter into thy chambers, they are all thine ; enter into thy chambers, let thine eye be there, let thy meditation be there, let thy soul be there every day ; there is thy portion, search it out and know it for thy good.

(2.) Delight. Fruition is the taking the pleasure of what we have. We cannot enjoy what we do not love, and love hath delight. We cannot enjoy that wherein we do not joy. " Delight thyself in the Lord," Psa. xxxvii. 4. " I sate me down under his

shadow with great delight," Cant. ii. 3. If his shadow be so pleasant, what will his sun-beams be!
" O taste and see that the Lord is good," Ps.
xxxiv. 8. Our senses help our understandings; we
cannot by the most rational discourse perceive what
the sweetness of honey is, taste it and you shall
perceive it. His fruit was sweet unto my taste.
Dwell in the light of the Lord, and let thy soul be
always ravished with his love. Get out the marrow
and the fatness that thy portion yields thee. Let
fools learn by beholding thy face, how dim their
blazes are to the brightness of thy day.

Let thy delights in God be pure and unmixed
delights. Let thy spirit be so filled with God, and
so raised above carnal joys, and the matters of them,
that it be no damp upon thee to have nothing but
God. Thy wine is the more sprightful when not
mixed with water. Live above in that serene air
which is not defiled with earthly exhalations. Sickly
bodies, and so sickly souls, cannot live in too pure
an air. Be so wholly spiritual, that spiritual joys,
spiritual delights, may be suited to thee, and sufficient
for thee. Do not say, I want the joy of the vintage
and of the harvest; I want the joy of the bridegroom and of the bride; I want the sound of the
millstones and the light of the candle, to make my
comfort full. Let the joy of the Lord be thy strength,
and thy life; say with the prophet, " Although the
fig-tree shall not blossom, neither shall fruit be in
the vines; the labour of the olive shall fail, and the
fields shall yield no meat; the flock shall be cut off
from the fold, and there shall be no herd in the stalls:
yet will I rejoice in the Lord, I will joy in the God
of my salvation," Hab. iii. 17, 18.

(3.) Satisfaction. The quiet, or resting of the

soul in its portion; therefore the schools say, it is only the last end, that is the proper object of fruition. The carnal world, whatever they possess, yet they cannot be said properly to enjoy it; though they be their gods that they live upon; as their drag is their god, their yarn is their god, their plough, and their plenty, and their pleasure is their god; they burn incense to them, yet they cannot enjoy them; there is no rest for them in their god. " What man is he that feareth the Lord? his soul shall dwell at ease," Psa. xxv. 12, 13. In the original it is " shall lodge in goodness." The soul is never at ease whilst it is in want, every want wrings; it can never take up its lodging where it cannot take its rest. His soul shall be at ease, shall lodge, that is, shall take up its rest in the goodness of God: and when we find rest in our beds, then we enjoy them. Is thy soul lodged in God? O enjoy thy lodging: " Soul, take thine ease, thou hast goods laid up for many years. Return to thy rest, O my soul, for the Lord hath dealt bountifully with thee." As it was said to, so let it be said by, the church and every saint, " This is my rest," here will I dwell for ever. Here thou mayest find rest when thou hast no other rock to lean upon; thou mayest be at rest in thy God, in thy most restless state, in a weary land, in a barren wilderness, in a tempestuous ocean. However it was in the vision of the prophet, yet thou mayest say, If the wind rise, the Lord is in the wind; if after the wind, an earthquake, the Lord is in the earthquake; if after the earthquake, a fire, the Lord God is in the fire; and wherever thou findest God, thou mayest find rest. If thou find God in a wilderness, thou wilt find rest in the wilderness; if thou find God in the earthquake, or the tempest, or the fire, even there also

thy soul shall find rest. When thou canst not rest in
thy bed, nor in thy house, nor in thy land, thou
mayest still rest in thy God. Say, christian, say
again, " Return to thy rest, O my soul, for the Lord
hath dealt bountifully with me." Though my helps
fail me, and my friends fail me, and my flesh and
my heart fail me, God is the strength of my heart,
and my portion for ever. This is my rest, here
will I dwell for ever.

To these I might add a fourth thing wherein
fruition stands; the making use of our portion.
He enjoys who uses what he hath. We then enjoy
our portion, when we have a power and heart to
make use of it on all occasions. I am thine, soul,
come and make use of me as thou wilt, thou mayest
freely; I have nothing but it is for thee; thou
mayest freely come to my store, and the oftener the
better welcome. Have thou not a God lying by
thee to no purpose; let not thy God be as others'
gods, serving only for a show. Have not a name
only that thou hast a God; since he allows thee,
having such a Friend, use him daily: " My God shall
supply all your wants;" never want whilst thou hast
a God, never fear or faint whilst thou hast a God:
go to thy treasure, and take whatever thou needest;
there is bread, and clothes, and health, and life, and
all that thou needest. O christian, learn the divine
skill to make God all things, to make bread of thy
God, and water, and health, and friends, and ease;
he can supply thee with all these; or, which is better, he can be, instead of all these, thy food, thy
clothing, thy friend, thy life to thee. All this he
hath said to thee in this one word, " I am thy God;"
and hereupon thou mayest say, I have no husband, and yet I am no widow; my Maker is my

husband. I have no father, nor friend, and yet I am neither fatherless nor friendless, my God is both my Father and my Friend. I have no child; but is not he better to me than ten children ? I have no house, but yet I have a home; I have made the Most High my habitation. I am left alone, but yet I am not alone; my God is good company for me; with him I can walk, with him I can take sweet counsel, find sweet repose; at my lying down, at my rising up, whilst I am in the house, as I walk by the way, my God is ever with me; with him I travel, I dwell, I lodge, I live, and shall live for ever.

2. Live up to your privilege. Live according to your rank and quality, according to your riches laid up for you in God. The rich men of this world live like rich men, they sort themselves with persons of their own quality, attend on the courts of princes, are employed about the palace, you may read their estates in the whole way of their life, they wear them on their backs, spread their tables with them ; they live sumptuously, and fare delicately. Christians, feed not on ashes or husks, you have better meat ; you have milk and honey, marrow and fat-ness, the hidden manna, the bread that comes down from heaven, the water of life ; you have blessed privileges, precious promises, lively hopes, living comforts, glorious joys, the fountain of life to feed your souls upon ; come eat, O friends ; drink, yea, drink abundantly, O my beloved ; out-fare the rich man, Luke xvi. who fared deliciously every day; you have enough to maintain it ; let every day be a glad-day, a feast-day with you.

Let your clothing be according to your feeding. Be clothed with the sun ; put on the Lord Jesus.

The King's daughter is, and so let all the King's sons be, all glorious within, let their clothing be of wrought gold. Be clothed with humility, put on love, bowels of compassion, gentleness, meekness; put on the garments of salvation.

Let your company and converse be according to your clothing. Live amongst the excellent, amongst the generation of the just. Get you up to the " general assembly and church of the first-born, to that innumerable company of angels, and the spirits of just men made perfect." Live in the courts of the great King, behold his face, wait at his throne, bear his name, show forth his virtues, set forth his praises, advance his honour, uphold his interest: let vile persons and vile ways be contemned in your eyes, be of more raised spirits than to be companions with them. Learn hence a holy elevation of spirit. Regard not their societies, nor their scorns, their flatteries or their frowns; rejoice not with their joys, fear not their fear, care not for their care, feed not on their dainties; get you up from among them, to your country, to your city, where no unclean thing can enter or annoy. Live by faith, in the power of the Spirit, in the beauty of holiness, in the hope of the gospel, in the joy of your God, in the magnificence, and yet the humility, of the children of the great King.

3. Their sun. He will discover and make manifest to them the riches and glory of their portion. He hath granted them himself for their portion, and he will reveal and make manifest to them what a portion he is. He will make manifest both the blessedness they shall enjoy in him, and the way to it, and also the dangers that lie in the way. " The Lord God is a sun," Psa. lxxxiv. 11. The sun is

the light of the world, it discovers itself, and all things else. We cannot see the glory of the sun but by its own light; the moon, the stars, the firmament, and all this lower world, would all disappear if the sun withdrew its light. Beauty and deformity, safety and danger, the right way and the wrong, are all brought to view by the light of the sun; the sun-light makes the day; night is spread over the world when the sun is set: God is glorious, but who would be ever the wiser did not this glory shine? "In thy light we shall see light," Psa. xxxvi. 9. Why is the glorious God apprehended, understood, admired, by so few amongst the sons of men? Why, he is out of sight, the sun is not risen upon them, nor shines unto them: they have moonlight, or star-light, some dimmer reflections of this glory at second-hand from the creatures, but they see not the sun.

What is the reason that truth and falsehood, good and evil, substances and shadows, things perishing, and things permanent, are no better distinguished? What is the reason that men are so mistaken and misguided in their judgments, in their choice, in their way? that they are at such a loss, such wanderers from their bliss? What is the reason that men's own sparks, the light of their own fires, their candle-light, or torch-light, their fleshly imaginations, their carnal prosperity, their pleasures, their ease, their earthly glory, and their carnal joys that hence flash up to them, are so adored and admired by them? Oh, they see not the sun. God is out of sight, and thence are all their dotages, and foolish mistakes and miscarriages. God will be a sun to his saints, their sun. "Thy sun shall no more go down." They shall have both the propriety

and the comfort of this glorious sun; he will show
them his face, he will cause his glory to appear, he
will lead them into himself by his own beams; he
will show them their end, and the means; the goal,
and their way to it; he will show them the good
part, and the right path; good and evil, duties and
sins, realities and delusions, helps and hinderances,
dangers and advantages, their snares and their suc-
cours, will all be discovered to them by the light of
the Lord.

Hearken, thou poor and dark soul, that hast
chosen, but thou knowest not what; that art going,
but thou knowest not whither; that art wandering
and stumbling on, but thou carest not how; that
complainest thou canst not see, thou canst not value,
thou canst not be affected with all the glory and joy
of the invisible world: that findest thy husks and
thy trash to be a greater pleasure to thee than all
the riches of immortality; that wouldest fain mind,
and choose, and love, and relish, and seek God, and
things above, but thou canst not: thou seest so little
of the beauty of them, that they do not entice thine
heart after them; and when thou art seeking, thou
art at a loss, and in the dark, as to the way that thou
shouldest take.   Hearken, soul, thy God calls to
thee; " Come unto me, look unto me, and I will be
thy sun : I will show thee all that glory, and the
right way that will bring thee to it : I promise thee
I will, trust me, I will be a light unto thee."

4. Their shield. " The Lord God is a sun and a
shield," Psa. lxxxiv. 11. The gods of the earth are
so styled, " The shields of the earth," Psa. xlvii. 9.
much more the God of glory. Faith is called a
shield: " Above all taking the shield of faith,"
Eph. vi. 16. it signifies the same, as God is a shield.

Faith is to the soul whatever God is. This is the grace that entitles the soul to God, and applies God to the soul. " Fear not, Abraham, I am thy shield," Gen. xv. 1. What is promised to the father of the faithful, stands sure to all the seed, Rom. iv. 16. The state of christians in this life is a militant state, a state full of hardships and hazards; by reason whereof, as richly as they are provided for, they are subject to fears of being undone, and spoiled of all. They are in fears about things eternal; they have spiritual adversaries that lie in wait for their souls, that fight against their souls, that are tempting them, and enticing them from their God; that watch their opportunities to steal away their God, by stealing away their hearts from him; and such dangerous attempts of this kind they meet withal, that they often are in great doubt what the issue may be. They are in fears about things temporal; their names are shot at, their liberties are invaded, their estates, with all the comforts of their lives, are in danger to be made a prey; to-day they are a praise, to-morrow a scorn; to day they are full and abound, but to-morrow they may have nothing left; they die daily; they are killed all the day long. But whatever their dangers and their fears thereupon are, here is sufficient provision made against all. God is their shield.

Christian, thou hast enough, and all that thou hast is in safety. Thou art compassed about with a shield, secured on all hands, there is no coming at thee. Whatever assaults are made, thy God is a wall of partition betwixt thee and harm. They are not shields of brass and iron thou art furnished with; the strong God is thy defence. Wherefore dost thou doubt, O thou of little faith? A christian, and yet afraid! shifting for thyself! taking care for the asses, and oxen, and sheep! vexing, and loading, and losing thyself, in thy cares and fears from day to day! Where is thy God, man? Doth not God take care for oxen, and asses, and all that thou hast?

But oh, what meanest thou in this, to be shifting thyself from danger, by shrinking back from thy God! securing thyself from affliction, by taking sanctuary in iniquity! What art thou doing, but throwing away thy shield to save thee from harm! making a breach in thy wall, to keep thee in safety! " Walk before me, and be thou perfect," Gen. xvii. 1. &c. follow thou me, stick to me, and then, " Fear not, Abraham, I am thy shield," Gen. xv. 1. This now is the first and great promise of the covenant, " I am thy God," and the second is like unto it.

Chapter II —*Christ in the Covenant*

God hath put Christ into the covenant, and made him over to his people, " I will give thee for a covenant," Isa. xlii. 6. He who is promised, as the chief matter, the mediator, surety, scope of the covenant, is by a metonymy* called, The Covenant. " I will give thee for a covenant ;" that is, I covenant to give thee to the people. Whatever glory and blessedness there is in the fruition of God, wo is me, there is a great gulf fixed between me and it, over which there· is no passing; there is a partition-wall raised, over which there is no climbing; there is a hand-writing against me, whilst that stands, all that is in God is nothing to me ; were this God mine, I had enough. Let me be put to labour, or suffering ; let me dig, or beg, or starve, and die ; whether I be rich or poor, have something or no-

---

* A figure of speech by which one thing is put for another.

thing, be a praise or a reproach, it matters not, so God were mine.

But oh how may I obtain? Who shall bring me to God? Why, the Lord God hath given thee his Son to undertake for thee, and to be thy way unto the Father, Heb. x. 19, 20.

Jesus Christ, who is the morning-star, the Sun of righteousness, the image of the invisible God, the first-born of every creature, by whom are all things, who is before all things, the head of the body the church, who is the beginning, the first-born from the dead, in whom dwells all fulness, even the fulness of the Godhead bodily; who hath made peace by the blood of his cross, Col. i. and ii. whose name is " Wonderful, Counsellor, the mighty God, the everlasting Father, the Prince of Peace," Isa. ix. 6. This Jesus is granted thee in the covenant, to bring thee to God. To which blessed and glorious purpose he is exhibited—

I. As the light of life.

II. As the Lord our righteousness.

III. As our Lord and King.

IV. As our Head and Husband.

I. As the light of life. " A light to lighten the Gentiles, and the glory of thy people Israel," Luke ii. 32. " In him was life, and the life was the light of men," John i. 4. " He that followeth me, shall have the light of life," John viii. 12. There is a light that serves to kill and destroy, to bring death and condemnation to light: the light of the law, that killing letter concerning which the apostle says, " When the commandment came, sin revived, and I died; the commandment which was ordained to life, I found to be unto death," Rom. vii. 9, 10. But Christ brings life and immortality to light; heaven, glory, the invisible God, which are lost, out of reach, and out of ken, are all discovered in the face of Jesus Christ; " To give us the knowledge of the glory of God in the face of Jesus Christ," 2 Cor. iv. 6. He is the image of the invisible God, the brightness of his Father's glory, the glass in which by reflection we see the sun. " Show us the Father, and it suffices us. Why," says he, " hast thou known me, Philip, and yet sayest, Show us the Father ? He that hath seen me, hath seen the Father, and this is the light of life," John xiv. 8, 9. " This is life eternal, that they might know thee the only true God, and Jesus Christ whom thou hast sent," John xvii. 3.

II. As the Lord our righteousness. This is his name, " He shall be called, The Lord our righteousness," Jer. xxiii. 6. To this end he is given to us,

1. As our propitiatory sacrifice; " The propitiation for our sins," 1 John ii. 2. " Christ our passover," 1 Cor. v. 7. "A lamb slain from the foundation of the world," Rev. xviii. 8. Our price, our ransom, to satisfy justice, pacify wrath, discharge from the curse ; to blot out the hand-writing, break down the wall of partition ; to finish the transgression, to make an end of sins, to make reconciliation for iniquity, to bring in everlasting righteousness, and so to bring us to God. Whatever difficulties there appear in thy way, whatever doubts arise in thy heart, from thy sins, from thy guilt, from thy poverty, from thy impotence ; whatever objections thy fears may hence put in, there is the blood of the Lamb, that will answer all. Christ our passover is sacrificed for us.

2. As a merciful and faithful High-priest, Heb.

ii. 17. who hath made an atonement for us in the earth, and appears for us in heaven; who hath made reconciliation for us, and makes intercession for us, " to appear in the presence of God for us," Heb. ix. 24. We read, Exod. xxviii. 12. 29. that Aaron as the type of Christ, was to bear the names of the children of Israel, engraven in stones, upon his shoulders, and upon his breast-plate, when he went into the holy place, for a memorial before the Lord continually. Our Lord is entered into the heavens, to appear in the presence of God, with our names upon his shoulders, and upon his heart, for a memorial before the Lord; there is not the least of saints, but there his name is engraven. Here is my ransom, Lord, and behold my ransomed ones. Here is my price and my purchase, my redemption and my redeemed. Whatever accusers there be, whatever charge be laid against them, whatever guilt lies upon them, here are the shoulders that have borne all that was their due, and paid all that they owe; and upon these shoulders and in this heart thou mayest read all their names; and when thou readest, remember what I have done for them, and acquit, absolve, and let them be accepted before thee for ever. Remember the tears of these eyes, the stripes on this back, the shame of this face, the groans of this body, the anguish of this soul, the blood of this heart; and when thou rememberest, whatever name thou findest engraven upon this heart, and upon these shoulders, they are the persons whose all these are; and whatever these are, whatever acceptance they have found with thee, whatever satisfaction thou hast found in them, put it upon their account; never let me be accounted the accepted, if they be rejected; never let me be accounted righteous, if they lie under the imputation of wicked. If they be not righteous in my righteousness, I must be guilty under their guilt. Whatever I am, whatever my satisfaction is, all is theirs; for them they plead, for them they pray; my tears, stripes, wounds, groans, anguish, soul, blood, they all cry and say, Father, forgive them, Father accept them.

Of all cries there are no such strong cries as the cry of blood, and that whether it be against, or for the guilty; its voice shall be heard on high. "Thy brother's blood crieth unto me from the ground," Gen. iv. And what followed? Wo to those persons against whom blood crieth; but where blood, such blood, cries for them, for pardon, for mercy, blessed are those souls.

Christian, this blood is for thee, it "speaks better things than the blood of Abel," Heb. xii. 24. It pleads, sues, presses for thy discharge from all that is upon thee. Thou hast many cries against thee; Satan cries, thy sins cry, thine own heart, thy conscience cries against thee; and thou art amazed at the dreadful noise they make; but behold! the blood of the Lamb, who is God, cries for thee. Thou hast an accuser, but thou hast an Acquitter: thou hast adversaries, but thou hast an Advocate. "An Advocate with the Father, Jesus Christ the righteous, who is the propitiation for thy sins," 1 John ii. 1, 2. "Who shall lay any thing to the charge of God's elect? It is God that justifieth; who is he that condemneth? it is Christ that died; yea, rather, that is risen again, who is even at the right hand of God, who also maketh intercession for us," Rom. viii. 33, 34.

Nay, further, thou hast not only a righteous but

a merciful High-Priest, that is provided with a sacrifice, and hath a heart to offer it for thee; thy name is in his heart as well as on his shoulders, in his bowels as well as on his back. He hath blood for thee, precious blood; and he hath bowels for thee, pitiful bowels. He can have pity and compassion on the miserable, Heb. v. 2. If he can find no other, he can find arguments enough from thy wo and thy misery to draw forth his soul towards thee. He is merciful, and his mercies are tender mercies; he is pitiful, and his compassions are tender compassions; thou art not so tender of the wife of thy bosom, of thine own child; thou art not so tender of thine own flesh, of the apple of thine eye, of thine own soul, as thy Lord is of thee. His Spirit is moved for thee, his soul melts over thee, he bleeds in thy wounds, he suffers in thy sorrows, his eye weeps, his heart breaks over thy broken and undone state; fear not his forgetting thee.

He is a merciful and a faithful High-Priest. No dignity to which he is exalted above thee, no distance to which he is removed from thee, can make him forget his friends; he is gone into the heavens, and there exalted far above all principalities and powers, and set down at the right hand of God. He is gone, but he hath carried thy name with him as a perpetual memorial for thee. Thou art unfaithful; shame to thee! thou forgettest thy Lord at every turn; every business that comes, every trouble that comes, every pleasure that comes, every companion that comes, makes thee forget thy Lord, forget his love, forget thy duty; oh, how small a matter will steel thy heart from him! yea, stir up tumults and rebellions against him. Thy comforts, thy hopes, thy needs, thou hast daily of him; will not all prevail to hold him in remembrance with thee. Thou forgettest thy Lord, but he will not forget thee; though thou hast been unfaithful in many things, yet he is in nothing. " Yet he abideth faithful, he cannot deny himself," 2 Tim. ii. 13. he should not be true to himself, if he be not faithful to thee; his interest lies in thee; thou art his, his possession, a member of his body, fear not; if he should be unfaithful to thy soul, he is therein unfaithful to his own body. If thy case be such that he can help thee, if there be any thing wherein he can stead thee; if all that he hath, his blood, his righteousness, his interest with the Father, will be sufficient for thy help, he hath undertaken to procure it for thee, and secure it to thee. Faithful is he that hath called you, and will do it.

This now is that Jesus who is given unto us, as our propitiatory Sacrifice, as our merciful and faithful High-Priest, who suffered on the earth, and is gone into the heavens for us; standing in his red robes, garments rolled in blood, with those glorious whites upon the red; pardon, peace, absolution, acceptance; with the names of his ransomed ones engraven upon his heart and upon his shoulders: this is that Jesus, who is THE LORD OUR RIGHTEOUSNESS.

III. As our Lord and King. A King shall reign in righteousness, and in him shall the Gentiles trust. " Shout, O daughter of Zion, behold thy King cometh," Zech. ix. 9. " The government shall be on his shoulder," Isa. ix. 6. God hath more care of his saints, than to leave the government of them on their shoulder. Is not her King in her ?

He is a King to gather them, a King to govern them, a King to defend and save them; to save them from their temporal enemies, the sons of violence, the men of this evil world; from their spiritual enemies, to save them from their sins. " Thou shalt call his name Jesus, for he shall save his people from their sins," Matt. i. 21. It is a mercy to be under government and under protection. What would become of us were there no king in Israel? Where there is no king, all are kings; more kings than men: Satan will be a king, every lust will be a lord, as many kings as there are devils and sins. Whither would our unruly hearts carry us? How easily would our wily and potent enemies ruin us! What tyranny would sin exercise within! what cruelty should we suffer from without! Whither should we wander! where should we fix! What peace, what order, what stability! Whence should counsel, and protection, and salvation come, were there no lord over us? It is a mercy to be under government; but to be under such a government, under a King, and such a King? such a wise and potent King, such a meek and merciful King, such a holy and righteous King? Oh what a wonder of mercy! " Rejoice greatly, O daughter of Zion; shout, O daughter of Jerusalem; behold, thy King cometh unto thee, he is just, and having salvation; lowly, and riding upon an ass's colt," &c. He is just, having salvation, as a Priest he hath purchased, as a King he bestows his salvation. He comes not to get, but to give; not to give laws only, but to give gifts unto men; and he gives like a king, palms, crowns, and thrones; salvation to his people by the remission of their sins. Oh how unthankful, oh how foolish is this rebellious world! Impatient of subjection! shake off the yoke! groan under duty! under discipline! We will not have this man

to rule over us! Who then shall save you? hard
to be a christian! strict laws, severe discipline, no
liberty! Is this thy complaint? that is, Wo is me,
I am so limited, and hedged in on all hands, that
there is no liberty left me to be miserable; if I will
be his, I must be happy.

Let fools inherit their own folly, but let Israel
rejoice in him that made him, let the children of
Zion be joyful in their King; for the Lord taketh
pleasure in his people, he will beautify the meek
with salvation. Lift up your heads, O ye gates, and
be ye lift up, ye everlasting doors, and the King
of glory shall come in. Who is this King of glory?
The Lord of hosts, yea, the Lord our righteousness, he is the King of glory. The Lord is our
Judge, the Lord is our Lawgiver, the Lord is our
King, he will save us. Praise ye the Lord. Come
all ye Nimrods, ye mighty hunters on the earth:
come all ye sons of Anak, ye seed of the giants:
come all ye sons of Belial, ye seed of the adulterer
and of the whore: come all ye Ishmaelites and
Ammonites, ye Moabites and Hagarenes, associate,
confederate, take counsel together, smite with the
tongue, bite with the teeth, push with the horn, kick
with the heel; come all ye gates of hell, and powers
of darkness: thou dragon with all thy armies, with
all thy fiery darts and instruments of death: come
thou king of terrors with thy fatal dart; the virgin,
the daughter of Zion, hath despised you all, she hath
laughed you to scorn; the daughter of Jerusalem
hath shaken her head at you; her King is in the
midst of her; the Lord is her King, he will save
her.

IV. As our Head and Husband. He that is
given to be Head over all things to the church is

given to be the Head of the church, Eph. i. 22, 23.
and of every member in particular, 1 Cor. xi. 3.
Believers are all joined to the Lord, 1 Cor. vi. 17.
United in Christ as fellow-members; united unto
Christ as their common Head; " From which all
the body, by joints and bands, having nourishment
ministered, and knit together, increaseth with the
increase of God," Col. ii. 19. They are married
to Christ, " I have espoused you to one Husband,"
2 Cor. xi. 2.

From this union follows :

1. A communication of influences.
2. A complication of interests.

1. A communication of influences. Having nourishment ministered. Christ our Head is our Fountain of Life. Our Head is our Heart also, out of it
are the issues of life; from him we live, and are
nourished and maintained in life. He is our Joseph,
all the treasures of the holy land are with him.
" In him are hid all the treasures of wisdom and
knowledge," Col. ii. 3. " It pleased the Father
that in him should all fulness dwell," Col. i. 19.
He is the only begotten Son of God, full of grace
and truth.

Here note. What grace there is in Christ. The
schools tell us, that in him there is a three-fold
grace.

(1.) The grace of union. The human nature of
Christ hath received the high grace or favour to be
personally united to the second Person in the Godhead; by virtue of which union the fulness of the
Godhead is said to dwell in him bodily: bodily, that
is personally, or substantially, in opposition to the
types and shadows of the Old Testament, in which
God, in a figure, is said to dwell. God is said to

dwell in the tabernacle, in the ark of the covenant, in the temple; but in these he dwelt only as figures, and shadows of the human nature of Christ. In Christ he dwells not in a figure, but personally and substantially. As Christ, Col. ii. 17. is called the body, in opposition to the types of old, which were but the shadow; so bodily here notes not a figurative, but a personal inhabitation. Christ is the body, not a shadow; and God dwells in him bodily, that is substantially, and not in a shadow.

(2.) Habitual grace. " All those moral perfections, wherein stands the holiness of his nature : the love and fear of God; his humility, meekness, patience; in sum, his perfect conformity to the image and whole will of God. " Such a high-priest became us, who is holy, harmless, undefiled, separate from sinners," Heb. vii. 26.

(3.) That honour which is given to him to be Head of the church.

Also observe, how Christ is said to be full of grace ; there is a two-fold fulness of grace. In respect of grace itself. Thus he is said to be full of grace, that hath all grace, and hath it in the greatest excellency and perfection of it. Also, in respect of the person that hath it : and thus a person is said to be full of grace, that hath as much grace as he is capable of. Christ is full of grace in both respects ; that grace which is in him, is grace in the highest perfection of it, and as much as his vessel can hold.

Observe also, that this fulness of Christ is ours, and for us; " Of his fulness do we receive grace for grace," John i. 16. " Your life is hid with Christ in God," Col. iii. 3. Your life, that is, both your spiritual life, grace, and your eternal life, glory. " This is the record, that God hath given to

us eternal life, and this life is in his Son," 1 John
v. 11. Our life is said to be in Christ in three
respects. 1. It is hid in Christ, as the effect in the
cause. As the life of the branches is hid in the root,
so is the life of a christian in Christ. He is our
root. 2. It is deposited with Christ; it is laid up
with him, committed to his trust and custody; with
him it is secured and put into safe hands. 3. The
dispensation of it is committed to him: from him it
is at his pleasure to be derived to us. Of his fulness we receive. The Son hath life in himself, and
he giveth it to whom, when, and in what measure
he pleaseth.

Christian, art thou nothing in thyself? Thou hast
enough in thy Jesus. Art thou dark? he is a fountain of light. Art thou dead? he is a fountain of
life. Art thou poor and low, weak in knowledge,
in faith, in love, in patience, &c.? he is a treasure
of all grace; and what he is, he is for thee. Is he
wise? he is wise for thee. Is he holy? he is holy
for thee. Is he meek, merciful, humble, patient?
he is so for thee. Is he strong? is he rich? is he
full? it is for thy sake. As he was empty for thee,
weak for thee, poor for thee; so for thee he is
mighty, he is rich and full. While thou bewailest
thine own poverty and weakness, O bless thyself in
thy Lord, in his riches, righteousness, and strength.

2. A complication of interests. As the head and
body, as the husband and wife, so Christ and his
saints are mutually concerned; are rich or poor,
must stand and fall, live and die together. As the
husband conveys to the wife a title to what he hath;
as the wife holds of the husband; so is it betwixt
Christ and his church; they have nothing but
through him; their whole tenure is in the Head;

they have nothing but through him; and whatso-ever is his, is theirs. His God is their God, his Father is their Father; his blood, his merits, his Spirit, his victories, all the spoils he hath gotten, all the revenue and income of his life and death, all is theirs. For them he obeyed, suffered, lived, died, rose, ascended, is set down in glory, at the right hand of God. He obeyed as their Head; died as their Head; rose, ascended, reigneth as their Head; and hath in their names taken possession of that inheritance which he purchased for them. This is that Jesus who is given to us, and thus is he granted and made over to all his saints in this cove-nant of God.

CHAPTER III —*The Spirit in the Covenant*

GOD hath put his Spirit into the covenant; the Almighty, the Eternal Spirit; the Holy Spirit, the Spirit of glory, and of God.

This Holy and Eternal Spirit is first poured forth on our Head, the Lord Jesus; to anoint him our Redeemer, to furnish and qualify him for that great undertaking, " The Spirit of the Lord God is upon me, because he hath anointed me to preach good tidings to the meek," &c. Isa. lxi. 1. Isa. xi. 2—4. " The Spirit of the Lord shall rest upon him, the Spirit of wisdom and understanding, and of the fear of the Lord," Isa. xi. 2.

And he is promised to each member, " I will put my Spirit within you," Ezek. xxxvi. 27. To all these he is granted,

I. As a Spirit of wisdom and revelation.

II. As a Spirit of holiness and sanctification.

III. As a Spirit of truth and direction.

IV. As a Spirit of comfort and consolation.

I. As a " Spirit of wisdom and revelation,"
Eph. i. 17, 18. To enlighten them, to open their
blind eyes, and to shine into their hearts ; to give
them the knowledge of the glory of God in the face
of Jesus Christ, that they may know what the hope
of his calling is, and what the riches of the glory of
his inheritance in the saints. To counterwork the
spirit of this world, whose work is to blind men's
eyes, " lest the light of the glorious gospel should
shine unto them," 2 Cor. iv. 4—6.

This is he by whom the Father hath " called us
out of darkness into his marvellous light," 1 Pet.
ii. 9. The light that the Spirit brings in is a marvellous light, and that in three respects :

1. It is a marvellous thing that ever light should
come into such dark souls. That those who were
born blind, and upon whom the god of this world
had, for many years together, been trying his skill
to thicken their darkness, to increase and seal them
up under it ; that ever such eyes should be opened,
and the light of life should shine in upon such
hearts ; this is a marvellous thing. When our
Lord Jesus in the days of his flesh, opened the eyes
of those who had been born blind, the people ran
together, and wondered at the sight. If you should
see stones live, if you should see dead stocks, or
dry bones walk up and down the streets, if you
should see trees, or houses, or mountains full of
eyes, this were not more full of wonder, than to behold blind sinners receiving their sight. Thou
wert once darkness ; art thou now light in the Lord ?
stand and wonder at thy cure.

2. They are marvellous things which this light
discovers. It is a wonder that such eyes should ever
see, and they see wonders. The gospel is a

mystery full of wonders: there are heights, and depths, and lengths, and breadths. We have seen strange things to-day. Strange love, strange grace, wonderful wisdom, wonderful pity, patience, mercy; wonderful providences, wonderful deliverances, incomprehensible excellences, unspeakable joy and glory. It is a wonder there should be such things every day before our eyes, and yet we could not see them till now; and it is a wonder, that when we did not see them before, we should ever see them now; that those things which we despised, derided, mocked at, stumbled at, as mere foolishness and fancy, we should now see and admire, even to astonishment; that that Jesus who was to the Jews a stumbling-block, to the Greeks foolishness, should be to the same men when called, the wisdom of God, and the power of God. Oh the deep things of God! Oh the unsearchable riches of Christ! which he that searcheth all things, reveals unto the saints! Oh the hidden treasures they now discover in this deep mine! To you that believe he is precious, a praise, an honour; all fair, all glorious; and you have seen his glory, as the glory of the only begotten Son of God, full of grace and truth.

Again, there are marvellous evils, as well as good things, which by this light are brought to light. Sin with all the hidden things of darkness, that lie below in those chambers of death; the secrets of the evil heart of man. Sin appears a wonder to the savingly enlightened soul; exceeding sinful, a world of wickedness.

There is death, and hell, and the devil, in every sin; unkindness, unthankfulness, folly, enmity, rebellion, spite, and the blackness of darkness. What once appeared as a pleasure, a delight, a beauty; or at least if an evil, yet but a trifle, a matter of nothing; is become a plague, a terror, a burden, a bondage, bitterness, shame, sorrow; and such a high provocation, that whereas once he swelled and murmured, and cried out of rigour, severity, cruelty in the least punishment of it; now he wonders at the clemency, and patience, and forbearance of God, that such an affront and provocation, had not long since turned the whole earth into a hell.

Christian, thou complainest thou canst not see, thou canst not feel, thou canst not mourn, thou canst not break under all the guilt that lies upon thee; thine heart is hard, thine eyes are dry, not a tear, not a groan, scarce a sigh, will all this evil fetch out from thee. Oh this blind and sottish mind! Oh this dead and senseless heart! what shall I do? what would I not do to get me a melting, mourning, broken spirit! but I cannot, I cannot; I cannot see, I cannot bleed, nor break. O beg the light of this Holy Spirit! and if the sight he will present thee with, of this wonderful evil, do not rend thy heart, and turn thee, and open all thy sluices, and let out thy soul in sighs and groans, in shame and sorrow, thou mayest then well be a wonder to thyself. But be not discouraged, be not dismayed; do not say, This rock will never break, this iron will never melt; I may go sighing for sighs, mourning after tears, groaning after groans, but all in vain, it will never be; past feeling, past feeling, sorrow flies still from me, repentance is hid from mine eyes. Do not thus discourage thyself; wait for this Spirit, open to it and thou shalt see flowing in such streams of self-shaming, self-confounding light, as shall flow forth in self-abasing, self-abhorring streams of tears.

3. These marvellous things are revealed with marvellous clearness; that is, in comparison of what they are to the purblind world, and in comparison of what they themselves once saw. They come to see the glory, and the beauty, and the reality of the wonderful things of God. "We have seen his glory," saith the apostle, John i. 14. The kindness of God our Saviour appeared, "but we all, with open face, behold, as in a glass, the glory of the Lord," 2 Cor. iii. 18. Out of Zion hath he appeared in perfect beauty.

It is prophesied, Isa. liii. 2. of the unbelieving world, that when they should see Christ, they should see no beauty in him. Strange! though he were all beauty, yet they should see him, and yet see no beauty; that is, they shall see him, and yet not see him. They see not wood for trees. What is thy beloved more than other beloveds? What is Christ more than an ordinary man? What is the gospel more than an ordinary story? What is the Spirit? What is truth? What is there in this faith and love, in this holiness and righteousness, in this peace of conscience, and joy of the Holy Ghost? What substance is there in them? Where is the glory, and wherein is the excellency of them? Which way came the Spirit of the Lord from me to thee? Thou shalt know in that day, when thou shalt call to the mountains to fall on thee, and the rocks to hide thee, from the face of God and the Lamb. We know whom we have believed. We know that we know him. We speak that which we know, and testify what we have seen. We have an unction from the Holy One, we know all things. God hath revealed them to us by his Spirit, for the Spirit searcheth all things, even the deep things of God. Now we have received not the spirit of this world, but the Spirit which is of God, that we might know the things that are freely given to us of God. We have a clear and certain sight. We do not see men as trees walking; with our eyes half open; we see men as men, Christ as Christ, truth as truth, in its full lustre and evidence. This we have seen, and do testify, neither deceiving, nor being deceived. We thank thee, O Father, Lord of heaven and earth, that thou hast hid these things from the wise and prudent, and hast revealed them unto babes.

And as they see truth, and holiness, and goodness, in their wonderful glory and beauty; so also folly, and falsehood, and sin, in its wonderful ugliness and deformity. Sin appears to be sin, to them, Rom. vii. Folly to be folly, falsehood to be falsehood; they see men as men, Christ as Christ, truth as truth, holiness as holiness; and they see beasts as beasts, fools as fools, sin as sin, devils as devils, hell as hell. They see all things as they are, temptations as they are, delusions as they are; they see what is under them, the hook under the bait, the sting in the locust's tail, the war in the devil's heart, carried on under his fawning face; we are not ignorant of his devices.

Sinners, cease your wondering at the saints, let them be no longer for signs and for wonders in Israel; cease your wondering at the saints, and come and wonder with them. Wonder not that they say not as you, live not as you, run not with you after the same follies and vanities; Oh! if ye

once come to see what they see, you will be a wonder to yourselves. Mock not at their blessedness;
blessed are their eyes, for they see. The blind
envy, but do not disdain the seeing. Say not,
These men are in a dream, or drunk, or mad; take
heed, blaspheme not the Holy Spirit, call not his
light darkness, put not your darkness for light.
Would you know, when these men testify what they
have seen and heard, whether they are sober or
beside themselves? Come and see; I say not,
stand and see, you cannot see at that distance you
stand; come near, come in and, you shall see; see
your blindness first, if ever you will see the light.
Oh! bewail your darkness, and seek light, seek and
you shall see it. "Son of David, have mercy on
me!" Why, what wilt thou man? "Lord, that I
may receive my sight." Shall that be thy cry?
O pity thy blind soul! O pray for eyes. They
that see, pity the blind; we have a little sister that
hath no breasts, we have a poor brother, yea a
world of them, that hath no eyes. What shall
we do for our poor brethren, in the day that they
shall be spoken for? Oh! be eyes to thy blind, be
a light to thy dark souls; let them that dwell in
darkness see thy great light. Sinners, those whom
you persecute, do thus pity, do thus pray for you,
"Lord, that their eyes might be opened." Will
you say, Amen, to their prayers? or will you say,
Lord, regard not their word, we desire not the knowledge of thy ways?

Christians, be marvels. You that have seen
marvellous things be marvellous persons, set the
world a wondering for something. Let your light
shine, let the light which hath shined into your
hearts, shine forth in all your paths: let the Spirit

of light within you be a Spirit of glory resting upon you. Once you were darkness, but now are ye light in the Lord; walk as children of the light. Be ye holy, harmless, the children of God, without rebuke in the midst of a crooked generation, amongst whom ye shine as lights in the world.

Beclouded christian, thou goest on bemoaning and bewailing thyself, complaining that thou art still blind; the light hath shined into thy darkness, but thy darkness comprehendeth it not; thine eye is yet but tender, at least, and thou canst see but little; but little of Christ, the sun is but as a spark to thee; but little of sin, that mountain looks yet but as a molehill; it is neither clear nor dark, neither night nor perfect day. Thou didst hope that long ere this, thy scales would have fallen off, the vail would have been removed, but they abide upon thee; thou waitest for light, but behold obscurity! for brightness, but thou walkest in darkness; thou goest on, adding darkness to darkness, the darkness of sorrow to the dimness of sight. Thou fearest that the gospel is hid from thee, thou doubtest it is still night, because it is not yet noon with thee. But hearken; as little as thou seest of Christ, dost thou see so much, that thou prizest, and lovest, and cleavest to him above all? as little as thou seest of sin, dost thou see so much that thou loathest and shunnest it above all things? dost thou walk in that little light thou hast? dost thou love, long, wait, cry for the light? "Send forth thy light and thy truth, lift up the light of thy countenance; Sun of righteousness shine upon me; why are the wheels of thy chariot so long a coming? when Lord? Make haste my beloved, O might I once see thy face, as the sun, looking over the mountains." Is this thy

voice? are these the breathings of thy soul? be of
good comfort, these are the glimmerings and groanings of that Holy Spirit within thee, who hath already
delivered thee from darkness, and will bring thee
forth into his marvellous light; thou shalt know, if
thou follow on to know the Lord. "Arise, shine,
thy light is come, the glory of the Lord is risen upon
thee." Though yet, as to thy sense, it be neither
clear nor dark, neither night nor perfect day, in the
evening there shall be light.

II. As a Spirit of holiness and sanctification. He
is given as a Holy Spirit, and as a sanctifying Spirit;
therefore sanctification is called the "sanctification
of the Spirit," 2 Thess. ii. 13. He comes to change
us into his own nature, to make us partakers of his
holiness; he is a refiner's fire, and fuller's soap,
Mal. iii. 2. to purge, and work, and wash off the
filth and corruption of our natures; what it is said
he shall be to the church, Isa. iv. 4. "a Spirit of
judgment, and a Spirit of burning," to wash away
the filth of the daughters of Sion and to purge the
blood of Jerusalem, from the midst thereof. "A
Spirit of judgment," that is, in the rulers of Israel;
stirring them up to do justice, and execute judgment, that so the guilt of blood may be taken away,
Isa. xxxii. 15, 16. and, "a Spirit of burning," that is,
in the hearts of the people of Israel, to consume and
destroy the inward lusts of their hearts, that no more
such wickedness be committed amongst them. This
he is to every saint; a Spirit of judgment, to give
sentence against their lusts, to condemn them to
the fire: these must be cast out; to the fire with
them; away with them, get ye hence ye sons of the
bond-woman, ye may not be heirs with the sons
of the free-woman. The Spirit of the Lord first

discovers and convinces of sin, judges betwixt light and darkness, grace and sin, and then gives sentence, — Away with these lusts, they may not be suffered to live.

A Spirit of burning, to execute the sentence, to consume them in the fire. The Spirit of sanctification is a Spirit of mortification. "If ye through the Spirit do mortify the deeds of the body," Rom. viii. 13. It is the Spirit that kills, the flesh profiteth nothing.

The Spirit implants the soul into Christ, gives it an interest in his death, brings it under the influence of his death. It is the death of Christ, that is the death of sin; these thieves are crucified with him; "Our old man is crucified with Christ, that the body of sin might be destroyed, that henceforth we should no longer serve sin," Rom. vi. 6. Hell knew not what they did when they crucified Christ; death with all its armies were put to death with him.

The Spirit raises up another party in the soul, a party against a party, an army against an army; brings grace in to take up arms against sin. Grace doth not only fight against sin, but is in the very nature of it the death of sin; as the generation of a new, is the corruption of the old form. Humility is pride dead; meekness is sinful passion and frowardness dead; patience is impatience slain.

The Spirit excites and stirs up the soul against sin, sets it a praying against it; the Spirit of grace is a Spirit of supplication, fetches down hail-stones and thunder-bolts from heaven to destroy these Amorites; sets a watch against it, presses the soul to deal wisely with it to keep it low, by cutting off all provision from the flesh, restraining and keeping it

short of all those fleshly objects, which would keep
it in heart, and so it is starved to death.   It is true,
our own greatest wisdom, watchfulness, abstinence,
self-denial, and all external means alone, will fall short
of killing one lust; it is the Spirit who killeth,
without it the flesh profiteth nothing.   All external
attempts for the mortification of the flesh, are but a
fleshly mortification.   But if ye, through the Spirit,
do mortify the flesh, pray in the Spirit, watch in the
Spirit, curb and keep short and keep under this body,
still taking in the assistance of the Spirit, then it
shall die.

Christian, thou livest in a weary land, and thou
hast but a weary life of it, briers and thorns are with
thee, the Canaanite is yet in the land, thou
sojournest in Mesech, and hast thine habitation in
the tents of Kedar; and thou hast a Mesech and
Kedar within thee; thou hast armies within thee of
fleshly lusts which fight against thy soul.   Thou
goest mourning daily, because of the oppressor,
those spiritual wickednesses which lie in thine heart,
and war in thy members.   Thou often groanest
and criest out to thy God, " Liberty, liberty; redemption, redemption.   Oh this proud heart! Oh
this vain heart! Oh this earthliness! Oh this flesh-
liness, this slothfulness, this enmity and rebellion
against the law of my mind, and my God! When I
would do good, evil is present with me.   I cannot,
I cannot do the things that I would.   I can with no
peace serve or enjoy my God and my soul: my
duties are either prevented or polluted, my comforts
are either wasted or made quite to vanish and disappear.   When I would serve my God, I must away
to serving my belly, or my back, or my friends;
when my soul is a little gotten upon the wing, and

soaring in the upper region, it is presently checked, pulled down again to the earth. Oh .my pinioned, imprisoned soul! Wo is me, wretched man that I am, who shall deliver me from the body of this death?" Why, yet comfort thine heart, the enemy flies upon thee as a flood, but the Spirit of the Lord shall lift up a standard against him. Thou complainest thy gold is become dross, thy wine is mixed with water, yea with mud and dirt, yet he will turn his hand upon thee, and purely purge away thy dross, and take away all thy tin. Though these briers and thorns be set in battle against thee, yea, and against him also, yet he will " go through them, he will burn them together," Isa. xxvii. 4. Thou complainest that thy garments are defiled, thy glory is stained, thy beauty is marred, the image of thy God is so defaced, that there is but here and there a spot of it left upon thee. Thou art black but not comely; while thy Lord says, " Thou art all fair, O my love ;" thou cryest out, " I am all foul, O my Lord:" thou wouldst be holiness to thy Lord, but thou art an offence to him ; holiness is still thy love, and thy desire, and thy longing, but it flies from thee ; it is rather thy wish than thy hope ; thou canst weep over, but thou canst not weep out thy deformity; thine iniquity is still marked before the Lord. If there be a little grace in thee, yet there is such a weakness in its sinews, such a paleness in its face, that it is not like to live ; or if it live, Oh! how little hope that ever it should thrive or flourish. Thus thou complainest, thus thou goest mourning, and sighing, and sinking, and fainting in thy mind, and now and then venturest out a desponding prayer : " Lord, pity ; Lord, look upon my sorrow, and my sin ; Lord, wash me

Lord, help me." Why, the Lord God hath sent thee his help out of his sanctuary, and his strength out of Zion. The eternal Spirit is come down on purpose to give battle to the flesh, to subdue thine iniquities, and bring all those that rise up within thee, under thy feet. Thou mistakest thyself and thine enemies, if thou thinkest they will be conquered by one blow of thine arm, this kind goeth not out so; not by might nor by power, much less by weakness and by flesh, by any weak attempts of thine own, but by my Spirit, saith the Lord. It is work for a God to relieve and cleanse such a heart, to turn such a hell into a heaven. What thou canst not do, being weak through the flesh, behold! he comes down to do it for thee; thou hast proved thine own weakness, now try everlasting strength; He stands at the door and knocks, hear his voice at the door; "Wilt thou be made clean? Wilt thou be made whole? Wilt thou be delivered?" Open to him, and with him deliverance comes in, he stands at the pool, stirring the waters for thee; put in thy cripple-soul, and be healed of all thy diseases; say to him, " Lord, if thou wilt, thou canst make me clean ;" and thou shalt soon have this answer, " I will, be thou clean."

III. As a Spirit of truth and direction, John xvi. 13. He shall guide them by his counsel, he shall lead them in the way that they shall go. " They shall hear a word behind them, saying, This is the way, walk ye in it, when they are turning to the right hand, or to the left," Isa. xxx. 21. He shall lead them into all truth, to prevent mistakes; and into all righteousness, to prevent miscarriages. Nay more, he shall not be only their star, but their strength too; he shall guide them on and help them

on, they shall be led by the Spirit, bound in the
Spirit, pressed in Spirit; they shall be excited,
assisted, carried on in the power of the Spirit, in
the way that they should go; he will cause them to
walk in the statutes of the Lord. Whatsoever thy
waywardness and thy wanderings have been, whatever thy feebleness and fickleness be, whatever false
lights and false ways are before thee, whatever temptations thou meetest with to turn thee aside out of
the right way, whatever doubts hence arise in thine
heart, " I shall one day or other perish from the way,
and be a lost sheep at last;" yet his conduct shall be
prosperous, and the event shall be sure; he shall
so guide thee by his counsel, that he shall bring thee
to glory. He shall gather his lambs with his arm
and carry them in his bosom, and gently lead those
that are with young.

IV. As a Spirit of comfort and consolation; he is
so called, John xvi. 7. The Comforter; " If I go
not away the Comforter will not come unto you;
but if I depart, I will send him unto you." He
shall come unto them, and abide with them, to supply the absence of their Redeemer, to support them
under their affliction, to witness their adoption, to
seal them up unto the day of redemption, and to be
the earnest of their inheritance, Eph. i. 13, 14.

" He shall take of mine, and show it unto you,"
John xvi. 14. " He shall take of mine," that is, not
only of the truths, those treasures of wisdom that are
in me, though that be specially intended, but of my
love, my righteousness, my holiness, and all those
treasures of grace and mercy that are laid up in me;
whatever there is in me, that may stand you in any
stead, yield you any relief or support, the Comforter
which I will send you, shall bring it down to you;

he shall take my blood, and the pardons it hath purchased for you; my compassions that are working in me towards you; my prayers and intercessions I am offering up for you; he shall take of all those treasures of grace, and everlasting consolations which are laid up for you with me: he shall take of mine, and show it unto you. As much as you have in the world to afflict and amaze you, as little as you have of your own to comfort you, either in your hearts, or in your houses, or among your friends, he shall show what I have for you to refresh you.

O christians, a sight of Christ in our sorrows, in our fears, in our thickest darkness, what day-light would it bring in! When thou lookest into thine heart, and art astonished and confounded at what thou findest there, at the blindness and the hardness, the poverty and the emptiness, the guilt and the guile, the pride and the peevishness, the evil thoughts, the vile affections, the filthy lusts, that are swarming and working in thee; when thou lookest into the world, and tremblest at what thou beholdest there; the malice, the craft, the power, that is engaged against thee; the furious spirits, the fiery tongues, the fierce looks, the violent hands, that are flying upon thee, and the little relief the earth will afford thee, when thy heart faints and dies within thee, at the sense of this thy woful and forlorn state; a sight of what thou hast in thy Lord presented to thee by his Spirit; look thee here, soul, what thy Jesus hath sent thee down, a glance from his eye, a drop from his heart, a mess from his table; and all to tell thee, Yet do I not forget thee; behold the care I take of thee, the treasures I have for thee, to encourage thy love, and reward thy faithfulness.

Oh! how will this make all thy darkness to depart, and turn the shadow of death into the morning?

Thus is the Holy Spirit given to the saints, to be the light of their eyes, the death of their sins, the guide of their ways, the stay of their hearts; to uphold their grace, and to maintain their peace; to subdue their enemies or their fears; to secure them from temptations, or succour them when tempted; to wipe off their reproach, or make it their crown; to heal their diseases, or make them their cure; to help their infirmities, to work their works, to make their yoke easy, and their burdens light; to turn their sighs into songs, to form their groans into prayers, to send them up to their Lord, and bring down their returns; to comfort their hearts, to establish, strengthen, settle them, that they be neither offended at the chain, nor moved from the hope of the gospel.

Ch. IV—*The Earth in the Covenant*

God hath put the earth into the covenant. Though the saints have not their reward in this life, their portion in this world, yet this world also is theirs, " The meek shall inherit the earth," Matt. v. 5. " Things present, and things to come, all are yours," 1 Cor. iii. 22.

I. The good things present.

II. The evil things present.

I. The good things present, " Houses and brethren, and sisters, and mothers, and children, and lands, now in this time," Mark x. 30. " Length of days are in her right hand, and in her left hand riches and honour," Prov. iii. 16. Houses, and lands, and riches, and honours, where are they?

Who are the poor of this world, the houseless, harbourless, and friendless? Who have wo, and want, and shame, and sorrow? Who are strangers and pilgrims, dwelling in tents, driven into corners, into dens, and caves, hunted up and down upon the mountains of the earth? To whom is hunger and thirst, cold and nakedness, but to the meek of the earth? Is this to inherit the earth? All theirs, when nothing theirs? yet they do inherit the earth. For:

1. They shall ever have as much as will suffice them, and that is as much as all. They shall not want any thing, but what they may want, " your Father knoweth that you have need of these things;" and he knows how much they need. More than needs, is more than enough; and more than enough is a prejudice. Many men have too much; too much money, too much esteem, too many friends; more than they can bear; so much as to sink them, and drown them in perdition and destruction.

Christians shall have enough; they shall never be in such a needy state, but whatever is necessary for them in all the earth they shall have it. " The earth is the Lord's, and the fulness thereof;" and he hath said, that those that seek him shall not want any thing that is good, Psa. xxxiv. 10. If the whole world can supply them out of all its store they shall be supplied.

2. What they have, they have a better and further title to, than any others in the world. Though the dominion be not founded in grace, yet, by grace, it is established. What they have descends upon them not barely by providence, but by promise, Heb. i. 2. Christ is heir of all things, and they are fellow-heirs with Christ. A little coming from the

promise hath more in it than the greatest abundance that is only handed down by common providence; that which comes in from the promise, comes in with a blessing; if thou hast but a handful, thou hast a blessing in thy hand; if thou hast but a corner, thou hast a blessing in thy corner. A little from love is a great blessing. Thou hast God in every morsel thou eatest, and in every drop that thou drinkest; a drop from heaven will turn thy bran into the finest flour, and thy water into wine.

Oh what serene and quiet lives, how void of care, distracting care, might the saints live in the world! What are the burdens that do gall our backs? what are the briers that tear our flesh? what are the thorns that pierce through our hearts ordinarily, but the cares of this life? What shall I eat? what shall I drink? wherewith shall I be clothed? where shall I dwell? how little have I for to-day? what for to-morrow? what for hereafter? how shall I secure what I have? when this is gone, whence shall I be supplied? Thus do we go on, piercing ourselves through with many sorrows. Our cares for supply eat up what we have; our thoughts cut deeper than our wants; we cannot at so cheap a rate fear, as we often bear the want of all things.

And why take ye thought? "The earth is the Lord's, and the fulness thereof;" and he hath said, "All this is yours, you shall want nothing." You have not only your providence to live upon; you have also the promise before you, and this hath all things in it; all is yours. What for to-morrow? what for hereafter? Why, what saith the promise? "Thou shalt want nothing, neither thou nor thine. Never saw I the righteous forsaken, nor their seed begging their bread."

Hast thou two worlds made sure to thee, and canst thou want? thou mayest as well whine, and make a pitiful cry at a full table, O where shall I have my next morsel? as under such a full promise, O where shall I have my next meal? Oh how much beneath the spirit of christianity are the carking anxious lives of too many christians, you do not believe, you do not believe; you talk of your covenant-right, of your part in the promise, of living by faith; but where is any such thing? Can you trust God for your souls, and can you not trust him for your bodies, for your children? Believe, and you will make as much, and be satisfied as well, with a penny in the promise, with a meal in the promise, with house in the promise, as with a penny in your purse, or a meal in your cupboard.

What dost thou get by all thy cares? "Which of you by taking thought can add one cubit to his stature?" one farthing to his store? If thou lose nothing by them, thou mayest surely put all thy gains into thine eyes; tears and trouble are all they will add to thee. Be quiet, and nothing will ail thee; let not any straits sting thee before they are; want not before thou wantest; let not the winter's frost nip thee, while it is yet summer.

Know when thou art well, and be content. All is thine; if thou inheritest thy God, thou inheritest the earth, nothing of all its store shall be kept back from thee, that is necessary for thee; only thou must not look to be thine own carver; thy God will carve out what thou needest. Let enough suffice thee, and thou shalt never have too little. Thou shalt never have so little, but thou mayest say, this little is enough.

What if what thou wantest in water, be made up

in wine? If thou hast but little in bran, but the more in flour? A short meal with a smile from Heaven, thou mayest count no fast, but a feast; a little oil in the cruse, how far will it go with a smile, the blessing of the covenant? If the upper spring run freely, thou mayest abate a nether spring.

Let my beloved comfort me with his apples, and stay me with his flagons; and let the rest be as little and as coarse as it will. Let the promise be my portion, let the pipes be kept open to my soul, and then the least pittance for this carcass shall suffice me. O, my Lord, let me feed with thee, and I will not quarrel whatever my fare be. Let my portion be from thy table, and then be it much or little,—let me hear thy voice, " I am thine, and with me all things ;" and I am content to be at thy allowance. Let thy deed of gift stand sure to me, put in my children's names there, and I ask no more for myself or them. Hold thy peace, keep silence, O my anxious soul, know when thou art well; be in nothing careful, the Lord is at hand.

II. The evil things of this earth are theirs. The cross is in the covenant. " If his children forsake my law, and walk not in my judgments ; if they break my statutes, and keep not my commandments ; then will I visit their transgressions with a rod, and their iniquity with stripes," Psa. lxxxix. 30—34.

1. The covenant hath its cross. The doctrine of the gospel is the doctrine of the cross, the preaching of the gospel is the preaching of the cross, 1 Cor. i. The mysteries of a crucified Jesus, and of his crucified saints, do fill up the whole New Testament. The cross is not only imposed upon the saints as their burden, but bequeathed unto them as a legacy. It is given unto them as an honour and a privilege.

" Unto you it is given in the behalf of Christ, not only to believe on him, but also to suffer for his sake." Phil. i. 29.   It is joined with the most glorious gift, the gift of faith.   Yea, and it is a greater gift than this.   To suffer in faith is more than barely to believe.

2. By virtue of the covenant the cross is a blessing.   The word is now changed ; it is no longer cursed, but blessed is every one that hangeth on this tree.   " Blessed are they which are persecuted for righteousness' sake ; blessed are ye when men shall revile you, and persecute you, and shall say all manner of evil against you falsely for my sake," Matt. v. 10, 11.   Why, where is the blessedness ? or wherein stands it ?   It stands in these things :

(1.) In the separation of the cross from the curse.

(2.) In the sanctification of the cross to its ends.

(3.) In the proportioning of the cross to their needs and strength.

(4.) In the special comforts of the cross.

(1.) The cross is separated from the curse.   There is something in this.   To be able to say under the sorest of afflictions, This scourge is no scorpion ; this is no curse, it is but a cross.   Our Lord bare both the cross and the curse together, and that made his cup so bitter ; but now he hath divided them ; the curse he hath left upon sinners, and laid only the naked cross on his saints.   The crosses of reprobate sinners are all curses.   Every affliction is a curse ; there is wrath in all their sufferings, there is venom upon every arrow, there is vengeance in every dart, every rod is a serpent to them.   Thou who art of the number of Christ's implacable enemies, when he comes to fall upon thee, and to grind thee under

his hand, thou wouldest have a word of comfort to
be spoken to thee in thy sorrow! no, no, there is no
comfort can be spoken; thou mayest say of every
dart he smites thee with, This is sent of God, to revenge himself upon me. The crosses of the impe-
nitent are all curses; but the saints' curses are all
come to be but crosses. Though men curse, the
Lord will not curse; whatever troubles come upon
thee, though there be vinegar in them, yet there is
no venom in them; though there be anguish in
them, yet there is no wrath in them; though they
be ill-looked, yet there is no ill-will in them; they
come upon no ill intent, nor shall have any evil
issue. The smitings of the wicked are to thee as the
smitings of the righteous were to the psalmist, a
precious balm. "Let the righteous smite me, it
shall be a kindness, it shall be an excellent oil; it
shall not break mine head," Psa. cxli. 5. And thou
mayest say, Let the wicked smite me; smite me with
the tongue, with the fist of wickedness, or what they
will, it shall not break mine head, much less mine
heart; it shall be a kindness to me, an excellent
oil.

(2.) The cross is sanctified to its ends. It hath
many holy and excellent ends, and it shall prosper;
it shall accomplish its ends. The cross is laid on
the saints, sometimes to prove them, sometimes to
reprove them; to humble them, to purge them, &c.
and whatever it is sent to them for, it shall not
return in vain. "As the word, so the rod, shall
accomplish that for which he pleases that sent it.
By this the iniquity of Jacob shall be purged."

(3.) The cross is proportioned to their needs and
strength. "I will correct thee in measure, but
I will not leave thee altogether unpunished,"

Jer. xxx. 11. Just so much as will serve shall suffice;
the wise physician hath respect both to the need,
and to the strength of the patient. " I will not contend for ever, neither will I be always wroth ; lest
the spirit should fail before me, and the souls which I
have made," Isa. lvii. 16. The apostle tells the
saints, Heb. x. 36. that they have need of patience ;
and their experience tells them, they have need of
something to exercise their patience. And their
needs are different; some are knotty pieces, and
need more ; others are tender, and upon them less
will serve. The stubborn child must have more
stripes ; the shaking of the rod will do more on
some spirits than the smart of it on others ; but all
need something. Let him only that is without sin,
say, I have no need of shame and sorrow. The
Lord will neither over, nor under do ; every one
shall have his load, and no more ; no more than
they can bear, and no less than their need requires.
The Lord delights not in his children's tears, he
doth not afflict willingly, nor grieve the children of
men ; but yet he had rather they cry than perish.
Wonder not, christians, that your tender Lord puts
you to pain, and that your pains are so sharp and
so many ; " Your heavenly Father knoweth that
you have need of all these things." It is a mercy
that he will chastise ; you may put your corrections
among your mercies. His breakings of you are his
blessings, his woundings are your cures ; and by
your own, as by your Lord's stripes, you are healed.
And when you shall review, and read over all his
darker providences, and behold the wisdom and
tenderness which is attempered with his severities,
evidenced in his laying on so much, and yet no more
than was needful, you will then write down with the

psalmist, "Thou in very faithfulness hast afflicted me."

O my Lord, let me not want thy staff nor thy rod; neither a friend nor an enemy; neither a calm nor a storm; neither food nor medicine: if my disease be too strong for my physic, let me have yet a stronger potion; if my wanton heart will not yet be tamed, put on more fetters, a heavier load; load upon load, weight upon weight, and till thou seest, let me never say it is enough. Let me never be sick of my remedy till I be cured of my disease. Let me rather suffer by the hand of a devil, than perish by the hand of a lust. Spare not, Lord, cease not, Lord, to smite thy servant, till thou hast thereby smitten down all mine enemies. Peace, plenty, ease; what! that I may have to spend upon my lusts! to wax wanton against my God! Such peace I will not have.

Pain, trouble, want, any thing rather than peace, upon such terms. Correct me, O Lord, yet in judgment, but not in thy fury, lest I be consumed and brought to nothing.

(4.) The cross hath its special comforts. " Blessed be God, even the Father of our Lord Jesus Christ, the Father of mercies, and the God of all comfort; who comforteth us in all our tribulation, that we may be able to comfort them which are in any trouble by the comfort wherewith we ourselves are comforted of God. For as the sufferings of Christ abound in us, so our consolation also aboundeth by Christ. And whether we be afflicted, it is for your consolation and salvation, which is effectual in the enduring of the same sufferings, which we also suffer; or whether we be comforted, it is for your consolation and salvation: and our hope of you is stedfast; knowing that as ye are partakers of the sufferings, so shall ye be also of the consolation," 2 Cor. i. 3—7.

The comforts of the cross are often the sweetest and the fullest that the saints ever taste on this side the crown. The first draught is often bitter: the green cross is heavy, and it is necessary it should be so. As it is with some medicinal waters, it works by its weight; it must be a heavy yoke that will tame an unruly neck; if it gall not, it will not heal; it is the smart of the rod that stills the child. Think not your burdens will lie easy, when first laid on, and think not much if they do not. The first conflict with temptations may put you to a harder brunt than you are aware. It must be so, that it may be for your good afterward. So my physic will work, I am content it make me sick. Tribulation worketh patience; that it cannot do unless it pains. It is observable that it is not said, that the cross worketh patience, but the tribulation, the pinching of the cross, or the pain the cross puts us to; this is patience, a quiet bearing that pain which the flesh when touched puts us to. When we feel the thorns and the nails, when the iron enters into our souls, when it pricks and smarts, then it will work. The green cross is heavy; a prison or a wilderness will look uncouth at the first, but when your Lord comes in and visits you, then the sweet, the pleasure comes: and the more frowns at the threshold, the more kisses you may expect afterwards. Christ doth not always meet his saints in the porch; the devil's parlour, the inner prison is his banqueting house, the dungeon his wine-cellar; there they drink and are satisfied. The stocks and the rack are the organs that make them the sweetest music. Many a saint hath been sadly disappointed at the first, hoping to meet with Christ at the door; but behold! a dreadful sight; behold! sin lieth at the door; all his sins, all that ever he did against Christ, all his unthankfulness, unfaithfulness, unkindness, rebellion against his Lord, stand forth and stare him in the face. Christians, beware of sin now; it will meet you in the day of adversity, the cross will tell you all that ever you did. I remember my faults this day: now I remember all my pleasant things; my sabbaths, my ordinances, my liberty, the dear society I once enjoyed, but trifled and wasted away. Oh my pride and my wantonness, my idleness, my earthliness, my hypocrisy, wherefore are you come thus to affright and torment me? Lord, whither am I come? Oh how dreadful is this place! Is this my prison-entertainment? Are these my prison-comforts? Oh what a hard lodging am I like to have with such companions! Oh the wormwood and the gall! a dark habitation, a bitter cup indeed is now given unto me. Is this the comfort of the cross? Are these the sweets so much talked of? Yet be not dismayed, as roughly as thou art handled at the door, it is better within; the devil is going out in this storm; thy sins meet thee now, but it is only to shake hands and part; after this agony, expect the angels to come and minister to thee. Complain not if thou yet find no sweet, thou hast not drank deep enough; the next draught the sugar may come; in the next room thou mayest meet thy Lord, and then tell me, if it be short of all that hath been told thee.

But shall I give you a more particular view of some of the special comforts of the cross, or our sufferings for Christ? I shall only first premise a word, to let you understand what I mean by the sufferings of Christ. We then suffer for Christ, when we suffer for Christ's cause; when we suffer because we will be christians, we will be holy and righteous; when we suffer because we will not sin; and when we suffer upon Christ's call, when he cuts out a cross for us, and lays it on. Then Christ calls us to suffering, when he puts us to this choice, either to suffer or to sin; when our backs or our consciences must suffer; when we must suffer, or he must suffer by us. " If any man will be my disciple, let him take up his cross." Christ is not, and christians must not be prodigal of their blood; their blood is his; their estates, their names, their liberties, are all his, and to him they must be accountable how they part with them. It is not every cross that thou canst call " thy" cross; we must not leave our way to seek a cross: when Christ hath laid a cross athwart a christian's way that he should go, and he must either make a stand, or turn aside, or submit his neck to it; then he says, There is thy cross, take it up and get thee gone. Whatever cross be before thee, if thou hast a way open to avoid it without sin; that is none of thy cross, thou mayest not take it up, or if thou dost, thou wilt have no thanks for thy pains.

Christians should be wary here. Though it be an argument of a gracious spirit, to be always of a ready and forward mind to suffer for Christ; and when he demands, Who will go with me? who will bear my cross? cheerfully to answer, I will go, Lord, let me bear it; yet should we take heed, that as we hang not back, when he says, Go, so that we run not before he send us. Though it be a high honour to suffer for the gospel, yet no man taketh this honour upon himself, but he that is called of God. I would not go to a prison without a mittimus from Heaven, lest, if my suffering be of myself, I be there left to shift for myself. If Christ should meet me in prison or in banishment, and demand of me, "What dost thou here, Elijah? Friend, how camest thou in hither?" What should I say, if I could not say this, Thou, Lord, hast brought me hither? my conscience, my duty hath brought me in?

But understand me here with this caution, that when the cause for the main is Christ's, but the call seems doubtful; yet when the sufferer hath carefully inquired the mind of God, truly follows the dictates of conscience, sincerely designs the honour of Christ and his gospel, although he should err in some circumstances of his case, and for fear of iniquity should choose affliction, when possibly he might have avoided both; God will surely wink at his mistakes, own his sufferings, and greatly accept and reward his readiness of mind.

Yet still take heed of careless or wilful errors: take heed of preparing nails for thine own cross; thorns, scourges, spears for thine own head or heart. Take heed both how thou shunnest, and how thou espousest a suffering state.

Go not in upon heedless mistakes; go not in for good company, much less upon any carnal designs; let not thy pride, or ostentation, or the bias of any fleshly respects, lead thee into the house of correction, lest thou find them the rods to lash thee when thou art there.

Christians consider, if there be not sometimes some uncomfortable miscarriages in this matter; and whether it hath not been the lot of some of

Christ's (with how much justice or charity let the
Lord be judge) to be censured and reproached as
unfaithful or as fearful on no other account but
for walking by this rule : not to go to prison without
a warrant, that is, not to cast themselves into a suffering state, whilst God hath left a way open to
escape, without sin.   I confess the more dangerous
and the more ordinary error is on the other hand ;
we are more apt (especially when afflictions are
more sharp and bite in earnest, and then will be
the great trial) rather sinfully to shift ourselves of
them, than unwarrantably to run ourselves upon
them ; but yet let it be considered, whether here be
not an error on this hand also.

It is true, where the cause is the same as to the
main, different circumstances may make that to be
one man's sin, which is another man's duty ; yea,
that may be a duty to the same man at one time,
which, supposing him in different circumstances,
might have been his sin at another.   And it is not
seldom, through the unavoidable difference of our
apprehensions, and the difficulty of discerning our
cases, that christians equally careful to know and
do the will of God, when the case and the circumstances also are mostly the same, do judge differ-
ently about their call to suffering.   Here let no man
be so tyrannical to others, as to expect that they
should go cross to their own, to comply with their
brethren's judgments and consciences.   Let us not
put one another on this unmerciful necessity, either
to break our peace with God, or our friends.   Let it
be sufficient to us, faithfully to follow our own light,
without judging or quarrelling with those who are
otherwise minded.   Beware of bitterness.   Be not
cruel to consciences ; smite not with the tongue,

nor let an evil thought arise in thine heart, upon any such account as this. Thine arrows will recoil and fly back in thine own face. Blemish not thine own sufferings by blasting thy brother's liberty. Let not the wariness of some be condemned for cowardice, nor the forwardness of others for pride or hypocrisy; but let us be clothed with humility, let us put on a spirit of self-suspicion and charity to our brethren; and let this christian frame be the more studiously maintained, by how much the more our differing practices, according to the variety of our apprehensions, seem to condemn each other, and so provoke to uncomfortable schisms and contentions; and by how much the more pernicious such schisms are likely to prove in the issue.

These things premised, I shall now show you what the special comforts of the cross are. You may expect your suffering state to be sweetened with,

[1.] A more plentiful diffusion of special grace. Grace is a comfort; it is never better with the saints than when that flourishes. The joy of the harvest is howling to the joy of grace; he is not a christian that cannot say, It is summer, when these flowers appear in their beauty. Flourishing faith and love have their glorious joys, 1 Pet. i. 8. The springs of grace are a resurrection from the dead; and there is no such spring as after a shower. Oh how green do the herbs then look! the withering flowers do then lift up the head; never so many stars appear, nor with such lustre as in a frosty night; grind the spices, and their fragrancy flows out. Saints are never more saints than in the house of bondage, or the land of their pilgrimage; our winter-weather makes us warm at heart. " As our outward man perishes, our inward man is renewed

day by day," 2 Cor. iv. 16.   Persecution is the
time of life.   "We are delivered to death for Jesus'
sake, that the life also of Jesus might be manifest in
our mortal flesh," 2 Cor. iv. 11.   Decayed soul,
comfort thine heart, the cross comes; now thou
shalt live, now thou shalt recover.   This weakness
will strengthen the things that remain, and are ready
to die.   Now faith, and love, and patience, and
courage, that have so long hung the wing, lift up
the head, the day of your redemption draweth nigh;
this night is your day of hope.

[2.] A more clear revelation of special love.
Lovest thou me, Lord? there is enough.   Let me
hear thy voice, let me see thy face.   Kiss me with
the kisses of thy mouth.   Thy loving-kindness
is better than life; send forth thy light and thy
truth, let these tell me, thou lovest me.   Thy love-
sick spouse is sick for love; O when wilt thou
say, "Thou knowest that I love thee?"   Why,
come up with me on the cross, that withered tree
bears more blossoms of love, than all the green trees
of the field.   The whole gospel is hung upon the
cross.   Where our Lord hung, there is sin nailed,
the curse vacated, death vanquished; pardon, peace,
joy, glory, showed forth in open sight.   There is
love with all its tokens, go up and take.   Fear not
to be baptized with thy Lord's baptism, nor to drink
of his cup; this cup also is the communion of the
blood of Christ.   Come with me into the wilderness,
there will I speak comfortably to thee.   When thou
most wantest it, where thou wilt most value it,
there will I show thee my loves.

Our Lord loves not to have love slighted; the
full soul loathes the honeycomb; thou hast yet too
many lovers to bid thy Lord welcome; he keeps his

best wine till all thine own be soured; then it will relish, and then thou shalt have it. His oil is for thy wounds. The child never knows so much of the parents' hearts and compassions as when it is sick, or in distress; then every look is love, every word is pity and compassion. O the compassion of Christ's heart towards his afflicted children! when thou knowest hatred, then look to know love. When thou art persecuted, when thou art cast out, and trodden under foot of men, then will he take thee in and cherish thee.

[3.] A more full manifestation of glory. There is not a prison into which the saints are cast, but hath a window in the palace. Calvary becomes a Tabor, where they have a sight of their Lord in his glory. Golgotha becomes a Pisgah, where they may look over Joidan into the land of promise. Hast thou known little of heaven? thou hast not yet been in the deep.

Of Stephen, the first gospel-martyr, it is said, "He looked up stedfastly into heaven, and saw the glory of God, and Jesus standing at the right hand of God," Acts vii. 55. And, "All that sat in the council, saw his face as it had been the face of an angel," chap. vi. 15. Such an admirable splendour and serenity in his countenance, as spake him rather an angel than a man. Oh what a heaven was there within that cast out such a divine lustre on his face! his joy was too big for his heart, his face must have its share; yea, his very adversaries, at second hand, behold the glory of God.

He looked up and saw heaven opened. Looking down, he might see hell opened, all his tormentors about him; the jaws of death ready to devour and swallow him up: but looking up, he saw heaven

opened, and Jesus standing at the right hand of
God. Oh there he is, for whose sake is all this.
My beloved, my beloved is yonder. Behold the
region of light, whither this dark tempest is wafting
me; his hell and his heaven meet, but the light
swallows up the dark. Hell ceases to be hell, where
heaven appears to be heaven. This is the portion
of suffering saints. When you read what is written
of those armies of martyrs that have gone before;
of their unspeakable joys, their undaunted courage,
their admirable boldness; of their cheering their
friends, confounding their foes, their rejoicing in
their stripes, singing in their stocks, leaping in their
chains, boasting of their bonds, kissing their stakes,
embracing the flames, riding up in triumph in their
chariots of fire, not repenting of their faith, nor
accepting of deliverance ;—what doth this speak, but
that their eyes, as well as their anchor, are within
the vail, whither Christ their fore-runner is gone
before them? Oh who would not be with them?
Who would fear sufferings?

Soul, what art thou afraid of? whither art thou
running? from what art thou hiding thyself? what is
thine ease, or thy liberty, or thy quiet? why so loth
to loose from this shore? launch forth into the
deep. Fear not transportation into thy house of
bondage; when thou art once there, it is but look
up and thou art in Paradise.

Such are the sufferings of Christ, this is the cross
of the covenant.

[4.] In sum; as that which comprehends all the
rest, a more manifest exhibition of Christ's special
presence, " I am with thee to save thee," Jer. xxx.
11. " When thou passest through the waters, I
will be with thee, and through the rivers, they shall

not overflow thee; when thou walkest through the
fire, thou shalt not be burnt, neither shall the flame
kindle upon thee," Isa. xliii. 2. Through fire and
water thou must go; (" we went through fire and
water into a wealthy place;") but wherever thou
goest, he will go with thee. When the bush was
on fire, the Lord was in the bush; when the three
children were in the furnace, the Son of God was
there with them. " In all their afflictions he was
afflicted, he saved them by the angel of his presence;
in his love and his pity, he redeemed them, and he
bare them, and carried them all the days of old,"
Isa. lxiii. 9. Though all men forsook me, the Lord
stood with me, and strengthened me, 2 Tim. iv. 16,
17. The saints shall never have this to charge
upon the Lord; " I was in prison, and thou visit-
edst me not."

He is ever with them; to bear their burdens, and
ease their shoulders; to plead their cause, and maintain their innocence; to wash their stripes, to wipe
off their tears, to heal their wounds, to bind up their
broken bones, to revive their weary spirits, to perfume their prisons, to lighten their dungeons, to
lead them in their wanderings, to converse with
them in their solitudes, to give down from above,
in divine smiles, in illapses of spiritual joys, assur-
ances of dearest love, tenderest care, melting sympathy, gracious acceptance, to give down from above
whatever is wanting beneath. In fine, to preserve
them from falling by the presence of his grace, till
he present them faultless before the presence of his
glory. Oh it is good being with Christ any where.

Tell me, O thou whom my soul loveth, where
thou feedest and causest thy flocks to rest at noon.
Where thou feedest? yea, where thou art, whether

feeding or fasting, whether rejoicing or mourning;
where thou causest thy flocks to rest at noon; yea,
and where thou sufferest thy flocks to be scattered
in the night. Where thy flocks are, thou art not
far away; tell me where thou feedest, tell me where
thou art.   My beloved that feedeth among the
lilies, feedeth sometimes among the thorns.   When
his love is a lily among thorns, there he feedeth.
He feedeth among thorns; he feedeth with his sheep,
ne feedeth with his lambs wherever they feed; when
darkness, and desolation, and devils, and death feed
upon them, even then he feedeth them, and takes
his feeding with them.

Oh wherever my Lord is, there let my lot fall.
Let me dwell amongst the thorns, so my dwelling
be with my Lord amongst the lilies.   Let me
wander amongst the mountains, whilst he is with me
telling all my wanderings.   Let me be scourged, so
he will wash my stripes; let me weep, so he will
wipe off my tears; I would not want wounds, whilst
I have such oil to pour in.   Come all ye thieves
and robbers, I fear you not, my dear Samaritan
comes by; come ye bulls of Bashan, ye boars of
the forest, let my Beloved kiss me with the kisses
of his mouth, and I regard it not, though you kick
me with the heel. O my Lord, bring me where thou
feedest, let me live in thy face, let me feel thy smiles
upon my heart, let me love thee, tell me thou lovest
me, rememberest, pitiest, acceptest, takest care for
me, and then choose my condition, my dwelling, and
entertainment for me.

Fainting christian, lift up thine eyes, comfort
thine heart; here is that thou fearest and tormentest
thyself withal. Here is the inside of that formidable
cross, the light side of those dark clouds, the sunny

side of that shady thorny hedge that so wounds
and afflicts thine heart. Fear not, be strong and
of a good courage. Thou still sayest, Woe is me,
I can find no such thing. Ah, Lord God, doth he
not speak parables? O that I were assured it might
be thus with me. Why art thou in covenant?
Believe, and all is thine. I believe, and therefore
have I spoken; believe, and thou shalt see the salvation of God; as sure as the cross is thine, all the
comforts of the cross are settled upon thee. Read
over all the gracious words thou hast before thine
eyes; view over all the instances of suffering saints
that have gone before thee, on whom these good
words have been made good; in conspicuous in-
creases of divine grace, in the signal discoveries of
divine love, in the clearest and fullest revelation of
divine glory, in the intimate sense of the divine
presence, quickening, enlarging, encouraging, sup-
porting their spirits in the darkest dens, in the
sharpest conflict, with reproaches, mockings, bonds.
banishments, torments, and deaths; and know that
all these things are written for thy learning, that
thou through patience and comfort of the scriptures
mayest have hope.

Read over Isa. li. "Hearken to me ye that follow after righteousness, ye that seek the Lord, look
unto the rock whence ye are hewn, and to the hole
of the pit whence ye are digged. For the Lord shall
comfort Sion, he will comfort all her waste places;
he will make her wilderness like Eden, and all her
deserts like the garden of the Lord; joy and gladness shall be found therein, thanksgiving and the
voice of melody, lift up your eyes to the heavens,"
&c. "Hearken unto me, ye that know righteousness, the people in whose heart is my law; fear ye

not the reproach of men, neither be ye afraid of
their revilings: for the moth shall eat them up like
a garment, and the worm shall eat them like wool ;
but my righteousness shall be for ever, and my salvation from generation to generation. I, even I,
am he that comforteth you: who art thou, that thou
shouldst be afraid of a man that shall die, and of the
son of man which shall be made as grass ? and forgettest the Lord thy Maker, that hath stretched forth
the heavens, and laid the foundations of the earth ,
and hast feared continually every day because of the
fury of the oppressor, as if he were ready to destroy ?
and where is the fury of the oppressor ?" ver. **7, 8.
12, 13.** " I, even I, am he," &c. " And where is the
fury of the oppressor ?" Where is the fury of the
oppressor ? Where is it not rather ? Is it not in the
house, and in the field ? Is it not in the city, and in
the villages ? Is it not upon my cattle, upon my
purse, upon my body, upon my children, upon my
friends ? Where is not the fury of the oppressor ?
But when thou rememberest the Lord thy Maker,
the oath, the promise, and covenant of God, the presence, protection, and comfort of thy God,—when
thou rememberest this, then, " Where is the fury of
the oppressor ?"

CHAPTER V —*The Angels of Light in the Covenant*

THE angels of light are in the covenant. " Are they
not all ministering spirits, sent forth to minister for
them who shall be heirs of salvation ?" Heb. i. 14.
Whilst our Lord himself was sent down to minister,
behold his servants are to be ministered unto, the
angels are made their ministers, " He shall give
his angels charge over thee, to keep thee in all

thy ways," Psa. xci. 11. they have received a charge, and they have great advantages for the keeping the charge of the Lord.

I. They are mighty. " Bless the Lord ye his angels that excel in strength," Psal. ciii. 20. An angel is more than an army ; what slaughters have the angels made in the armies of the aliens ! A hundred fourscore and five thousand Assyrians are slain by one angel of the Lord, when encamped against Judah, Isa. xxxvii. 36. It is hard service indeed that is too hard for an angel.

II. They are numerous. There are great multitudes of them. " Thousands of angels," Psal. lxviii. 17. " A multitude of the heavenly host," Luke ii. 13. An angel is more than an army ; but what then are an army of angels !

III. They are faithful. They can do much for the saints, but will they do it ? yes, they are faithful ; " They do the commandments of God," Psa ciii. 20. God bids them keep, and they are faithful, they will keep his sheep ; we are taught to pray, that " the will of God may be done on earth, as it is in heaven ;" that men may be faithful as the angels of God.

IV. They are favourites, they behold the face of God, they dwell in his presence, they are admitted to stand before his throne, they can be heard ; they have favour in heaven, and therefore such power on earth. " Take heed ye despise not one of these little ones, for I say unto you, that in heaven their angels do always behold the face of my Father which is in heaven," Matt. xviii. 10. Touch not mine anointed, let alone my little ones, take heed how you offend them, their angels are before my Father, and are mighty with him, to engage his power for their aid and deliverance.

Oh the great security of the least of saints! These mighty ones, these multitudes, these faithful ones, these favourites of heaven, the holy angels of God, have all received a charge from the Lord, to preserve and defend them; " Lord, open their eyes that they may see. Behold the mountains full of chariots and horses of fire round about Elisha," 2 Kings vi. 17.

Should a mighty prince commit any subject of his to a potent and faithful life-guard, with this charge: Look to this man, keep him in safety, see that he come to no harm; whoever offends, do you defend him; wherever he goes, go you with him; wherever he lodges, stand you as a guard about the house; while he sleeps do you watch; see that he want for nothing, nor hurt come to him: if this were thy case, in what great security wouldest thou count thyself? But oh, what is a life-guard of men to a guard of mighty angels! Fear not, little flock, in heaven your angels behold the face of God, and in earth have they pitched their tents round about you.

CHAPTER VI —*The Powers of Darkness delivered over in the Covenant*

THE powers of darkness are delivered over in the covenant; Satan and all his instruments. We are naturally in bondage to Satan, held " captive by him at his will," 2 Tim. ii. 26. His prisoners, his slaves, his vassals. By the blood of the covenant, the Lord hath brought forth his prisoners, and redeemed his captives, Zech. ix. 11. and also hath spoiled principalities and powers, and led captivity captive. In this covenant there is deliverance of the prisoners, and a delivery over of them by whom they were held; a jail-delivery, and a delivery of the jailers too, into their hands; and they are delivered over bound, the god of this world in chains, limited, spoiled, banished, and cast out. "The gates of hell shall not prevail against it," Matt. xvi. 18. The gates of cities were anciently their special strength, and in them were their great councils held, for the contriving and managing of all their concernments. By hell understand the whole infernal corporation, all that belong to that dark region, Satan and all his instruments, the dragon with his armies, the serpent and all his seed. By the gates of hell understand the power and policy, the combination and counsels of Satan and his whole party. These gates of hell shall not prevail against it, that is, against the church; neither against head, nor any member of it; they shall not prevail, that notes two things.

I. They shall fight against it; they are all combined and listed against the church, making a war upon it. Raze it, raze it, even to the foundation thereof. Down with it, root and branch, let it not have a being, let it not have so much as a name under heaven. Particular quarrels there may be betwixt devil and devil; Herod against Pilate, and Pilate against Herod; yet the tails of these smoking fire-brands are united against the Lord and his anointed ones; against their profession, against their religion, against the soul of every saint. Whatever vails or specious pretences they varnish their quarrel with, this is it that lies at the bottom of all their counsels and machinations, wherein all their aims are concentred, to root out godliness, and the professors of it, out of the earth; to deceive and destroy souls for ever.

II. Though they shall fight against them, yet they shall not overcome. They shall not prevail against it; that is, not finally, in the end the victory shall be the saints; Jerusalem shall be " a burdensome stone to all people," Zech. xii. **3**.

1. Such a stone that they shall not be able to lift, or move it out of its place; it shall stand as a rock, against which the impetuous waves may dash themselves, but they cannot move it.

2. They shall not be able to bear it. It shall crush those who burden themselves with it; those who shake the church are pulling a house about their ears, a rock upon their loins; it shall break the backs of all those who contend against it; they shall be cut in pieces (saith the text) that burden themselves with it; though all the earth, yea, and hell too, be gathered together against it. It is a vain design that Satan and his partakers are driving on. " Why do the heathen rage, and the people imagine a vain thing ?" Psa. ii. **1**. It is a vain design, and it is a fatal design to themselves : " Thou shalt break them with a rod of iron, thou shalt dash them in pieces like a potter's vessel."

In the first dawning of this glorious day-light, it is promised that the Seed of the woman shall break the serpent's head. " I will put enmity between thee and the woman, and between thy seed and her seed; it shall bruise thy head, and thou shalt bruise his heel," Gen. iii. **15**. " Now is the judgment of this world, now shall the prince of this world be cast out," John xii. **31**. Cast out, whence ? Why, cast out of his kingdom, out of his hold, cast down from his throne and dominion. His prison is broken, and now the prey is taken from the strong, the captives of the mighty are taken away.

But how was this now done, at the death of Christ, to which these words refer? Doth not Satan still reign? Is he not still the god of this world, and the prince of the power of the air? Yea, what hold hath he yet of the saints that are in the earth! What a tyrant is he to them! how doth he entangle and ensnare them! what havoc doth he make in their conscience! lording it over them, leading them captives by lusts and temptations; what a strong party hath he still within them, bearing arms against their Lord, fighting against their souls! What sad spoil doth he make upon their grace, upon their peace! they cannot rest for him day nor night, abroad nor at home, alone nor in company; he is ever following them; whithersoever they go, the devil is at their backs; they cannot pray, nor read, nor spend a thought, nor cast a look, nor despatch a sigh towards the Lord, but Satan stands by to resist, and hinder them. What a yoke hath he still upon their neck! what clogs and weights hath he still upon their loins! how do they mourn in their souls whilst he vexes them from day to day! how do they groan, and travail in pain, sighing in themselves, and waiting for their redemption! How is it then said, Now is he cast out? Why, now he hath received his judgment? "The prince of this world is judged," John xvi. Now is the fatal blow given, now is the serpent's head broken, though he still may bruise and hang on the saints. The blow he levelled at our Lord hath rebounded on his own head. Though he be as Gad, a serpent in the way, yet you may now tread upon this serpent, and it shall not hurt you. The strong man is now bound; if he be a god still, he is a god in chains, a prince in fetters; he must ask leave of your Father ere he can touch one hair of your heads. He cannot tempt you, nor cast a bank against you, nor shoot an arrow at you, without a commission from Heaven. The devils are subject to you. He is cast out, and in your Lord's name you may cast him out. " In my name shall ye cast out devils ;" out of possessed bodies, out of possessed souls ; you may be instruments to bring many a soul to repentance, that they may recover themselves out of the snares of the devil, who are held captive by him at his will. Every sinner that is converted by you, you have cast out a devil out of that soul.

Though he be an adversary still, yet such an adversary as may be resisted ; " Whom resist stedfast in the faith," 1 Pet. v. 9. And if you will resist, he shall flee from you, James iv. 7. Stand, and your enemy runs.

Nay, more ; he is not only a conquered enemy, but made your servant. This viper shall yield you medicine against his own poison. His smitings shall be an excellent oil ; his messengers he sends to buffet you, his thorns he sticks in your flesh, shall be a prevention of greater evils. The very destruction he intends to bring upon you shall promote your salvation. " Deliver such an one to Satan for the destruction of the flesh, that the spirit may be saved in the day of the Lord Jesus," 1 Cor. v. 5. Behold, the devil is the church's servant, and such a servant as in their present state they cannot well want. The execution of their censures. A commonwealth may as well want a jailer, or a hangman, as the church a devil. Behold Satan divided against Satan ; the devil without, against the devil within ; the destroyer of souls become the destroyer of sin. " Deliver such an one to Satan for the destruction of the flesh." Though much against his mind, his hand is against his own party. He is made to kill his own friends, which otherwise would kill the soul. Whether he will or not, the very tormentor is made a saviour; " that the spirit may be saved in the day of the Lord Jesus." Christians, as much as you feel of the devil's malice, you could ill want his service; there is many a soul lost and undone by a sleeping, that might have been recovered and roused by a raging devil. His winds shall blow off your chaff, his floods shall wash away your filth, his earthquakes shall open your prison-doors, his tempests shall drive you to harbour. Some men want a tempest to save them from a wreck.

Nay, once more; he is not low enough yet; he shall be yet brought lower. You have assurance of his total and final overthrow. " The God of peace shall bruise Satan under your feet shortly," Rom. xvi. 20. " The devil shall be cast into the lake of fire and brimstone," Rev. xx. 10. It is but a little while, and when he hath done his work he shall be sent to his place, where he shall be shut up, and a seal set upon him; whence he shall come out no more for ever. He shall tempt no more, vex no more, deceive no more, destroy no more, torment you no more; he shall be thrust out, he shall be chained up; the tormentor shall be tormented day and night for ever and ever.

Stand, christians, stand your ground a little while; follow your work, hold up your holy profession, hold on your holy course; keep your hearts, keep your garments, keep on your armour, keep under corruption, resist temptation, bear your affliction; hold out faith and patience, fight again your adversaries, watch with your Lord this one hour, and behold, he that shall come, will come; he cometh quickly, and he that is in the world shall be consumed with the breath of his mouth, and destroyed with the brightness of his appearing. He shall be cast out, he shall be cast down, and rise no more for ever.

CHAPTER VII — *Death in the Covenant*

GOD hath put death into the covenant. " Whether Paul, or Apollos, or Cephas, or the world, or life, or death, all are yours," 1 Cor. iii. 21. Death! there is a great purchase, you will say; what advantage is that? Yes, death is advantage. To die is gain. For,

I. The commission of death is changed. It was once, Take him jailer; away with him, carry him down, to prison with him, there to be reserved to the judgment of the great day. It is now, Take him, janitor; take him, porter; take him in, give him an entrance into his master's joy. Death doth but take the bride when she is ready, and lodges her in the chamber of the bridegroom; this made death the apostle's desire; " I desire to depart, and to be with Christ, which is far better," Phil. i. 23.

II. Death is conquered. What does this mean? Your enemy is yours; other than this, your enemy is conquered to you; a conquered enemy is made a tributary; death is disarmed, it hath lost its sting. When a serpent hath lost its sting, you may take it into your bosom.

He that can say, " Death, where is thy sting?" may go on and add, "Thanks be to God, which hath given me the victory." A signet sent from heaven, with a death's head, is a precious token. Come, christians, be of good courage, set your feet on the neck of this king of terrors.

III. Death is at once the destruction of all their enemies. When once death hath done its office upon them, then farewell Edom, and Ammon, and Amalek, and Egypt; farewell the pricking brier and the grieving thorn; then farewell sin and sorrow for ever; the Egyptians they have seen, and feared, and felt to-day, they shall never see again for ever. It destroys itself, their last enemy, by destroying them; it hath its welcome and farewell the same moment; it is but welcome death, and farewell death for ever. Death dies with them; once dead, they die no more for ever; mortality is swallowed up of life, death is cast into the lake of fire; that is its region; there, there they die, and die, and die again: over and over, for ever and ever; but for the saints—it doth but set them on the banks of that good land, whither it cannot follow them. Our Lord by death, by ours as well as his own, hath delivered those who, for fear of death, were all their life-time subject to bondage.

Christians, you may now not only with patience, but with desire, expect the assault of this king of terrors. What! shall tribulation, and persecution, and famine, and nakedness, and peril, and sword; shall sorrows, and fears, and mortality die with me? Yea, shall sin die with me? then welcome death. Lord strengthen me this once, let me die with the Philistines. Would it be good for thee to be with thy Father? in the bosom of thy bridegroom? the presence-chamber of thy Lord and love? would it be a mercy to thee, to weep no more, fear no more, suffer no more, be tempted no more, sin no more; to be unclothed of corruption, and be clothed upon with immortality and incorruption? Then bid death welcome.

Blessed souls, when you come ashore, and see the light, the love, the joy, the rest, the glory, that is on the other side, you will then more fully understand what this meaneth, Death is yours. He knew something, who said, I cannot tell you what sweet pain and delightsome torments are in Christ's love; I often challenge time, that holdeth us asunder; I have for the present a sick life, much pain, and much love-sickness for Christ; O what would I give to have a bed made to my wearied soul in his bosom! O when shall we meet! O how long is it to the dawning of the marriage-day! O sweet Lord Jesus, take wide steps: come over the mountains at one stride. O my beloved, flee as a roe, or a young hart upon the mountains of separation! O if he would fold the heavens together like an old cloak, and shovel time and days out of the way, and come away!

Chapter VIII —*The Kingdom in the Covenant*

God hath put the kingdom into this covenant; "Theirs is the kingdom of heaven," Matt. v. 3. "It is your Father's good pleasure to give you the kingdom," Luke xii. 32. Glorious things are spoken of thee, O thou city of God. I might here enlarge in describing the glory of this kingdom; but when I have said all, I must at last leave it within the vail; and therefore shall only tell you from the apostle, "Eye hath not seen, nor ear heard, neither have entered into the heart of man, the things which God hath prepared for them that love him," &c. 1 Cor. ii. 9. When by the Spirit of wisdom and revelation, the eyes of your understandings are opened, ye shall know "what is the hope of his calling, and what the riches of the glory of his inheritance in the saints," Eph. i. 18.

CHAPTER IX —*All the means of Salvation in the Covenant, hath outward and inward; in special, the blessing of a new heart*

LASTLY, God hath put into the covenant all the means of salvation; and all things on their parts necessary, to the obtaining the everlasting kingdom.

I. All the *outward* means of salvation. Ordinances, word, sacraments, and prayer; officers; prophets, apostles, evangelists, pastors, and teachers, Eph. iv. 11, 12. 1 Cor. iii. 22.

II. All the *inward* means of salvation. Every grace, every duty; their obtaining the one, and performing the other, and perseverance in both, these are all comprehended in the second part of that great promise, " They shall be my people." Which, though it be properly the matter of their own stipulation, yet for this also the Lord himself undertakes.

You shall be my people. Two things are hereby signified :

1. I will account you, and reckon you for mine. You shall have the privilege and the blessing of my people. I will set you apart, and separate you to myself, out of all the tribes and kindreds of the earth ; and will avouch you for my portion and peculiar possession. I will set you as the apple of mine eye, as a seal upon my heart, and upon mine arm.

I will mark you out for the people of my love; of you will I take care, for you will I provide, with you are my delights, over you will I rejoice, with you will I dwell, and you shall dwell with me for ever.

2 I will not only reckon you for my people, but I will undertake for you, that you shall consent to me, accept of me, own me, follow me, and cleave to me as my people. I will not only separate you to myself, but I will fashion you for myself; I will sanctify you, and guide you, and teach you, and help you. I will fulfil in you all the good pleasure of my will; I will work all your works in you; I will avouch you for my people, and you shall avouch me for your God. You shall love me, fear me, obey me; I will keep you from falling, and preserve you to my heavenly kingdom.

Particularly, the Lord hath promised to give them,

First. A new heart. Second. A heart to know the Lord. Third. One heart. Fourth. A heart of flesh. Fifth. A heart to love the Lord. Sixth. A heart to fear the Lord. Seventh. A heart to obey the Lord. Eighth. A heart to persevere to the end.

First. A new heart. " A new heart will I give you, and a new spirit will I put within you," Ezek. xxxvi. 26.

This new heart (I take it) is the genus of all the following graces; and therefore the less shall suffice to be spoken of it here. A new heart, that is, not physically new, in regard of substance, but morally only, in regard of qualities.

This new heart signifies both another heart, and a more excellent heart. It is said of Caleb, Num. xiv. 24. that he had another heart. And this other heart is declared to be a more excellent heart than was in the rest of the people. Whilst they either followed not the Lord, or but haltingly, he followed the Lord fully, " A man of understanding is of an excellent spirit," Prov. xvii. 27.

There is another heart that is not a new heart.

Nebuchadnezzar had another, but no new heart : the heart of a beast for the heart of a man ; an evil heart grown worse is not a new heart, but the old heart grown older.

We read, 1 Sam. x. 9. that when Saul was anointed king, God gave him another heart; this was a more excellent heart than he had before, and yet not the heart here promised. He gave to him another heart, that is, the spirit of government ; the heart of a king for the heart of a private person ; a more public, raised, heroic heart ; the heart of a king, fitted to the station and office of a king.

The excellences of this new heart are not natural but spiritual excellences, as will appear more in the handling of the particular graces promised ; and are such as fit them for their new state, work, and reward.

I. For their new state. Christians are made the children of God, vessels of honour, a royal priesthood, a holy nation, a peculiar people ; and God gives them a heart answering to the dignity of their high calling.

II. For their new work. A christian hath other work to do than other men ; whilst their business lies all here below, in this earth, in their fields, and vineyards, &c., christians' work lies above, with their God and their Jesus, and within about their nobler and immortal part ; their work is spiritual, and such is the heart that is given to them.

III. For their new reward. God intends better things to them ; a better portion, a better hope, better comforts, joys, delights here, and a better inheritance hereafter ; and he prepares them better hearts to receive these better things ; he will not put his new wine into old bottles.

The excellences of this new heart may be reduced to these three :

1. A new light, discovering the dignity of their state, the spirituality of their work, the glory of their reward.

2. A new law, or frame, or bent of spirit, inclining, disposing, and fitting them to all that which they are made for. And this is the meaning of God's writing his law in the heart. The law written in the heart signifies, not only the law made known in the heart, but the heart made suitable to the law, and adapted to the obedience of it. There is a kind of connaturalness betwixt the new heart and all that the law requires.

3. A new power, enabling them for their new work. We have all these mentioned in one scripture, 2 Tim. i. 7. God hath not given us a " spirit of fear, but of power, and of love, and of a sound mind." A sound mind, there is the new light ; a spirit of love, there is the new law, or frame, and with these a spirit of power.

In sum, this new heart is the divine nature ; the image of God renewed ; the life of God begotten, Christ formed in them. A heart after God's own heart, containing in it all those graces of the Spirit, wherein stands their likeness to God, and their capacity of serving and enjoying of him. This is the heart the Lord will give ; " A new heart will I give unto you."

Against all those glorious things promised before, it would be objected; A kingdom promised! glory, and honour, and everlasting blessedness granted ! Alas, what is all this to me? to whom is it promised? or upon what terms? when I consider what is required, it is all one to me, as if there had been nothing promised. The way to this blessedness is too narrow, the gate is too straight for me ever to hope to enter. Whatever the price be, the strictness and severities of a christian course, the very foresight of them does amaze and confound me. Live a new life; deny myself, take up my cross, follow Christ, spend my days in fasting, and praying, and mourning! live by rule, look to every step, to every word, to every thought, &c. all these things are against me! A new life, a new course! if this be it, I shall never bear it. No man having tasted of the old, will endure this new way; for he saith, the old is better. It is all one to me, as if there had been no Christ, no gospel, no kingdom promised, if it cannot be obtained upon other terms than these. I had even as good sit down as I am, and run the venture of what follows, as to feed myself with hopes of that which I see I can never obtain. If I do but move heavenwards, the stream carries me down; if I do but take up a thought, make an essay, set a foot forward towards this new course, I find my old things hang in my heels. My old customs, my old companions, my old pleasures, and ease, and liberties, quickly pull me back. O what shall I do? I must be undone, I must be a lost and condemned wretch. Fain I would be happy, but I cannot be holy. I dread, I often tremble to think of losing Christ, and the blessings of his gospel; but this wretched heart is too hard for me, and will not come on towards it. I am ashamed, I am plagued to think, what I am likely to lose, and for how little; but I cannot help it; the way is such, that this foolish heart will never endure it.

Why, hearken soul; the Lord who hath called

thee to this new course, will give thee a new heart.
And there is not anything required in a holy life
so irksome, and so contrary to thee; but this new
heart is so fitted and suited to it, that it will become
easy to thee. Its pain will be pleasant, its severity
will be liberty, its very drudgery, as thou countest
it, will be a great delight. " I delight to do thy
will, O God, thy law is within mine heart," Psa.
xl. 8. And of the renewed soul it is said, " His
delight is in the law of the Lord," Psa. i. 2. In
the original, his will, his heart, is in the law. The
law is in the heart, and his heart is in the law.
God's will and his are the same. Whatever God
bids him do, his heart bids him do, and his hand will
never say his heart nay. He that delights in the
law, and as it is a law commanding such things,
will never grudge to do what it commands.

Where it is a pleasure to be commanded, it is no
pain to obey. Whatever work the law cuts him
out, it is work he loves. Bid him pray, bid him
watch, bid him walk humbly with his God; it is
work he loves; it is in his heart to do it. Bid a
saint draw nigh to God in any duty; it is as if you
bid the hungry to eat, or the thirsty to drink, the
naked to be clothed, the beggar to come for an alms,
or the poor labourer for a day's work. Bid a christian deny himself, or crucify his flesh; it is the
same as if you bade him deny his enemy, revenge
himself on his enemy; such revenge is sweet: but
O how pleasant is it to him to be called to a life of
praise! to live above in the light, in the love, in
the joy of the Lord! to be searching, and studying,
and looking into, and admiring those everlasting
treasures of spiritual and heavenly delights laid up
in God! to behold his face, to live in his presence,

and to dwell in the light of his countenance! It is true, there is some remaining difficulty and irksomeness in the sweetest works of religion, as far forth as the heart is unrenewed and is yet carnal—Deny myself! mortify lust! forsake my companions! withdraw from iniquity! Why what is this but to cut off my hand? to pluck out mine eyes? to tear my flesh? walk with God! seek his face! dwell in his presence! it is all one, as to bid me feed on the air, wander on the mountains, dwell in the wilderness; and as much pleasure can I find in the one as in the other. It is so indeed, as far as thou remainest carnal; the Lord God and all his ways are a wilderness, a land of darkness to thee; but as much as thou hast of this new heart, so much ease and pleasure thou wilt find herein.

Desponding soul, thou sayest, thou art yet ignorant, and hast little knowledge of the way of the Lord; but behold a new light to lead thee. Thou art yet carnal, and thy heart is contrary, and ever quarrelling at it; but the new nature will end the old quarrel. Thou art weak and impotent, the work is too hard for thee, if thou lovedst it ever so well; but what will this be when thou art endued with power from on high?

O friend, wouldst thou indeed live this new life, get this new heart. But oh there lies the difficulty; how or where shall I get it? Why, have recourse to the covenant; there it lies for thee. But how shall I get it thence? Why, hath the Lord promised to give it thee? take the word from his mouth, and put it into thine own; turn the word of promise into a prayer. Doth he say, I will give? let thy soul answer, Give, Lord, give me this new heart. I am weary Lord, and thou art weary also of this wicked heart, at once ease thyself and me; take away this and give me a better heart. Turn the word of promise into a prayer, and then turn the word of prayer into a word of faith. He says, I will give, let thy faith say, Thou wilt give, I shall have it; since thou hast said, thy servant may also boldly say, Thou wilt do it. Thou wilt give me a better heart. Farewell my old sins, lusts, and companions; farewell my old pleasures and ways; now for heaven in earnest, now welcome the straight gate, the new and living way. Old things are passed away, all things shall become new. Turn the word of promise into a prayer, turn thy prayer into a word of faith, and God will turn the word of faith into a word of command. Be it according to thy word. Let there be a new light, let there be a new law, let there be a new power, let there no more be a spirit of fear in this heart, but a spirit of power, of love, and of a sound mind. And as when he said in the creation of the great world, " Let there be light," let there be a firmament, let there be a sun and moon, it was so; so when he shall say, in the new creation of this little world, Let there be light, let there be love, let there be power; let us again make man in our image, after our own likeness, it shall be so. The Lord hath said, I will; let thy prayer say, Do it Lord. Let thy faith say, Thou wilt do it, and God will say, Amen. So be it.

Chapter X —*A heart to know the Lord*

" I WILL give them a heart to know me," Jer. xxiv. 7. The knowledge of God is the first excellency of the new heart. As in the old, so in the new creation, as was said before, the first word is, " Let there be light." There is not so glorious a preeminence of day above night, as of the knowledge above the ignorance of God. As the firmament without a sun, as the body without an eye, so is the soul without knowledge. What this knowledge of God here promised is, will appear, if we consider,

I. Its object.

II. Its act.

I. The object of this knowledge is God, not only the nature or being of God, manifested in his essential perfections, his glorious attributes, his infiniteness, eternity, omnipotency, &c., in his personal relations, the subsistences in the Godhead ; but God in Christ, God in covenant ; yea the whole mind and will of God, all that which God hath revealed to us as our duty or happiness.

God known in the heart, is the whole bible opened ; the law opened, the gospel opened ; duties, comforts, privileges made manifest. Christ opened in his sufferings, in his satisfaction, in his Spirit, in all the riches of his glory ; the whole mystery of godliness revealed. The heart opened, man made known to himself, all the depths of the heart, all the deceits of the heart, all the faculties and powers of the heart ; with their motions, operations, inclinations, the rectitude or obliquities of them. Heaven opened, the crown, the kingdom known ; everlasting rest, glory, honour, immortality brought to light. Hell opened, sin known, the devil known, wrath, temptation, the curse, eternal fire known. All this, even all that God is, and all that he hath revealed in his word and works, are the object of this knowledge of God.

II. The act. To know, is to apprehend, or

understand God, and the things of God ; " Let him
that glorieth, glory in this, that he understandeth
and knoweth me," Jer. ix. 24. " That ye may
comprehend with all saints, what is the height, and
length, and breadth, and depth, that ye may know
the love of Christ," Eph. iii. 18, 19. This apprehension of God, doth not barely note our having
received some natural or metaphysical notions of
God, and the truths that are in him : but further it
notes—

1. An approbation of him ; an approving or
liking the things that are excellent ; " That your love
may abound more and more in knowledge, and in
all judgment, that ye may approve the things that
are excellent," Phil. i. 9, 10.

2. Appropriation. The knowing of God as a reconciled God ; a God, and a God to me ; good, and
good to me ; wise, and wise for me ; my Lord and
my God. To know God in Christ, reconciled
through Christ, propitious through Christ, this is
saving knowledge. To know and not possess, to
see and not eat, to know an angry God, a wrathful
God, a God lost ; to know goodness, mercy, loving-
kindness, compassion, all-sufficiency, and to have
the heart recur, What is this to thee ? this is none of
thine ; the damned thus know and die.

3. Affection. As " those that know thy name,
shall trust in thee," Psa. ix. 10. so those that
know thy name will love thee, and fear thee, and
rejoice in thee, and bless thy name. To know and
hate God, to know and contemn God, to know and
fly from God, to know and blaspheme and curse
God, the devils thus know and tremble.

But especially that which distinguishes this saying
from common knowledge ; is,

Its power, and its savour.

(1.) Its power, the knowledge of God is mighty; my preaching was not weak, but mighty in you, 2 Cor. xiii. 3. it hath

A transforming and a fructifying power.

[1.] A transforming power. " We all with open face, beholding as in a glass, the glory of the Lord, are changed into the same image," 2 Cor. iii. 18. " Be ye not conformed to this present world, but be ye transformed, by the renewing of your minds," Rom. xii. 2. By the renewing of your minds, the renovation of the mind, both is this change, and works it further upon the whole soul, this new light is the new creature ; old things pass away, all things become new, where the mind is savingly enlightened. God known in the soul, is God united in the soul ; Christ revealed in the heart, is Christ formed upon the heart ; there is life in this light, it is no other than the light of life. The knowledge of God comprehends in it, and is involved in, and spirits and animates every grace and duty. As the same soul in the eye sees, in the ear hears, in the palate tastes ; as the same juice which is in the olive fatness, in the fig-tree sweetness, in the oak strength, in the rose fragrancy, in the lily beauty ; so the same grace, which is in the mind, light, in the heart is love, holy desire, holy fear, holy joy. And one says, that as feeling is inseparable to all the organs of sense ; the eye feels and sees, the ear feels and hears, the palate feels and tastes, the nostrils feel and smell ; so knowledge is involved in every grace. Faith knows and believes, charity knows and loves, temperance knows and abstains, patience knows and suffers, humility knows and stoops, repentance knows and mourns, obedience knows and

does, compassion knows and pities, hope knows and
expects, confidence knows and rejoices; and therefore we believe, and love, and obey, and hope, and
rejoice, because we know. God gives us this knowledge as the eye of our souls, and by that eye he
enters with all his power and glory; " That ye may
know the love of Christ, which passeth knowledge,
and be filled with all the fulness of God," Eph. iii.
19. Daylight is not that light we receive by reflection from the moon and stars, at second-hand:
when the sun is risen and come in amongst us, then
it is day; when the Sun of Righteousness is risen
in the heart, there is the light of life; God is, and
God dwells in this light, and where God dwells,
every unclean thing vanishes. Can darkness dwell
with the sun? can death dwell with life? according
to the measure of the manifestation of God in us,
so far forth is sin necessarily vanished. Thou art
but the carcass of a christian, the light that is in
thee is darkness, the life that is in thee is death, if
thou be not in the whole man renewed, after the
image of him that created thee. If Christ be not
formed in thy heart, if the love, the humility, the
meekness, the patience, the compassion, the holiness of the Lord Jesus, be not begotten in thee,
whatever thou knowest, thou knowest nothing as
thou oughtest to know; if thou hast all knowledge,
and hast not charity, (and so if thou hast all knowledge, and hast not humility, meekness, holiness,
thou art nothing,) thou art but as sounding brass,
or a tinkling cymbal. Doubting christian, that
complainest of, and bewailest thine ignorance, and
fearest that thou knowest not God, look upwards,
where his glory dwells; lift up thine eyes and see;
or if thou canst not see, lift up thy heart for eyes;

Lord, where dwellest thou? let me see thy face, show me thy glory, pity the blind, let the eyes of this blind be opened, and the tongue of this dumb shall be loosed, and speak forth thy praise. Look upward, and if yet thou seest not thy God, look inward; canst thou see his face in thy soul? canst thou see his image on thy heart? canst thou behold in this glass the glory of the Lord, and find thyself changed into his image? comfort thine heart, how short-sighted soever thou seemest to be, how dim soever thy candle burns, how weak soever in the knowledge of God thou complainest thou art; thou hast seen God, thou hast seen his face in peace. God that commanded the light to shine out of darkness, hath shined into thine heart, and given thee the knowledge of his glory in the face of Jesus Christ.

[2.] A fructifying power. This sunshine makes a fruitful soil. My desire for you, saith the apostle, is, " That ye might be filled with the knowledge of his will; in all wisdom and spiritual understanding: that ye might walk worthy of the Lord, unto all pleasing, being fruitful unto every good work, and increasing in the knowledge of God; strengthened with all might, according to his glorious power, unto all patience and long-suffering, with joyfulness," Col. i. 9—11. And, " Being filled with the fruits of righteousness, which are by Jesus Christ, unto the glory and praise of God," Phil. i. 11. Full of light and full of love, of faith, of patience, of humility, and fruitful in every good work; " A good man out of the good treasure of the heart, bringeth forth good things; an evil man out of the evil treasure, bringeth forth evil things," Matt. xii. 35. A good man hath a good treasure within him; a treasure of heavenly wisdom, of divine truth; a treasure of light; God hath shined into his heart; he is filled with all the fulness of God. And what is laid up within, he brings forth without; an evil man hath an evil treasure, Satan hath been filling his heart. "Why hath Satan filled thine heart?" Acts v. 3. The treasures of darkness are there; a treasure of lust and lies; falsehood and folly are found with him, these treasures of darkness within bring forth darkness; dark souls lead dark lives; their way is dark, their deeds are darkness. Oh how fruitful are sinners in their unfruitful works! " filled with all unrighteousness, fornication, wickedness, covetousness, maliciousness, envy, murder, debate, deceit, malignity," &c. Rom. i. 29, 30. Their hearts are full, and thereupon their mouths full, their eyes full, their hands full; mouths full of cursings, eyes full of adultery, hands full of violence, filled with all unrighteousness. "O generation of vipers, how can ye, being evil, (having such hearts,) speak good things?" All is evil that comes from you, and how can it be otherwise? Out of the abundance of the heart the mouth speaks: and in like manner, O generation of believers! how can ye, being good, but bring forth good things? or how can you say or think there is a treasure of grace, a fountain of light within, when no streams spring forth? penury in the life, speaks no great plenty in the heart; the truths of God within you are the seed of God; the good seed that he sows in his fields; where there is good seed sown in good ground, you will expect a fruitful harvest; a barren crop, speaks a barren soil, or no good seed sown there.

" Hereby we do know that we know him, if we

keep his commandments," 1 John ii. 3. We know
God : but are you sure of it ? are you not mistaken ?
No, we are not mistaken, we know that we know
him : but how do you know it ? Why, how are
trees known ? " By their fruits ye shall know
them." How do ye know that this is indeed the tree
of knowledge ? Why, see what fruits are hanging
upon it ; we keep the commandments ; here is obedience growing, here is holiness, and righteousness,
and mercy. Doubtless, this is the right tree, for
behold all the commandments, the two tables hanging upon the boughs of it, and not broken, but kept
and observed. We may as well say, obedience is
no obedience, duty is no duty, faith, and love, and
humility, and patience are not what they are, as that
the tree that brings forth this fruit is not the tree of
knowledge. " We know that we know him, because
we keep his commandments." Yea, and the tree of
life too, both in one ; " A tree of life to them that
lay hold upon her," Prov. iii. 18. Where these
fruits are not found, where there are nothing but
shows, and sounds, painted fruits ; where there are
nothing but the fruits of unrighteousness, contention, strife, covetousness, sensuality, and the like :
he is very ignorant indeed that is not able to say,
Whatever I am ignorant of, this one thing I know,
that I know not God. Christian, boast not of what
thou hast, but consider what thou doest, try thy head
by thy heart, and thy heart by thy hand ; judge of
thy light by thy love, and thy love by thy life ; say not
that God hath shined into thine heart, unless thy
light shine, thy works shine before men ; " The path
of the just shineth," Prov. iv. 18. It is but a form of
knowledge that brings forth but a form of godliness ;
he that holdeth the truth in unrighteousness, hath

not the truth in him. Thou sayest thou knowest the Lord, but what say thy ways? Do these speak the same things? Action is the best interpreter of the inner man; feel the pulses of thy heart, what watchfulness, what holiness hath thy knowledge brought forth? Hast thou received the Spirit, who yet walkest in the flesh? What! heaven in thy heart, and nought but earth in thy hand! Truth in thy heart, and lies in thy mouth! Holiness in thy heart, glory in thy heart, and in thy tongue nothing but filth or froth! What! a heart so full, and a life so empty! how can these things be? hath the light in thy heart given laws only to thy heart? or doth thy heart submit, whilst thy tongue rebels, and thou kickest with the heel?

Woe to us christians, that sinners should be so full, and saints so empty; that they should speak what they have seen with their Father, and we should speak no more what we have seen with our Father; that oaths, and lies, and blasphemies, and scoffs, and cursing, should be so rife in theirs; and that truth, and goodness, and holiness, blessings and praises, should be no more in our mouths; that there should be so much guile in theirs, and so little grace in our lips; that the shade should be more fruitful than the sun; that the good should be only the barren ground, that their habitations should be so full of violence, and oppression, and wantonness, and no more mercy, and righteousness, and sobriety in ours.

Woe to us that we know so much to so little purpose; that we should be bushels to hide, and not father candlesticks to hold forth the candle of the Lord he hath lighted up in us! O, how many dark souls might our candle lead on to the sun!

The light that is in Israel might do much to the turning Egypt into a Goshen. Speak, christians, speak what you have seen, and testify what you have believed : bring forth out of your treasure ; pity the blind world ; or at least be more helpful one to another. Instruct as you have been instructed ; convince as you have been convinced, comfort as you have been comforted of God. Outvie sinners, let not their mouths be so full of cursing as yours of blessing : whilst theirs are so full of blasphemies, let it be said of you as of your Lord, Full of grace are their lips. Good words are not wind, you may reckon them not amongst the leaves, but the fruit. Whilst you are speaking of the things of God, you are therein doing the will of God. I confess the proverb is true, The greatest talkers are not always the greatest doers. But, it is true also, he is seldom a great doer that hath nothing to say. There is a speaking which is our doing ; there is a speaking in a way of boasting, to magnify and set up ourselves, beware of that ; and there is a speaking to the use of edifying, to build up our brethren. When we are thus speaking to instruct, to convince, to awaken, and whet on our own and other spirits to our work, we are then in doing our work. Speak, christians, and speak often the things that you know ; but let me add, let your lives speak also, and not only your lips. If you would not be vain-talkers, be all tongue, let your lips speak, and your hands speak, and your feet speak, let your works and your ways speak the wonderful things of God. Bring forth what you have received ; he that is all inside, and he that is all outside, are equally nothing. The one is a shadow without substance, the other's substance is but a shadow; the one is a deceiver, the other a deceived soul; the one boasts himself, the other thinks himself something, but neither is anything.

Christians, be full of good fruits, and you will make full proof that your wisdom is from above. "If ye know these things, happy are ye if ye do them."

Weakling christian, that knowest but little of God, and calling that little nothing; whilst thou doubtest the light hath not shined into thee, dost thou walk in that little light thou hast? dost thou shine as a light in the world? dost thou know how to be holy, and humble, and harmless, and honest? dost thou live under the power of those truths thou knowest? dost thou fear the Lord, and obey the voice of his servants? Trust in the Lord, and stay thyself on thy God; thou art a child of light, though, through thy trembling heart, thou walkest in darkness. Having not seen thou lovest, and believing thou shalt rejoice with joy unspeakable and full of glory.

(2.) Its savour. "And maketh manifest the savour of his knowledge by us in every place," 2 Cor. ii. 14. The knowledge of God is sweet-scented; it casts forth a fragrancy where it comes. It hath a gratefulness to the heart, leaves sweet impressions on the senses of the saints. They taste that the Lord is gracious. As their breathings go up as sweet incense, so his beams come down with like sweetness to them, as it was said of Christ, so of God. The name of the Lord is "as ointment poured forth," Cant. i. 3. Why what is his name? This is his name; "The Lord, the Lord God, merciful and gracious, long-suffering, and abundant in goodness and truth; keeping mercy for thousands. forgiving iniquity, transgression, and sin," Exod.

xxxiv. 6, 7. Oh, what a bundle of myrrh, what a garden of spices is here inclosed! What a sweet-smelling savour doth it send forth to those who have their senses exercised to discern both good and evil!

The name of the Lord is a precious ointment, and the knowledge of God is this ointment poured forth. Where God is known in the soul, there his sweet savour is shed abroad. The thoughts of God are precious, the ways of God are pleasant to them that understand them. His fruit was sweet unto my taste. Oh the ineffable pleasures of religion! the carnal world count it a jejune and insipid thing; they cannot taste; and no wonder, for they do not see the things of God, nor can they, because they are spiritually discerned. Let God be savingly known, and then you will find what the savour of his knowledge is. This light is sweet, it is a plea-sant thing to behold the sun. O my soul, let thy walks, let thy dwellings be in this garden of the Lord; let the sun shine, and the smell of his spices shall flow forth unto thee. O my Lord, shed abroad thy sweet ointment, let the smell of thy garments refresh my soul. Let me taste and see, let me see, and I shall taste that the Lord is gracious.

Vanish all ye carnal pleasures, and sensual de-lights; these rose-buds rot, the flowers of your gar-dens wither, dead flies are in all your ointments, the light of the Lord hath shined all your glories into darkness. The waters of the sanctuary have made all your waters brackish; there remains no pleasure in them.

He that hath known the Lord, hath more or less, according to the measure of his knowledge, received in the relish and sweetness of it; and what he hath received in, he sends forth before men; he hath received, and he is a sweet savour. As the preachers, so the practitioners of piety, are a sweet savour of Christ unto God, and hand down the sweetness of God unto men. They are of savoury lips, and of savoury lives; the savour of their graces is shed abroad in the churches of Christ. Carnal hearts send forth a stench instead of a sweet smell; they are all rottenness, the savour of a sepulchre is all they have; their ways stink, their words stink, their very breath smells of a rotten heart; yea, the very best they have, their pleasures stink, their garments, their gallantry, their powders, and perfumes, and sweet odours stink of their proud, and vain, and sensual hearts. But oh what a scent do their oaths, and their curses, and their scoffs, and their lies send forth! Sinners, learn to know the Lord, and this will quickly change your savour. And you that know anything of God, think not that your knowledge is saving, till your souls have received in, and your ways do send forth the savour of his knowledge.

The last of these, the savour of this knowledge, the pleasure that it brings into the soul, though taken alone, it is but of uncertain signification; there may be some pleasure and joy arise from the common knowledge of God; and sometimes but little taste, where there is the truth of religion. But, taken in conjunction with the former, where is found both the power and the savour, the evidence of its soundness will be more full. Find all together, this transforming, this fructifying, this savoury knowledge, and you may rest satisfied that this is the saving knowledge of God. And of this is the promise, " I will give them a heart to know me."

Oh! how much need have we still to wait, and beg for the accomplishment of this promise! how little sound knowledge is there found among us! Some are weak in knowledge, who have been long taught of God, and yet are not taught of God. God hath been teaching them, but they have not learned of him ; they have had a good master, but have been ill scholars ; weak men, so we call a man of low understanding a weak man. Oh ! how many weak souls are there, even among professing christians, who, though for their time they might have been teachers of others, had yet need be taught the first principles of the oracles of God ! "Some men have not the knowledge of God ; I speak this to their shame," 1 Cor. xv. 34.

Others are men of knowledge, but of weak knowledge, who know much but to little purpose ; their great knowledge hath little power in them ; their lusts are too strong for their light, "I spake unto thee with a strong hand, and instructed thee," Isa. viii. 11. If God have spoken to these men, yet his hand hath not instructed them ; the nail hath not been struck deep enough, it dwells in the head only, it hath not reached their heart ; they have an eye, but far enough from having a heart to know the Lord. Their knowledge doth not lead them on to religion, but must serve them instead of religion ; it is all the religion they have, to know what it is : it is made to serve, and not suffered to guide and govern ; to serve their turns, to serve their interest, to serve their pride and their covetousness. Their knowledge of God makes them devils, it helps them to play the hypocrites, to be deceivers of others, yea, and of their own souls. It will seek them out acceptable words, put prayers into their mouths, praises into their lips, spiritualize their language, furnish them with savoury discourses, carry them

plausibly through duties, wherein, though God hath
the name, though souls have the name, yet are they
all but sacrifices to their lusts; the knowledge of
God humbleth, but this knowledge puffeth up, and
lifteth up; puffeth them up in their own, and lifteth
them up in other's thoughts; and when it hath done
this, it hath done them all the service they have for
it to do, unless, it may be, they have some worse
work for it; to make rents and divisions in the
church of Christ, to maintain disputes, to cavil and
quarrel, to divide and make parties, to make twenty
religions out of one, till at length they make that
one to be none. Whilst the apostle says, " Some
men have not the knowledge of God; I speak this
to your shame;" I may say also, Some men have
the knowledge of God, I speak this to their
shame. What! the knowledge of God, and no
more humility! the knowledge of God, and no
more charity! I speak this to your shame. Have
the faith of Christ in respect of persons! have
the knowledge of God in respect of parties! know
God! and yet divide, and scatter, and confound them
that are of God! yea, and contend and quarrel
about such small differences, as sometimes is seen,
here is God, and not there; with us, and not with
you; when, it may be, a little charity would tell you,
for the main, he may be with both; and so much
uncharitableness makes it a question whether with
either! The more such men pretend to the knowledge of God, the greater their shame.

Friends, beware you be not undone, either by
your ignorance, or your knowledge. Love not
darkness, and call not darkness light; call not that
the knowledge of God, which is not; misuse not
that which is. Hast thou no knowledge? What!

and such a promise before thee! " I will give
them a heart to know me, they shall all know me !"
What! and such a gospel before thee, the work
whereof is to open blind eyes, and to turn from darkness to light ! Open thy mouth sinner, and God will
open thine eyes ; " Ask, and thou shalt have ; seek,
and thou shalt find ;" see, wink not at the light that
shines round about thee ; love not darkness, if thou
love not death. " This is eternal life to know thee."
What then is ignorance ? there's death in thine
heart, if there be no light in thine eye.

Hast thou knowledge ? be thankful, and be humble ; be not high-minded, but fear ; prize it, but do
not abuse it.   Hast thou received the knowledge of
the truth ?   Live under the power of the truth thou
knowest ; resign up thyself to it, to its transforming
power ; give it leave to work, and to change thee
into its own image.   Let this new light make thee
a new man, to its governing power ; let it teach
thee and rule thee ; let it teach as one that hath
authority ; let it rule till it hath put all thine enemies under thy feet ; till every thought, imagination,
every high thing be made low, and brought into
captivity to Christ.   Let not the light of the Lord
help thee to do the devil's work ; let it not be fod-
der for thy flesh, lest it be fuel for thy flames ;
let it not repent thy God nor thee, that ever thou
hadst such a talent committed to thee ; let it neither
be loss to God, nor the eternal loss of thine own
soul.   He that hath appeared on earth in beams of
light will be revealed from heaven in flames of fire,
rendering vengeance to all that know God and obey
not the gospel of Christ.   Woe to those that neither know nor obey, but oh ! what to those that
obey not, though they know !

Christians, know the Lord, but know and fear;
know and serve, know and honour thy God; know
God, and know thyself, thy sin and thy misery, thy
dangers and thy temptations; know and mourn;
know and be ashamed; know, and fear, and watch,
and fight, and overcome. Know God, and know
his will; thy duty and thy way; thy privileges and
opportunities; thy race and thy crown. Know, and
do, and run, and suffer, and wait, and hope, and rejoice, in hope of the glory of God. Know God, but
God in Christ, God reconciled; pardoning, absolv-
ing, accepting, through him. Know, and believe,
accept, adventure upon, resign, commit thyself to
him. Know thy God, and behold him; look upon
thy God, in his power, in his wisdom, in his holiness, in his goodness, in his loving-kindness, in his
mercy. Behold him in his word, in his works, in
his providence, in his saints, in thy soul, in his Son;
set him before thine eyes, look upon thy God, and
never leave looking till thou art changed into his
image, and satisfied with his visage; and when thou
art brought up to this, then he hath done for thee
what he hath said: " I will give them an heart to
know me."

Chapter XI —*One heart*

" I will give them one heart," Ezek. xi. 19. We
read, " Ephraim is like a silly dove, without heart,"
Hos. vii. 11. hath no heart at all; none for his
God, that is, as good as none: and, Psa. xii. 2.
we read that Israel had a double heart, a heart, and
a heart; more hearts than one; but says the Lord,
" I will give them a heart, and it shall be but one,
and no more."

For the opening of this, (to let pass the signification it hath, as it respects christians collectively,)

as it respects each particular christian. This one heart may be taken as opposed

To a wavering—a divided—and a double heart.

1. As opposed to a wavering, unstable heart, Jam. i. 6. 8. Wavering-minded men have almost as many hearts as they live days, or meet with cases; a heart that changes with the weather, and tacks about with every wind, that resolves and repents, that chooses and changes, that, like a wave of the sea, is tossed about with every wind. This you may call either many hearts, or no heart, as you will. Thus this one heart is a fixed, established, resolved heart; " It is good that the heart be established with grace," Heb. xiii. 9. Grace fixes and establishes the heart, brings it to a consistency in itself, which before was any thing, or nothing.

2. As opposed to a divided heart, Hos. x. 2. a heart cut in two, as it were. Some talk that the devil hath a cloven foot, but whatever the devil's foot be, to be sure his sons have a cloven heart, one half for God, the other half for sin; one half for Christ, the other half for this present world; God hath a corner in it, and the rest is for sin and the devil. Thus this one heart is an entire heart; all the powers of it are united within itself, and go the same way; God hath the whole heart. " Bless the Lord, O my soul, and all that is within me, bless his holy name," Psa. ciii. 1. All its springs are in him, and thither do all its streams bend their course.

3. As opposed to a double heart, or a hypocritical heart, properly so called, Psa. xii. 2, 3. that is it which is called a heart, and a heart; a heart in the breast, and another in the tongue. Our outside is presumed to be an expression of our inside; what we speak, we pretend to be our very hearts. It is

the very heart in the tongue that speaks, the heart in the eye that weeps, the heart in the hand that works, the heart in the foot that walks; no, it is not so with the hypocrite, he shows another heart in his tongue, in his ways, than that which is within him. He hath a heart, and a heart; one in his tongue or life, and quite another in his breast. His course speaks him another man than he is. And thus one heart signifies a single or a plain heart.

To sum up all together; this one heart is such as

I. Pitches on one end.

II. Has but one thing to do.

III. Does what it does.

I. Pitches on one end. God is its end. There it wholly bestows itself: "I am thine," Psa. cxix. 94. And there only it takes up its rest. "And now, Lord, what wait I for? my hope is in thee," Psa. xxxix. 7. God is both its work and its wages. To please God, this is its whole business; and to enjoy God, this is its happiness. This is the mark it hath in its eye, this is the scope of all its motions, to honour and enjoy God. This it wills, this it loves, this it desires, designs, hopes, labours for, that the Lord may possess, and be the possession of it. Particularly, it gives God,

1. The place; 2. The power of the end.

1. The place of the end. God is its first and last. He is first in the eye, and it looks no further. It makes him not only the chief, but in a sense its only aim. It will have no other God, and therefore no other end, but the Lord. It makes all things else, not only to stoop and stand by, but to serve him. Get you hence, stand off, is its language to all that stands up in his room, or stands in his way. Evil men, whatever honour they pretend to have of

the Lord, they do but make him a servant to their other gods. Religion they will take up, but it is only to serve their own turns, to bring about their carnal ends; " They serve not the Lord, but their own bellies," saith the apostle, Rom. xvi. 18. Phil. iii. 19. Nay, they make the Lord their fellow-servant; they serve, and their religion must serve their sensual appetites. He that will have so much religion only as he may live upon, (which is the measure of the most) makes the Lord no longer his God, but his servant. A sincere christian will set God upon the throne, and make all things else his servants or his footstool. Whatever will not be serviceable, must be trodden in the dirt. Nothing will be loved and embraced, but what will set God higher, or bring God nearer to his heart.

2. The power of the end. The end hath a four-fold power: 1. It draws; 2. It directs; 3. It governs; 4. It rewards.

(1.) It draws the heart to it; God, who is a christian's end, is also his beginning. Our first step heaven-ward we owe to the influence of heaven upon us; "Draw me, we will run after thee," Cant. i. 4. "No man can come unto me, unless the Father, which hath sent me, draw him." Nothing but God will do it, as nothing will draw the soul another way; the pleasures of sin, the wages of unrighteousness, are poor and low baits to entice a soul away from God; that is, so far as it is renewed; so it is nothing but God that draws the soul on its way, and he will do it. God draws the soul not by an act of power only, but by moral suasion, that is the proper casualty of the end. Not by efficiency only, but by sympathy; as by the water, the thirsty soul is drawn to the water-brooks.

It is God who draws hearts after him ; there are instruments, as his word and ministers ; and there are arguments by which God draws ; but whatever the instruments or arguments are, it is God who does it. What is the work of either word, or ministers, but to set God before them ? and this draws. Instruments can do nothing, unless God be the preacher by them ; arguments can do nothing unless he be the medium of them ; as it was said concerning the people's following Saul, so much more concerning those who follow the Lord.

Those only follow him whose hearts God hath touched. It is not man's touching, but God's touching the heart, that draws it heaven-ward. The tongue of man may touch the ear, it is God only that touches the heart. And when he touches, then the heart will follow. As you know the needle, when it is touched with a loadstone, then it turns after it. The loadstone is not more naturally attractive of the needle than God is of that heart which he hath touched. " My beloved put in his hand by the hole of the door, and my bowels were moved in me," Cant. v. 4. He did but touch the door, and her heart felt him, and moved towards him.

O christians, when you have been waiting upon God in prayer, hearing, or any other spiritual duty, or ordinance ; consider, Hath mine heart been touched this day ? My tongue hath been touched, mine ear hath been touched, my heart hath been treated with, but hath the Lord touched it ? hath there virtue come forth from him, which hath enticed and drawn my soul after him ? Sometimes by a message, or visit from heaven, the Lord hath drawn a good word from the lip, a tear from the eye ; but

O, for touches upon souls, for turning of bowels, for the flowings out of hearts after the Lord; he is the only loadstone that prevails on gracious souls.

Others who have many hearts, have many attractives; every heart hath its peculiar god, twenty gods, it may be, in one man, because so many hearts. Their pleasures are their gods, their profits their gods, their belly their god; their wives, or their children, their gods; and so many gods so many ends. And every end is a loadstone to draw them after them. Every heart will go after its god. A christian that hath but one heart hath but one God, and this is he that draws it on its way. Thou sayest, the Lord is thy God, thou acknowledgest, thou ownest, thou hast chosen him for thine; but what doth thy God, whom thou hast chosen, do upon thine heart? what will the sight of God, or thy love to God, or thy hope in God, do upon thee? how far will it carry thee? which way runs thy heart? which way dost thou bend thy course? dost thou feel thy God drawing thee? and is thy heart running after him? Running denotes motion, and a swift or violent motion.

I shall lay before you these six or seven expressions the scripture uses, to note the running of those hearts after God whom he hath drawn.

[1.] The desiring of the soul after God. "The desire of our soul is to thy name. With my soul have I desired thee in the night; yea, with my spirit within me will I seek thee early," Isa. xxvi. 8, 9. Desire is the soul in motion Godwards. Towards him are their desires, and they come deep; from the bottom of the heart. "With my soul have I desired thee, with my spirit within me will I seek thee." Lord, all my desire is before thee,"

Psa. xxxviii. 9. It is not, All my desires, but " my desire ;" thou seest all, and it is all but one desire. He desires pardon, he desires peace, he desires help, and the healing of his wounds ; but all this is but one desire. God is all. " One thing have I desired," Psa. xxvii. 4.

[2.] The thirsting of the soul. " My soul thirsteth for God, for the living God," Psa. xlii. 2. Thirsting is the extremity of desire ; hunger and thirst are the appetite of desire heightened ; violent and painful appetites ; my soul thirsteth and is in pain till it be satisfied.

[3.] The longing of the soul. " O God, thou art my God, early will I seek thee : my flesh longeth for thee in the dry and thirsty land, where no water is," Psa. lxiii. 1. Longing causeth languishing, and pain, if it be not satisfied. " My soul breaketh for the longing desire it hath to thy judgments," Psa. cxix. 20. " My heart panteth, my flesh faileth, the light of mine eyes is gone from me," Psa. xxxviii. 10.

[4.] Calling after God. " Hear me when I call, O God of my righteousness," Psa. iv. 1. Calling upon God, is the voice of desires. The desiring soul will not keep silence; the tongue, the eyes, the ears, the hands, the knees, must all be orators, when the flame is once kindled within.

[5.] Crying after the Lord. This is an expression answering the thirsting of the soul. Crying is a passionate and importunate praying. " I cried unto the Lord with my whole heart," Psa. cxix. 145.

[6.] Crying out after God. This is the manner of the longing soul. Crying out denotes more than bare crying ; loud cries, strong cries, forced out by a paroxysm of love, or an agony the soul is in.

" My soul longeth, yea even fainteth for the courts of the Lord ; my heart and my flesh crieth out for the living Lord," Psa. lxxxiv. 2.

[7.] Following hard after the Lord. " My soul followeth hard after thee," Psa. lxiii. 8. This expression is more comprehensive; it denotes, both all the workings, and breakings, and breathings of the soul within, and its diligent pursuing in the use of all outward means, and pressing on after the Lord. All those labourings, and watchings, and runnings, all that holy violence, wherewith a saint presses into the kingdom of God.

Put all this together, and you will see the power and influence the Lord hath on holy souls, to the drawing of them after him; they are in motion heaven-ward, desiring, thirsting, longing, calling, crying, crying out, following hard after him. What aileth these souls ? what is the matter with them ? what would they have ? " What aileth thee," said the Danites once to Micah, " that thou comest thus after us ? What aileth thee ? Why, you have taken away my gods, and what have I more," Judg. xviii. 23. What aileth these crying, longing, running souls ? Why, it is after their God they cry, it is after their God they run. Go back, Elisha, said once the prophet to him, when he had cast his mantle on him ; " Go back, for what have I done unto thee ?" 1 Kings xix. 20. What hast thou done ? enough to hold me from going back : there went virtue with the mantle ; the mantle fell on his heart as well as his back, and drew it after the prophet. Should you say thus to these, Go back, soul, go back from following thy God, for what hath he done unto thee ? Oh he hath gotten my heart ; No, no ; I cannot go back, he is my God, and what have I more ?

(2.) The end guides and directs to means. " Whither shall I go from thee ? thou hast the words of eternal life."

(3.) The end governs. I shall put these both together   What is it that governs sinners but their ends ? this points them out their work, and their way ; this holds them to their work, and keeps them in their way : whatever fetters and chains their lusts are to them, it is their carnal ends to which they are in bondage.   These are they that lord it over them, and hereupon it is impossible to persuade a sinner to make a thorough change of his way, till he hath changed his ends.   Herein stands the conversion of a sinner, in the changing of his ends ; when he ceases to be any longer to himself, to his flesh, to the world, and for a worldly happiness, and is brought about to pitch on God as his portion and happiness, to whom he devotes and dedicates himself ; there is conversion.   Sin is our turning away, and conversion is turning back to our God.   Beloved, consider not barely how, but to what you live ; not only what you do, but what you would have ; and never count yourselves truly godly, whatever of God be in your way, till God be in your heart and eye.   He that hath first chosen God, and therefore a godly life, whose godliness of life springs forth as the fruit of his choice of the Lord—that is a godly man.

God governs as our king, and as our end ; as our king by his sovereignty, as our end by his excellency, by his worthiness and goodness ; as our king by laws, as our end by love.   Love will find out our way, will tell all our wanderings, will check us for our sins, sweeten our labours, quicken us on our course, cut out our way through dangers and diffi-

culties, and keep us in our way, till we come to the
fruition of our end.   Therefore it is said by the
apostle, " The law is not for a righteous man,"
1 Tim. i 9.   Love will save the law a labour ; " The
law is not for a righteous man," not so much, at
least, as for sinners ; not as to the coercion of it,
though still as to its obligation ; the constraint of
love will much supersede the coercion of laws.

(4.) The end rewards. " They have their reward,"
Matt. vi. that is, they have their end ; the reputation
for devout and charitable men was the end of their
devotion and charity.   They prayed, and fasted,
and gave alms for no other end ; and the obtaining
that reputation was their reward. " Verily I say
unto you, They have their reward."

God is the reward of his saints ; " I am thy exceeding great reward," Gen. xv. 1. " My judgment
is with the Lord, and my reward with my God," Isa.
xlix. 4.   God is the reward they shall receive, and
the reward they look to receive. Moses " had respect
to the recompense of reward," Heb. xi. 26.

And therefore the argument is weighty, which
Christ used to dissuade his disciples from being in
their devotions, in their alms-deeds, as the pharisees
and hypocrites are, who disfigured their countenances in their fasts, who sounded a trumpet to proclaim their alms ; " Be ye not like them, for they have
their reward."   The argument was strong to the
disciples, who being men of another spirit, could not
be satisfied with such a reward.

In these two things saints greatly differ from the
men of this world.   1. They are not willing to defer
their duties till hereafter. And, 2. They dread it to
have their reward here ; they would dispatch their
work, and are willing to go upon trust for their

wages. Sinners would have their wages in hand, and be trusted for their work till hereafter; they would be happy here, and can be content to stay for holiness till hereafter; it is soon enough to be saints in heaven. But oh! it would be a dreadful word to saints, There are thy good things, take them, these are thy reward. These are not their end, and therefore they cannot take them for their reward.

Poor foolish worldlings, how are you disjointed! How are your weary hearts scattered through the ends of the earth! how many masters do you serve! how many matters have you to mind! you weary yourselves in the greatness of your way, and what is your reward? What the fields can give, you have; what your sheep or your oxen can give, you have; what your beds, or your tables, or your houses, or your clothes can give, you have; here a little and there a little; you get up, your beds give you ease, your houses shelter, your sports and companions pleasure, your parasites honour, and that little you can pick up here and there, this is your reward. Verily I say unto you, you have your reward; unhappy souls! you are troubled and careful about many things for nothing; one thing is needful; and if yet ye will be wise, choose that good part, which shall not be taken from you.

This one heart hath but one thing to do. "This one thing I do," Phil. iii. 13. There are all things in that one thing; all things needful. How many things soever his hand findeth to do, all is but one. He intends in all, God. A renewed heart designs God, and is making Godwards in all he does. Whatever journey he goes, it is God is his home; whatever race he runs, it is God is his mark and prize; whatever battle he fights against flesh and blood, against principalities and powers, it is that he may cut his way through all to his God; whatever he does, he does it for God; whatever he suffers, he suffers for God. When he hears, or fasts, or prays, it is all for God. When ye fasted, did ye at all fast to me? Yes, to thee, a christian is able to say; he hath many things to pray for, and fast for; he hath bread, and clothes, and friends, and health, and safety, and liberty, to pray for; but in all, he prays for God: he entitles God to all he has and marks it up for him, and he sees and enjoys God in all he has. He will not own that for a mercy, that hath not God in it, and is not a foot or wing, to carry him on towards him. And therefore whatever he begs to himself, it is that he may have it for God. What he gives, he gives to God; whom he forgives, it is for the Lord's sake; whether he eats, or drinks, or works, or buys, or sells, or whatever else he does, he does it all to the glory of God, 1 Cor. x. 31. For him he prays, for him he waits, for him he labours, for him he suffers, for him he lives, to him he dies. "To me to live is Christ," Phil. i. 21. "According to my earnest expectation and my hope, that in nothing I shall be ashamed, but that with all boldness, as always, so now also Christ may be magnified in my body, whether it be by life or by death." This is the one thing he intends, this is the one thing he seeks in all, take his whole course together; he can say with the apostle, "This one thing I do, forgetting those things which are behind, and reaching forth unto those things which are before, I press toward the mark, for the prize of the high calling of God in Christ Jesus."

He does what he does: and that, 1. Not feignedly, but really; 2. Not faintly, but heartily.

1. Really. He pursues this end, in a plain and honest way. He that hath this one heart, hath but one way. Heart and life go hand in hand; he makes straight steps to his heart, and his heart makes straight steps to his feet. As he looks straight on, so he walks straight on to his mark. He doth not look one way and row another. He is a Jacob, a plain man, a plain-dealing man; a Nathanael, in whom is no guile : he turns his inside outward; his life is not a cloak but a commentary on his heart. The expositors of his inward man. His end is in his heart, and his heart is in his face, in his tongue, in his duties, and all his ways. He is no politician, not in fleshly wisdom, 2 Cor. i. 12. his religion is not a blind or a device to delude the simple; he is downright and in earnest in all he does. He does the same thing he seems to do ; his praying is praying indeed ; his fasting and alms are such indeed ; his very profession is practice ; he would not believe, nor make others believe, but that he is what he is. He seeks not commendation from men, but approbation with God. His design is not inordinately to commend nimself to the good opinion, though he would be made. manifest in the consciences of others. He would not be a lie or a cheat. He abhors all lying, but most of all a religious lie. He would not lie for God, much less against him ; such a lie is as blasphemy to him. He loves not images ; he would have a soul in all his practices. A prayer without a soul, a sacrifice without a heart, a religious carcass is an abomination to him. He would not make such a noble medium as religion, serve so base an end, as the serving of the flesh.

He hath other work to do than to serve times or tables ; than to please himself or men ; than to

serve wills, or humours, or lusts; he hath a soul,
a conscience, a God to look after; he hath but one
business to do, but one master to serve. If he be a
magistrate, he rules for God; if he be a minister, he
preaches for God; if he be a parent, he educates for
God; if he be a master, he governs for God; to him
he dedicates himself and his house; he writes on his
doors, This is Bethel, this is none other but the
house of God. If he be a child or a servant, he
obeys in the Lord, and for the Lord. He knows
he hath to do with God in all he does; when he is
dealing with men, with his friends, with his family,
in his calling, in his recreations, in all he hath to
do with God; and he can take comfort in nothing
but what God will take pleasure in. Thou hast no
pleasure in iniquity. Thou lovest truth in the inward parts. And there is no truth in the inward
parts, but when there is truth also in the outward
parts, when the heart, and tongue, and ways agree.
It is in vain to say, My heart is good, when the
ways are naught. A false tongue, deceitful ways,
will give the lie to the heart. He cannot subsist
longer than he hath smiles from Heaven. Communion with God is his life, his all is in God. His
heart dies, when that fountain is stopped. If he
cannot have clearness and boldness in the presence
of God, he can no longer look himself in the face,
but blushes and hangs down his head with shame.
He values not either the applause or the scorns of
men, so he may have a witness of his acceptance
with God. O Lord, dost thou regard? wilt thou
accept of me? It is enough. Let all the world call
me, Thou fool, thou pharisee, thou hypocrite, so the
Lord will say, My child, it is well. It is falsely
spoken, it is foolishly, it is weakly done; it is

pride, it is singularity, it is scrupulosity : thus the world cry.   Let them alone, O my soul; I will hearken what the Lord God will say, if he says, Thou hast been faithful; I will hearken what conscience will say, if it says, Well done, let all else say what they please; this is my rejoicing, my only rejoicing, the testimony of my conscience, that in all simplicity and godly sincerity, not in fleshly wisdom, but by the grace of God, I had my conversation in the world.

2. Heartily. Whatever he does for God, he does it with a good will.   He hath cast up all his business into one, and he is intent upon it.   He works righteousness, as sinners work wickedness, " with both hands earnestly," Micah vii. 3.   He is religious in good earnest, he prays in good earnest, he hears in good earnest, he runs in good earnest : the power of his soul being all united in one channel, run more strongly, his many springs falling all into one stream, make a river, that bears down all bays before it.   The psalmist prays, " Unite my heart to fear thy name," Psa. lxxxvi. 11.   Unite my heart to thee, and unite my heart in itself, that it may all run towards thee.   Unite my heart to fear, and so unite my heart to love thy name; unite my heart to serve, and follow, and live to thee. As if he should have said, O my God, my heart is divided, and discomposed, scattered up and down, I know not where ; my pleasures have a part, my estate hath a part, my friends have a part, my family hath a part, there is little or none left for God.   I have too many things to fear, too many things to love and care for, too many things to serve and follow, to follow the Lord with any strength or intention of mind.   Call in all, Lord, all my parts, all

my powers, command their joint and united attendance upon thee. " Gird up the loins of your mind and be sober, and hope to the end (in the original it is *hope perfectly*) for the grace that is to be brought unto you at the revelation of Jesus Christ. As obedient children, not fashioning yourselves according to the former lusts in your ignorance, but as he which hath called you is holy, so be ye holy in all manner of conversation," 1 Pet. i. 13—15. Gird up the loins of your minds. Gird and be sober, gird and hope perfectly, gird and be obedient, gird and be holy. Here it is true, ungirt and unblest, ungirt and unholy ; the girding is the gathering in the strength of the heart to its work. " Stand with your loins girt," Eph. vi. 14. Stand, do not gird and ungirt, stand always girt; call in your hearts and hold them in ; be always in a readiness to every duty, in a readiness against every temptation. Oh how loose are we! What loose praying, and loose hearing, and loose meditation, and loose walkings, do we satisfy ourselves with ! Our hearts are to seek, our thoughts and affections are gadding abroad, we know not where to find them, and our work is done thereafter. We excuse our non-proficiency in religion, by our many hinderances, by the difficulties of our work; but the great hinderance lies here, our loins are ungirded, our hearts are not united in our work, nor intent upon it. When God and the things of eternity get so deep into the heart, when there is such a deep sense of the weight and importance of the things that are eternal abiding upon us, as overpowers carnal objects, and loosens the heart from them ; when we feel the evidence and the consequence of these things commanding our whole souls after them, then there is religion in earnest; then we go on and prosper. And thus it is with this one heart, there are not some light touches only upon it; God is gotten deep into it, eternity is gotten deep into it, this is all; this is all I have to mind or do. My hope, my comforts, my life, my soul, all hang upon this one thing; if I speed well here, I am made for ever. What have I to do in the way of Egypt, or to drink of the waters of Siher? what have I to do in the way of Assyria? what have I to do in the way of pleasure? what have I to do in the way of the world? To build tabernacles for myself here below, or to drink the waters of my one cistern? How little am I concerned in the interest of this flesh? What matters it what becomes of it, or which way it goes? My God, my God, my soul, my soul, there lies my concernment; of these let my care only be. Get thee behind me, Satan, hold thy peace sinful flesh, keep silence worldly cares; hinder me not, speak no more to me of hearkening to you, away from me ye evil doers, I will keep the commandments of my God. Let others do what they will, run whither they please, choose whom they will serve, what they will follow after; come my soul follow thou the Lord, gird up thy loins and come away; for the other world, for the other world; make haste, linger not; let others loiter as they will, escape for thy life, look not behind thee, get thee up to the mountain and live.

Objection. One heart! why, it is evermore two: two men, a new man and an old; two nations, two selfs; there are twins in the womb of every saint; the ungodly seem more one than they, all for sin, and for hell; all dark, all hard, all but one stone.

Answer. Yet it is true, the saints, and they only, have but this one heart; for,

1. The old heart is not a heart, the old self is not the self; this old man is not the man, this is not he, that is the heart which hath gotten the dominion, and the rule in the man. The new heart hath the dominion; though sin, as Esau, be the first-born, yet the elder must now serve the younger; the old man is but a dead man, Col. iii. 3. Ye are dead, that is, your old man is dead, your sin is slain, and crucified with Christ, and when it is dead you may say it is not.

2. The meaning plainly is, I will give them one heart; that is, a single, sincere, upright heart; they shall be no longer a hypocritical people. If there be something of hypocrisy in them, yet hypocrites they shall no longer be; their hearts shall be upright before me; sincerity stands in pitching upon, choosing, and giving up our hearts to God, as our chief good, and last end. When God is our all, there is perfection; and when God is our chief, there is sincerity. I say, when God is our all, when the world hath nothing left in us to entice or draw out our souls after it, but God carries them wholly without any the least liking, or lusting after sinful objects, there is perfection. This is not attainable here; the heart cannot be thus perfectly one till corruption hath put on incorruption. But though it be not perfectly yet, it may be sincerely one, and then it is so, when however the flesh hath too great an interest in it, and influence upon it, and often pulls it aside, and puts it back; yet it still bends its course heaven-wards, and that way the stream and strength of the soul is running the flesh will be putting in for a part; it would have all, it would not take its turns with God. God will not take his turns with the flesh, he will have all or none. And the

flesh would not take its turns with him; it is not contented with now and then, it would not be served in the fields, or in the shop, or at the table, or in the bed only, but in the church, in the chamber, in the closet ; it would carry away all from God, but if it cannot have all, it will divide with God; wherever God is served, the flesh will be putting in for its share. The best of christians feel too great a truth in this ; their frequent humblings, and mournings, and breakings, and self-shamings before the Lord, are mostly upon this account. This is the voice of their deepest groanings and bitterest tears ; the burdens of their mournful groans, I cannot do the things that I would ; when I would do good, evil is present with me : with my mind I serve the law of God, but with my flesh the law of sin ! Woe is me, my soul, how am I straitened ! how am I divided ! Whither am I hurried ? wherewithal do I come before the Lord ? Oh ! what halting, and heartless, and distracted duties, do I serve my God withal ! This flesh eats up the fat, and the best ; and only the lame, and the lean, and the sick, are left for a sacrifice to the Lord. Woe is me, my leanness, my leanness ; my God, my God, how art thou served ! how art thou robbed of thy due ! these strangers are gotten into thy sanctuary, and eat up all thy pleasant things, and what have they left thee ?

Such are their complaints, and their very complaints are their comfort, and the witness of their sincerity, whilst they can with openness of heart make their approach and appeal to God : yet thou art my Lord, thou art my God, and I will serve thee. I have chosen thee as my heritage for ever, and I will wait for thy salvation. Hear the sighing of thy

prisoner, deliver thy captive: my heart is with
thee, let not this flesh entrench upon thy right, let
sin no longer reign in my mortal body; let me have
no more to do with the throne of iniquity, untie the
cords, loose the fetters, bring my soul out of prison.
Search me, O Lord, and know my heart; prove
me, and know my thoughts. Is there any way of
wickedness in me? Do I willingly go after the
commandments? Do I regard iniquity in my
heart? Here it lies, it is true; it wars, and raises
tumults and insurrections against thee; but do I
resign up myself to it? is it a pleasure to me? am
I at peace with it? O Lord, thou knowest. I cannot get rid of it, I cannot do the things that I would,
I cannot pray as I would, nor hear as I would, nor
think, nor speak, nor live as I would. whither I go,
sin goes with me; where I lodge, it lodges; if I sit
still, it abides with me; if I run from it, it follows
me; I can neither rest nor work, I can do nothing
for it. I can do nothing for it; and yet, blessed be
thy name, this one thing I do; what I cannot at-
tain, I follow after; I cannot conquer, yet I fight
against it; I wrestle with it, though it so often
give me the fall. I trust it not, though it flatter
me; I love it not, though it feed me; my heart is
with thee, Lord, my foot is making after thee; I
groan, I travail in pain, waiting for thy redemption;
till I die, I will not give over. I will die fighting,
I will die hoping, I will die praying, Save me, O
Lord, make no long tarrying, O my God.

And thus you have the description of this one
heart. It pitches on one end, and God is that end.
It gives him the place of the end; he is its first and
last. It gives him the power of the end: this one
thing, the obtaining of God to be theirs, draws them

on, guides, governs them in their whole course, and is accepted by them as their only and exceeding great reward. This instructs them, this rules and encourages them, calls them off from sin, calls them on to duty, carries them out in suffering; all their powers are united in this one business, all their arguments are resolved into this one argument, all their rewards are summed up in this one reward, God shall be glorified, and therein my soul shall be satisfied; God shall be mine, and glory shall be his.

In all this we see what this one heart means, but, oh, how little of this grace have we received! how many hearts have we! how many gods have we to divide these hearts betwixt them! how small a corner.

How low a place must the Lord take up with us, if he will have any at all! how often is he made to stand aside, or to stoop to a lust! God made to give place to the devil! Is God our all indeed? have we none else to please, have we none else to serve? have we no portion, no inheritance, no other God but the Lord? Is he our alpha and omega, our first and our last, our spring and our ocean, our sum and our scope, the rise and the rest of all our motions? Whatever our tongues speak, do our hearts also and our lives say, "To me to live is Christ?" None but God, none but Christ, nothing but heaven and glory? When we are driving so hard for our flesh, for our pride, for our ease, for our gain; when we are so busy this way, and so hearty and so zealous this way; when these must have so great a share in our religion, is this still the voice, "To me to live is Christ?" Oh how little power hath the Lord with us! How far is it that the single interest of God will carry our souls?

How little is done purely for God! We have often many strings to our bow. There are some services wherein there is something coming to the flesh, as well as to the name of God: some credit or honour, some outward advantage to be gotten by religion; but when all the other strings crack but this one, when there is nothing to move us but God, oh how weak do our motions grow! The flesh often goes partner with God: there is a double trade driving in the same actions; a trade for heaven, and a trade for earth together; there is something to be got by our religion besides what is coming to God; there are fields, and vineyards, and oliveyards, friends, and honours, and preferments; as it sometimes falls out, when godliness is in the rising side: and when it is thus, we go smoothly and vigorously on. Come, see the zeal that I have for the Lord of hosts. But when the interest of God and the flesh divide, and part asunder; when the flesh is like to be a loser by our religion; when God puts us on such duty, as will spend upon the flesh, and eat out and devour its interest; when our hearts tell us, as Deborah did Barak, "This will not be for thine honour," Judg. iv. 9. or this will not be for thine ease, or thy safety; then what becomes of our zeal? Oh how heavily do we then drive on! how seldom is it that this word, "Yet God shall be glorified," will balance all the prejudices, and confute all the cross reasonings of the flesh, and carry us on our way, without and against it!

How little hath the Lord of the government of us! If he doth govern as a king, yet how little as our end! How little doth goodness govern! how little will love do with us! we must have rigour and severity; we must have spurs, and goads, and rods, and stripes, and scorpions too, and all little enough, to drive us back from those other gods which we have chosen, and to bring us on after the Lord. If the law be not made for the righteous, if they need not a law, then what are we, whom a law will not suffice? If commands, threatenings, terrors, penalties, judgments, can do no more upon us; if we are yet so loose, and so carnal, and so earthly, and so froward, and so false, and so formal, under severest discipline; if we will not be whipped into more humility, spirituality, self-denial, watchfulness, care, activity, zeal; but are such drones and such sleepers, such earth-worms and such sensualists still, under all the corrections and compulsions of the law;—oh what should we be did we want a law? were there nothing but love to restrain us from sin, and constrain and quicken us to duty?

Christians, have we but one thing to do in all we do? sometimes we are busy in doing nothing. Though there be a prayer in our mouths, the praises of God in our mouths, Christ, heaven, holiness, glory, a new heart, a new life upon our tongues, there is nothing within: no prayer, no praise, no Christ, nor heaven; what have we been often doing in the closet, in the family, in the congregation, when we seemed to have been praying? Nothing, nothing, but sowing wind and good words. Sometimes we have too many things in our hearts; what a world of carnal devices and fleshly projects have we wrapt up in the garment of our religion! Peter's sheet had not a more heterogeneous miscellany of creatures, "four-footed beasts, wild beasts, creeping things, and fowls of the air," than our religious duties have of designs and ends. We have men to please; our pride, our bellies, to offer sacrifice to; we bring our farms, and our oxen, and our trades before the Lord. Are not our hearts, which should be the houses of prayer, the houses of merchandise? are we not taking, or pursuing, or in a journey, or asleep, or driving bargains? O christians, if we were privy to one another's hearts, as God is privy to them, what abominations should we see brought into the holy places! What monsters would our most sacred services appear! which, whilst the outside is only viewed, are applauded and admired. Is this our singleness of heart? Oh! for shame, and blushing, and confusion of face. Oh! for a vail to hide such hearts from the jealous eyes of the holy God: a varnish, a fair outside, hides all from men; but nothing but a dark vail of shame, and sorrow, and tears, and repentance; a vail dipt in blood, in the blood of Christ, will hide them from the eyes of the Lord.

Oh, how little plainness and singleness of heart is there in our ordinary course, in our dealings and conversings in the world! How little faith, or truth, is there in us! How little trust is there to us! What doubling, what deceitful dealing, defrauding, over-reaching, undermining are we guilty of! how false are we in our promises! how insignificant are our words! what an uncertain sound do they give! Our yea may often stand for nay, and our nay for yea. "They speak vanity every one with his neighbour, with flattering lips and a double heart do they speak," Psa. xii. 2. Trust ye not in a friend, put not confidence in a guide.

Blessed be God, the Lord hath a generation, on whom this cannot be charged. Children that will not lie, nor deceive: though Satan and this evil world bind up all in a bundle, they are all naught, they are all false, vain boasters, and deceitful workers; there is none upright, no not one : but, thanks be to God, Satan is a liar; the accuser of the brethren, is a false accuser. God hath his children that will not lie. But wo be to those professors, by reason of whom the offence cometh.

Christians, hath God promised to give you one heart? Let it be once said, " This day is the scripture fulfilled." O may you be the accomplishment of this good word. Hath God promised to give you one heart? Do not you say, But I will not take it; two are better than one: I have found so much the sweet of deceit, that there is no life like it. Hath God said, " I will give one heart?" let not any one among you say, But I fear he will not. Make not the promise of God of none effect, either by your impiety or unbelief. Doth God promise to give this one heart? he that promised it doth also require it. Be thyself, christian. Let it be said thou art what thou art, be true, be but one, have but one heart, and let thy one heart have but one tongue, but one face, and but one thing to do. Beware of hypocrisy, beware of carnal policy; make not thy God to serve thy flesh; call not the serving of thy flesh a serving of God, and make not thy serving of God to be a serving of the flesh. Be not divided betwixt God and the world. Oh how easy would our lives be did we find our whole souls running one way! taking up with God as the adequate object of all our powers, the mark of all our motions, and the reward of all our labours ! did all our streams empty themselves into this ocean, and all our lines meet in this one centre! Did God only draw and allure our hearts, and the sincerity of our hearts give motion to all our wheels! Guide our

eyes, govern our tongues, order our steps, animate
our duties, direct and quicken us in all our goings!
Oh how sweet, oh how beautiful, were such a life!
the sympathy betwixt our hearts and end, there is
sweetness; the harmony of our hearts and ways,
there is beauty. Oh how sweet are the drawings of
love, the free and full closure of our spirits with
God, dissolving themselves into his will, acquiescing,
resting satisfied in his goodness, is a sweetness
which no man knows but he who tastes it; the harmony of the power of the soul within itself, of its
motions and actions in the life, there is the beauty
which will eclipse the glory of the world. Christian,
be it thus with thee, and thou hast the blessing; that
covenant blessing which the Lord hath promised,
in saying, " I will give them one heart."

Chapter XII —*A heart of flesh*

" I will take away the stony heart out of your
flesh, and I will give you a heart of flesh," Ezek.
xxxvi. 26. The old heart is a stone, cold as a stone,
dead as a stone, hard as a stone; but I will take
away the stone, and give a heart of flesh.

A heart of flesh is a soft and tender heart; flesh
can feel any thing that is contrary to it, puts it to
pain. Sin makes it smart; it cannot kick, but it is
against the pricks, by its rebellion and resistance
against the Lord, it receives a wound; it cannot hit,
but it hurts itself. A soft hand gets nothing by
laying on, on a hedge of thorns. A soft heart, when
it hath been meddling with sin, is sure to smart for
it. It can neither escape the pain, nor yet endure
it; and what it cannot bear, it will take warning to
avoid.

Flesh will bleed. A soft heart will mourn, and melt, and grieve, when hard hearts are moved at nothing. Flesh will yield. It is apt to receive impressions. The power of God will awe it ; his justice alarm it ; his mercy melt it ; his holiness humble it, and leave the stamp and image of it upon it. And as the attributes, so the word and works of God will make sign upon it. Who sets a seal upon a stone ? or what print will it receive ? upon the wax, the print will abide. God speaks once and twice, but man, hardened man, will not regard it. Neither his word nor his rod, neither his speaking nor his smiting will make any sign on such hearts. It is the heart of flesh that hears and yields. And with such hearts the Lord delights to be dealing. " The heart of this people is waxed gross," Acts xxviii. 27. they will not hear, they will not understand ; and the next word is, Away to the Gentiles, they will hear. He will no more write his law on tables of stone : he will write in flesh ; there the impression will take, and go the deeper : and, therefore, wherever he intends to write, he prepares his table makes this stone flesh, and then engraves upon it Particularly this tenderness admits of a double distinction.

I. Respecting the object of it ; so there is a tenderness, 1. Of sin. 2. Of duty. 3. Of suffering.

1. Of sin ; and that is twofold, such as discovers itself, before the commission, and after the commission of it.

(1.) Before the commission. Whilst it is under a temptation, or feels the first motion to sin. A tender heart startles, starts back at the sight of a sin, as at the sight of a devil ; " How shall I do this great wickedness, and sin against God ?" Gen.

xxxix. 9. The manner of the speech presents Joseph as a man in a fright, startled at the ugliness of the motion. So David when he had an opportunity, and a temptation to slay Saul, rejects it with God forbid. "The Lord forbid that I should stretch forth my hand against the Lord's anointed," 1 Sam. xxvi. 11. And that not only at the higher and greater, but it resists the little ones, the smallest of sins. Is it not a little one? is no plea with it. Little or great, it is a sin, and that is enough.

(2.) After the commission; if it hath been brought on upon sin, yet it cannot go out with it. The skirt of Saul's garment was too heavy for David's heart to bear. His heart smote him presently, 1 Sam. xxiv. 5. Sin in the review, looks dreadful. Its pleasant flowers quickly turn to thorns; it pricks the heart, how much soever it pleased the eye. It ordinarily enters by the eye; and often runs out the same way it came in; runs out in tears. When he thought thereon, he wept. At least, it warns and makes more watchful after. Thou seest what it is, take heed; take it for a warning, and do no more. The pain of sin, if it do not force a tear, it will set a watch.

2. Of duty. A tender heart will neither slight a sin, nor neglect a duty. It is loath to grieve and offend, and careful to serve and please the Lord. It would not that he should suffer by it, nor so much as lose his due. It watches against sin, and unto duty. It cares how to please the Lord, and its care is tender. It would not displease by its neglects or performances; all must be done that ought, and as it ought to be done. It will neither stand out with its offering, nor will it offer an unclean thing. It considers not only what, but how. Both matter

and manner, substance and circumstance, all must be right, or it is not at ease. It will keep time, and as much as may be, keep touch* with the Lord in every point. It is not satisfied that it prays sometimes, it would not lose a praying time. God will not, and it cannot lose a duty. It would neither lose by non-performance, nor lose what is performed. It would neither leave undone, nor do amiss; any failing, not only in the matter, but in the principle, end, affection, intention; any failing pains.

3. In point of suffering. A soft heart will not be careful, what, or how much, but why and upon what account, he suffers. Will neither sinfully shun the cross, nor run upon it unwarrantably. He waits for a call, and then follows. He is patient under the hand of the Lord, but not insensible; can be touched with an affliction, though not offended at it. "The hand of the Lord hath touched me." He suffers more than his own, his brethren's sufferings. His brethren's burdens all lie on his shoulders. He weeps in their sorrows, bleeds in their wounds, his heart is bound in their chains. As the care, so the trouble of all the churches comes daily upon him. " Who is weak, and I am not weak ? who is offended, and I burn not ?" he espouses all the sufferings of Christ as his own. In all his afflictions he is afflicted.

II. Tenderness may be distinguished in respect of the subject of it; and so there is a tenderness of the conscience, the will, the affections.

1. Tenderness of conscience stands in these three things. 1. Clearness of judgment. 2. Quickness of sight. 3. Uprightness or faithfulness.

* Engagement.

(1.) Clearness of judgment. When it is well instructed, and understands the rule, and can thence discern betwixt good and evil, Heb. v. 14. There is a tenderness that proceeds from cloudiness; scrupulosity, that fears every thing, stumbles at straws, starts at shadows; makes sins; picks quarrels at duties; and so sometimes dares not please for fear of offending God. This is the sickness, or soreness of conscience, not its soundness. It is the sound conscience that is truly tender.

(2.) Quickness of sight, and watchfulness. I sleep, but my heart waketh. It can espy the least sins, and smallest duties. It can see sin in the very temptation; it can discover the least sin under the fairest face, and the least duty under the foulest vizor. Call it singularity, nicety, cloud it with reproaches; yet conscience can discover light shining through all the clouds; duty within, whatsoever unhandsome face it be presented in, the former stands in consciences understanding the rule, as was said, this in strait applying the rule to cases: and distinguishing them by it. The truly tender hath his eyes in his head; and his eyes open, to discover and discern all that comes, be it good or evil, little or great. If but a thought comes in, What comes there? says conscience; what art thou? a friend or an enemy? whence art thou? from God, or from beneath? It will examine whatever knocks, before any free admission. Oh what a crowd of evils do thrust into loose and careless hearts; the devil comes in in the crowd, and is never discovered. If the eye be either dim or asleep, there is entrance for anything. Little do we think oftimes, who hath been with us, what losses and mischiefs we have sustained, while our hearts have been asleep; which, had they been wakeful and watchful, might have been prevented.

(3.) Uprightness and faithfulness: which discovers itself, 1. In giving charge concerning duty; 2 In giving warning of sin; 3. In giving check for sin when committed.

[1.] In giving charge concerning duty, look to it soul, there is a duty before thee, which God calls thee to; do not say, It is no great hurt to let it alone, it is no great hurt to do it, it is questionable whether it be a duty or not; many wiser than I think otherwise. Do not say, It is a nicety, it is but a punctilio, it is mere folly and preciseness; and there will be no end of standing upon such small matters; see to it, it is thy duty, beware thou neglect it not; the balking of the least duty, is the neglecting of the great God of glory.

[2.] In giving warning of sin. Take heed to thyself, sin lies at the door, thou art under a temptation, the devil is entering upon thee. Do not say, it is but a little sin; as little as it is, there is death and hell in it; look to it, it is sin, have thou nothing to do with it, keep thyself pure, and though it run upon thee, shake it off.

[3.] After commission, it gives check for it; reproving, judging, and lashing the soul for it: " Where hast thou been Gehazi?" say not, thou hast been nowhere; went not this heart with thee, and saw thee running after thy covetousness, gadding after thy pleasures, feeding thy pride, dandling thy lusts, playing the hypocrite, playing the harlot from thy God, pampering thy flesh, pleasing thine appetite? and where hast thou been? What hast thou done, soul? think not to excuse or mince the matter, it cannot be excused; thou hast sinned against thy

God, and now bear thy shame. This is our heart smiting us, 2 Sam. xxiv. 10. our heart condemning us; "If our hearts condemn us, God is greater than our hearts, and knoweth all things." 1 John iii. 20.

2. Tenderness of the will, that stands in its flexibleness, and pliableness to the will of God. And this is that tenderness wherein chiefly stands the blessing of a soft heart; a hard heart is stubborn and obstinate. Thy neck is as an iron sinew, and thy brow brass. Thou wilt not be ruled, there is no bending thee, or turning thee out of thy course, thine iron is too hard for the fire, it will not be melted; and for the hammer, it will not be broken; there is no dealing with thee, thou art an untractable piece, thou wilt go neither led nor driven; thy heart is set in thee to do evil, thy will is set upon sin, and thou art set upon thine own will. The word which thou hast spoken to us in the name of the Lord, we will not do, but we will do whatsoever proceeds out of our own mouth; we will do what we will do, Jer. xliv 16, 17. "Who is Lord over us?" Psa. xii. 4. And Jer. ii. 25. "Thou saidst, There is no hope:" no, for we have loved strangers, and after them we will go, come what will of it, say what thou wilt against it; be silent, scriptures; hold thy peace, conscience; it is to no purpose to speak more, there is no hope of prevailing; we are at a point, we will take our own course. These are hard hearts, stubborn, obstinate hearts.

When the iron sinew is broken, when the rebellion and stubbornness of the spirit is subdued and tamed, and made gentle and pliable, then it becomes a tender heart.

There may be some tenderness in the conscience,

and yet the will be a very stone ; and as long as the will stands out, there is no broken heart. Conscience may be scared and frighted. Conscience may fly upon the sinner, What dost thou mean soul? whither are thy rebellions carrying thee? look to thyself, hearken, or thou wilt be lost ere thou art aware. But however God hath gotten conscience on his side, yet the devil still rides the will ; and there sin takes up its rest. There is a double resting of sin in the soul: in peace, and in power.

(1.) In peace ; when it dwells and rules in the soul without disturbance or contradiction ; when it carries all smoothly before it. When God lets it alone, and conscience speaks not a word against it ; when notwithstanding those armies of lusts, fighting against the soul, there is not so much as one weapon lifted up against them ; not a prayer, nor a tear, nor a wish for freedom, nor the least fear concerning the issue ; this is the most dreadful hardness.

(2.) In power: when, though it can have no peace, yet it hath still a place in the heart. Though it can have no quiet, but conscience is still quarrelling with it, and warning it away, yet it still holds its power over the will ; the master of the house is content to be its servant. Oh how many persons are there, even amongst the professors of religion, who cannot sin in quiet: they are proud, or passionate, or intemperate, or covetous, or false in their words, in their dealings ; they are formal, and hypocritical, and slight in their duties, but they cannot go out with it with any quiet. Conscience smites them for it, they feel many a pang and deadly twinge in their heart, insomuch that sometimes they cry, and groan, and roar in their spirits, O for redemption, O for deliverance from this false, this

proud, this covetous and wicked heart! And yet after
all this, the will remains a captive still, sin holds its
power there, though it cannot carry it on in peace,
though it cannot be proud, or play the hypocrite, or
be covetous, or an oppressor, without some galls,
and gripes in the soul, yet on it goes, the same
trade is kept up, the same course is held on.   God
commands, Cast ye out, cast ye out, come off from
all your wickedness and evil ways, and I will receive
you: no, though conscience would, the will cannot
come, whatever rendings and tearings; whatever
terrors, and torments, and worryings such souls are
at any time under; whatever stings, and plagues,
and fires, they find their sins to be in their souls
and bones; whatever wishings and wouldings they
wring forth, that they were well rid of these plagues;
whilst the will is still from them, there is a hard
heart, desperately hard; there is none of this heart
of flesh.   When the will is once broken loose from
sin; when it will be content to let all go, and give
up itself to the dominion of the Lord, there is a
broken heart.   Now speak Lord, and I will hear.
Now call Lord, and I will answer.   Now command
me, impose on me what thou wilt, I will submit.
None but the Lord; none but Christ; no other
Lord nor lover.   I am thine, Lord, thine own, do
with thine own, demand of thine own, whatever thou
pleasest.   What God will have me be, what God
will have me do, that will I do, and be.   No longer
what I will, but the will of the Lord be done.   When
it is come to this, there is a tender heart; there is
the blessing of a broken spirit; the stone he hath
taken away, he hath given a heart of flesh.

Christians, never trust to tears, never talk of
terrors, trouble of conscience, of the passionate

workings and meltings, which at any time you feel upon your spirits, though there be something in these, as you shall see more by and by; yet these are not the things you are to look at. A subdued, tractable, willing, obedient heart, that is the tender heart. " If ye be willing and obedient, ye shall eat the good of the land; but if ye refuse and rebel, ye shall be slain with the sword; the mouth of the Lord hath spoken it," Isa. i. 19.

3. Tenderness of the affections. I shall instance only in three; namely, love, fear, sorrow.

(1.) The tenderness of love. This is seen in its benevolence and in its jealousy.

[1.] In its benevolence. Our goodness extends not to the Lord, but our good will does. Our love can add nothing to him; " Can a man be profitable to God ?" Job xxii. 2. " If thou be righteous, what givest thou to him ?" chap. xxxv. 7. Yet though it can add nothing, it would not that anything be detracted from him; whilst he can have no more, it would that he should have his own, all that is due, his due praise, his due honour, and homage, and worship, and subjection, from every creature; it would have no abatement, not the least spot or stain upon all his glory. What is an affront to God, is an offence to love. " Love beareth all things," saith the apostle, 1 Cor. xiii. 7. all things from God, all things from men. And yet there are two things the love of God cannot bear,—his dishonour—his displeasure.

His *dishonour*. Love would have God to be God, to live in the glory of his majesty, in the hearts and eyes of all the world. His reproach is grievous to him that loves, for this is the cloud that takes God out of sight. He loves and honours, and would that God should be loved and honoured of

all ; he fears, and would that the whole world should
fear him. He would receive in his own breast,
every arrow that is shot against his Maker ; he
would that his own name and soul might stand
betwixt his God and all reproach and dishonour.
He would be vile, so the Lord may be glorious ; so
God may increase, he is content to decrease. He
is not so tender of his own heart and bowels, as of
the holiness of his God. He would suffer, and die,
and be nothing, rather than that God should not be all
in all. He would rather never think, nor speak, nor
be, rather than not be in word, and thought, and
life, holiness to the Lord. But oh what, or where
would he be, rather than his own hand should be
lifted up against him !

To see the Lord robbed of his holiness, wronged
in his wisdom or his truth, or his sovereignty, to see
sin, that devil, to see the world, that idol, set up in
the throne, and the God of glory made to stand aside
as insignificant ; to hear that blasphemy, God is
not worth this lust, or not worthy this labour, (and
what is said less in every sin ?) is a sword in his
breast. The reproaches of them that reproached
thee, are fallen upon me. Love hath tasted of God,
it hath fed on his fulness, it hath its nourishment
from his sweetness, it hath been warmed in his
bosom, all his goodness hath passed before it ; upon
this it lives and feeds ; and, having found and felt
what the Lord is, it is impatient that all his goodness should be clouded or belied. Love kindled
from heaven, is keen ; and the keen is a tender
edge ; the least touch of what offends, will turn it.
" I am in distress, my bowels are troubled, mine
heart is turned within me, for I have grievously re-
belled," Lam. i. 20. " My tears have been my

meat continually, while they daily say unto me, Where is thy God?" Psa. xlii. 3. Where is that care, and help, and that salvation of thy God, thou trustedst in? Thy God is not such a one as thou boastedst him to be: when I remember, when I hear such things, my soul is poured out within me. Love is large; he that loves hath a large heart, he can never receive or do too much; he would have all he can, and he would give all he hath to the Lord. He is tender how any thing be withheld that is due, how anything be wasted elsewhere, that might be useful to the Lord.

His *displeasure*. The displeasure of men it bears and rejoices; the wrath and rage of Satan, it bears and triumphs; though all the world, and hell to boot, be displeased, and provoked, so God smiles, it is well enough. Lord lift thou up the light of thy countenance upon me, and my heart shall be glad, Psa. iv. " Thou didst hide thy face, and I was troubled," Psa. xxx. 7.

Let him correct me, but oh not in fury; let him smite, but not frown; let him kill me, so he will but love me. And though he smite, though he kill me, yet will I love and trust in him. O my God, let me rather die in thy love, than live in thy displeasure; there is life in that death, this life is death to me. Let me not be dead whilst alive; turn away thine anger which kills my heart.

It is impatient of divine displeasure, and thence it is grievous to it that it does displease; thence it quarrels with sin, and falls so foul with itself for it. Is this thy kindness to thy friend? lovest thou God, soul? what! and yet provokest him thus daily? love! and yet neglect to seek and follow thy God? love! and yet so lame- and so slow, and so heavy, and so sparing in thy services to him? Is this all thy love will do? not deny thine ease, or thy pleasure, or thy liberty, or thine appetite, or thy companion, for the sake of the Lord? choose rather to pleasure thy friend, or thy flesh, than to please God? Is this thy love? Is this thy kindness to thy friend? O false heart, O unworthy, unworthy spirit! how canst thou look thy God in the face? how canst thou say I love thee, when thy heart is no more with him?

[2.] In its jealousy. He that loves the Lord is jealous, and jealousy hath a tender edge; he is jealous not of, but for the Lord, not of his God, but of himself, lest any thing should steal away his heart from God. Love would be chaste, would not bestow itself elsewhere; and yet is in great jealousy, it may be enticed and drawn away. He that loves the Lord, there is not any thing, whether wife, or child, or friend, or estate, or esteem, that gets near his heart, but he is jealous of them, lest they steal it away. Get you down, keep you lower, this heart is neither yours nor mine; O my God, it is thine, it is thine Lord, take it wholly to thee, keep it to thyself, let no other lovers be sharers with thee.

(2.) There is a tenderness of fear. The tender heart is a trembling heart: the tenderness of fear is manifested in its suspicion,—and caution.

[1.] In its suspicion. The fearful are suspicious: they look further than they see; he that is in dread, will be in doubt what may befall him, he suspects a surprisal; every bush is a thief, every bait he fears may have a hook under. There is a foolish and a causeless fear, and there is a prudent and a holy fear; this fear is a principle of wisdom, Psa. cxi. 10. " The prudent man foreseeth the evil,"

Prov. xxii. 3. but fools go on; the snare is never nearer, than to the secure; bold, venturous sinners never want woe, the devil may spare his cunning, when he hath to do with such. Nothing that looks like sin offers itself to a tender heart, but he presently suspects it; every pleasant morsel, every pleasant cup, every pleasant companion that comes, anything that tickles and gratifies the flesh, he looks through it ere he will touch with it, lest it betray his soul from God. There may be a snare in the dish, a snare in my cup, a snare in my company; and what if there should? he feeds himself with fear, dwells, walks, converses, works, recreates himself, with a trembling heart and jealous eye.

[2.] In its caution. Fear is wary; some com manders have set their scout-watches unarmed, that fear might make them watchful. A fearful christian will take heed what and whom he trusts; he dares not trust himself in such company as may be a snare unto him. He dares not trust his heart among temptations, he will keep the devil at a distance, he will not come near where his nets do lie. Blessed is he that thus feareth always. Oh the unspeakable mischief! Oh the multitudes of sins that we run upon, through our secure hearts! I never thought of it, I never dreamed of any such danger. Oh I am undermined, I am over-reached, I am surprised; my foot is in the snare, the gin hath taken me by the heel, my soul is among lions, sin hath gotten hold on me, my heart is gone ere I was aware, the enemy hath come in and carried it away, hath given it to lust, to the world, to pleasure, to divide it amongst themselves, my faith hath failed, my conscience is defiled, my love is grown cold, my grace withered, my comforts wasted, my peace broken!

and my God, Oh where is he gone? Woe is me, the evil that I feared not is come upon me; had I feared, I had not fallen: O that I had been wise, had kept my watch, had stood upon my guard; had I thought, had I thought, I had escaped all this danger! O christians be wise in season, and take heed of the fool's too late "had I known it."

(3.) There is a tenderness of sorrow. Sorrow is the melting of the heart, the stone dissolved, sorrow is the wound of the heart, a wound is tender, love is tender, and therefore godly sorrow, which is the sorrow of love; you may call it a love-sickness. Love is both the pain and pleasure of a mourning heart, it is love that wounds, and love that heals; it is both the weapon and the oil; this sorrow hath its joy, the melted is the most joyful heart; it is love that makes it sad, it therefore weeps because it loves, and it is love that makes it glad too; it therefore joys because in its sorrows it sees it loves. It is love that makes the wound, the matter of this sorrow being love abused; what hast thou done soul? whom hast thou despised? against whom hast thou lifted up thyself? Thou hast sinned, thou hast sinned, and hast thereby smitten and grieved thy God that loves thee, and whom thou lovest. Thou hast but one friend in heaven and earth, and him thou hast abused; to pleasure thy lust, thou hast pierced thy Lord, thou hast transgressed his commandments, and trampled upon his compassions; hast broken his bonds, and kicked at his compassion; his greatness and his goodness; his law and his very love hath been despised by thee; him who loved thee hast thou smitten. Is this thy kindness to thy friend? O vile, ungracious, unkind, unthankful, unnatural heart; what hast thou done?

Put all this now together, and you have the heart
of flesh which the covenant promises, a tender heart,
a heart that is tender of sin and duty, that carefully
shuns sin, or is sure to smart for it; that neither
slights sin nor duty; that says not of the one or the
other, It is but a little one; that can feel sufferings,
but not fret at them: a tender conscience, that will
neither wink at sin, nor excuse the sinner; that will
not hold the sinner guiltless, nor say unto the
wicked, Thou art righteous; that will not be smitten,
but it will smite again; that will give due warning
and due correction: a flexible, tractable heart, that
will not resist and rebel; that says unto the Lord,
What wilt thou have me to do? and will not say
of anything he will have, Any thing but this: a
willing, ductile heart, stiff against nothing but sin,
that a word from Heaven will lead to anything: a
heart of love, that bears goodwill to the Lord, and
all that he does or requires; in which good will lies,
radically, every good work; that says not of any
duties or sufferings, This is too great; or of any
sin, This is nothing; that would be anything or
nothing, so God may be all; that would rather
be displeased than displease; that is not displeased
when God is pleased: a trembling heart, that fears
more than it sees, and flies from what it fears,
whom fear makes to beware: a melting heart, a
mourning heart, that wounds itself in the wounds it
hath given to the Lord, and his name; that can
grieve in love, and can love and grieve, where it
cannot weep. In sum, it is a heart that can feel,
that can bleed, that can weep; or at least that can
yield and stoop, where it cannot weep, nor feel but
little; that will easily be commanded, where it is not
sensibly melted; this is a soft heart, this is the heart

ot flesh: I will take away the stone, and give them
a heart of flesh.

Oh what a blessing is such a heart! what a
plague is a hard heart! Oh what prisoners are the
men of this world : in prison under Satan, in prison
under sin, bound under a curse, shut up under unbelief and impenitence : the hard heart is the iron
gate that shuts them in that they cannot get out,
Rom. ii. 5. Oh what a hospital is this world become of
blind, and lame, and sick, and cripples, and wounded
creatures! Whence are all the calamities and distresses that befall them, but from the hardness of
their hearts? The stone in their hearts breeds all
their diseases, brings all their calamities : hath
blinded their eyes, and broken their bones, and
wasted their estates : there is not one misery that
befalls them, but they may write up over it, This is
the hardness of my heart. Oh what a Sodom is this
world become, for wickedness as well as for wrath!
what drunkenness, what adulteries, what oaths,
what blasphemies, and all sorts of monstrous sins do
every where abound! whence is all this, but from
the hardness of men's hearts? if you say, It is from
other causes ; it is from unbelief, from ignorance,
from impotence, from temptations ; lot it be granted :
yet still it is from hardness of heart. They are wilfully ignorant, wilfully weak, wilfully run into temptations; they shut their eyes, and stop their ears,
they will not see, they will not believe. Oh what
losses do they sustain! how many sabbaths are lost!
how many sermons are lost! how many reproofs,
counsels, corrections, are lost! a gospel lost, and
souls thereby like to be lost for ever! Oh what
prodigies are they become! under all this sin and
misery ! and yet merry, jolly, laughing, and singing,

and sporting, and feasting, and braving it out, as if nothing ailed them. Feeling nothing of all that is come upon them, and fearing nothing of all that is coming. Warn them, reprove them, beseech them, it is all but preaching to a stone. It may be you have sometimes wondered to see a company of thieves in prison, to be drinking and carousing, and making merry, when they know that, in a few days, they must be brought out and hanged. When thou wonderest at these, wonder at thyself. What bitter complaints do we sometimes hear, even from the best of saints! Oh this hard heart, oh this stubborn spirit! I cannot mourn, I cannot stoop, I cannot submit. "Why hast thou hardened our heart from thy fear?" Isa. lxiii. 17. Or why hast thou left us, or given us up to a hard heart? why hast thou not softened, and humbled, and broken us? thou hast humbled us, and we are not humbled; broken us, and we are not broken; thou hast broken our land, broken our peace, broken our backs, but the stone is not yet broken; oh for one breach more, Lord; our hearts, our hearts, let these be once broken; our streets mourn, the cities of our solemnities mourn, the waves of Sion mourn: oh when wilt thou give us a mourning Spirit?

Oh what sorrow-bitten souls are the saints for want of sorrow! I mourn, Lord, I lament, I weep, but it is because I cannot mourn, or lament, as I should: if I could mourn as I ought, I could be comforted: if I could weep, I could rejoice; if I could sigh, I could sing; if I could lament, I could live; I die, I die, my heart dies within me, because I cannot cry: I cry Lord, but not for sin, but for tears for sin; I cry, Lord, my calamities cry, my bowels cry, my bones cry, my soul cries, my sins cry,

Lord, for a broken heart; and behold, yet I am not broken.

The rocks rend, the earth quakes, the heavens drop, the clouds weep, the sun will blush, the moon be ashamed, the foundations of the earth will tremble at the presence of the Lord, but this heart will neither break nor tremble. O for a broken heart! If this were once done, might my soul have this wish, thenceforth my God might have his will; what would be hard if my heart were tender? Labour would be easy, pains would be a pleasure, burdens would be light. Neither the command nor the cross would be any longer grievous, nothing would be hard but sin. Fear, where art thou? come and plough up this rock; love, where art thou? come and thaw this ice, come and warm this dead lump, come and enlarge this straitened spirit, then shall I run the way of his commandments.

O brethren, how little, how very little of this tenderness is there to be found amongst the most of christians! The sacrifice of God is a broken heart; Oh how far must the Lord go to find himself such a sacrifice! we do but cast stones up to heaven when we lift up our hearts; it is a wonder that such hearts as we carry do not break themselves; that our marble weeps not; that if nothing else will do it, our hardness doth not make us relent; that we should so labour under, and complain of, and yet not be sick of the stone.

Broken hearts, yielding and relenting spirits, tender consciences, oh where are they? afraid of sin, tender of transgressing, or mourning under it? when shall it once be? our lusts no more broken; our pride, our passion, our envy, our earthliness no more broken. So venturous on temptation, so bold on sin, such liberty taken to transgress, such mincing, and palliating, and excusing of sin, as we find. Is this our brokenness? We are tender, it is true; but of what?—Of dishonouring God, of abusing grace, of neglecting duty, of defiling conscience, of wounding our souls? No, it is of our flesh that we are so tender; tender of labour, tender of trouble, tender of our carcases, of our credit, of our names and reputations; a tender shoulder, a tender hand, a tender foot; they can bear nothing, and do nothing; nothing can touch our flesh, nothing can touch our idols, our ease, or our estates, but we shrink, and smart, and are put to pain. God may be smitten, and we feel it not; the gospel may be smitten, the church may be smitten, conscience may be smitten, and it moves us not; we can fear an affliction, fear a reproach. Oh did we so much fear a temptation, or a sin! We cannot want bread, but we feel it; we cannot want clothes, or a house, or a friend, but we feel it; we cannot want our sleep, our quiet, our pleasure, our respects from men, but we feel it; any thing that pinches our flesh pierces our heart. We cannot pine, or languish in our bodies, but we feel it; a fever, or an ague, or a consumption, or dropsy, or a bodily sickness, oh it makes us sick at heart! a froward yokefellow, an unthrifty servant, an ill neighbour, a scoff, a slight cannot be borne, but oh! how much sin can be borne! while our flesh will bear nothing, oh how can conscience bear, and never complain!

Christians consider, when our flesh must be thus tendered, whatever come of it; must be tenderly fed, must have soft raiment, soft lodging, soft usage; be dealt gently with, though to maintain it conscience must be racked, and racked, and wasted.

When our wills cannot be crossed, our appetites cannot be denied, but a tumult follows, the soul is an uproar; and conscience, meanwhile, must be denied, rated, and must go away in silence. When the word works no more, when the prints of it are not received, the power of it is resisted; when the rod works no more; when our stripes make no sign, when the lashes on our backs fall all beside our hearts; when we remain so vain, and so wanton, so wilful, and so carnal, and so earthly; after the Lord hath been preaching, and whipping us into a better frame, when we stand upon our terms, keep our distances, our animosities, our heats, and heights of spirit, our censurings, our quarrellings one with another, christian with christian, professor with professor, after the Lord hath been heating us together to make us friends, and all to teach us more humility and charity :—is this our brokenness? is this our tenderness? when upon any the Lord's rougher dealing with us, smiting our faces, throwing us on our backs, trampling us in the dirt, we are yet no more brought on our knees. Is this our brokenness? when the Lord hath been awakening us out of sleep, putting his spurs and goads in our sides, to quicken us on our way; calling to us, Arise, sleepers, put on, sluggards, stir up your spirits, mend your pace: I will not be put off as I have been; no more such loitering, and idling, and trifling, and halting, as hath been; I must have other manner of service, other manner of praying, and hearing, and walking, and working, than hath been: be zealous and amend, more labour, more care, more watchfulness, more activity, more of the spirit and soul of what you profess. When the Lord hath been thus goading, and spurring us on, and

though our flesh feels, yet our hearts will not feel,
nor answer the goad or spur; is this an argument
of tenderness?

When great duties are little, and lesser are none;
when great sins are infirmities, and little ones are
nothing; when lying and defrauding; when false
weights, false wares, and false dealings; when de-
faming, back-biting, tale-bearing, railing, reviling,
do stand for little more than ciphers; when fellowship and familiarity with evil men in their sins;
when compliance with, or connivance at their
wickedness; when sinful courtings and compli-
mentings of such, to the fleshing them, and harden-
ing them in their ways, do pass for virtues and
civilities; when frothy, wanton discourse and communication; when scoffing and making a sport at
the sins, or infirmities of others; when sinful, vain
jesting, wherein rather conscience than wit must be
denied;—when all these pass for our ornaments
rather than our evils, where is our tenderness?

When, upon the auditing of our accounts, the
examining our books, and reckoning up our scores;
where a talent is owing, we bid conscience take thy
bill, and write down a shekel; where twenty or a
hundred sins are to be reckoned for, Take thy bill,
and write down ten, or but one, and that a little one:
when we are so free in multiplying, and so false in
numbering our iniquities, where is our tenderness?

Well, christians, the Lord hath promised a tender
heart, to make these stones flesh; and something
possibly is done already upon you towards it. O
let this sad sight now laid before you, this view of
what is wanting, have some influence upon the
making it up. Let the sense of no more done
work what is yet undone; as is said before, let your

unbrokenness break your hearts; let the stone that yet remains make your flesh to bleed. If you yet feel no more, may you at least feel this, that you feel not.

CHAPTER XIII —*A heart to love the Lord*

" THE Lord thy God will circumcise thine heart. and the heart of thy seed, to love the Lord thy God, with all thine heart, and with all thy soul," Deut. xxx. 6. Love is the soul of the new creature; the closure of the soul with God. He that hath most of God, is most a christian; and he that hath most of love, hath most of God. God is love.

In the opening of this love to God, we shall consider its object and its act.

I. Its object. The object of divine love is God. God is good, and good is amiable. God is all good: there is none good but one, that is God. God is essentially good. goodness in the abstract; he is infinitely excellent, he is all perfection. In this one attribute all the rest of the attributes of God are included, and this in each of them. However, the scriptures speaking to our capacities, describe God and his glorious attributes, in several and distinct notions; yet in each one all are included; each one is infinite, and infinite perfection is essentially all perfection. God is originally good, the fountain and pattern of all that moral good which is in the creatures; he is bountiful and gracious, ready to do them good; and he is the felicitating end, or the blessedness of the soul. The goodness of God to his creatures, according to its different respects to them, hath its different and various appellations. As it is freely bestowed, it is grace; as it respects

them as needy, so it is bounty; as in misery, so it
is mercy and compassion; as provoking, so it is
patience; as it intends their good, so it is love; as
it answers both their necessities and capacities, so it
is all-sufficiency. All these, his bounty, mercy,
compassion, patience, love, all-sufficiency, all these
are in one word his goodness, and goodness calls
for love. The object of this love is God, particularly, 1. God in himself; 2. God in Christ; 3.
God in all the things of God.

1. God in himself, as he is infinitely excellent,
(as before,) and so worthy of all love. God is to be
loved in himself, and for himself, for his own worthiness; God is good in himself, and therefore to be
loved for himself.

2. God in Christ. In whom alone, considering
us as sinners, he can be said to be good to us.

There is a four-fold incentive of love:—Perception—Proportion—Propriety—Possession.

(1.) Perception; or the apprehension or understanding of the object to be loved. We must know
before we can love; now God cannot immediately
be seen by mortals; he dwelleth in light, but that
light is to us invisible. Christ is the glass, in which
this glory may be seen. We cannot see God but
through a vail of flesh, in the face of Jesus Christ,
2 Cor. iv. 6. "No man hath seen God at any time,
but the only begotten of the Father," who is in the
bosom of the Father, he hath revealed him. John i.18.

(2.) Proportion. And there is a double proportion requisite. 1. In respect of quantity, there must
be sufficiency; 2. In respect of quality, there must
be suitableness. God himself is proportioned to us,
consider us as rational creatures, and in our state
of innocency; is both a sufficient and a suitable

good; but God in Christ only, being considered as lapsed creatures, in a state of sin.

God in Christ, is a God of pity and compassion to us; a God of patience, a God of mercy, with whom is plenteous redemption. A God, pardoning iniquity, and passing by transgression; loving us in our low estate, loving us and pitying us, loving us and pardoning us, loving us and washing us, loving us and saving us from our sins, and from the wrath to come. And such love is the great flame that kindles love; love breaking forth out of a cloud of wrath, and fury, and displeasure; abused love, provoked love, and yet forgiving love; to whom much is forgiven, they will love much.

(3.) Propriety. What is good, good for us, and our own good, that carries our hearts. We must love our own good, because we most love ourselves. Our love to God is heightened from our due self-love; there is a sinful self-love; when either we love that for a self, which is not ourself; when we love our flesh and fleshly interest; or when we love ourselves inordinately, more than God, and God only for ourselves: and there is a lawful self-love; when we love ourselves, in the Lord, and for the Lord. And the more we thus love ourselves, the more is the Lord loved by us; and the more he is our own, the more love he hath. Now in Christ the Lord is our God. Our own God; even our own God. "O God, thou art my God, and I will praise thee. Thou art my God, and I will love thee," Psa. cxviii. 28.

The Lord is God, and we therefore love him; the Lord is good, gracious, merciful, and we therefore love him, yea, and ought to love him, whether he be ours or not; but when both meet, he is God, and our God; he is good and our good; gracious, merciful, all-sufficient, and all this to us: hence is our love made perfect in us.

(4.) Possession. We can love a distant, an absent good; a good that is only possible; there is love in hope; but by how much the nearer good is to us that is really so, by so much the more attractive and acceptable it is. It is then most in our hearts, when it is most in our hands. Indeed those things which are fancied good; or those things that are finite good; and good over-rated; that are judged better than they are, are loved most at a distance; because when they come to hand, we see our mistakes. But that which is what it seemed; much more, that which is above our thoughts, beyond our expectations infinite good; by how much the nearer, it is ever the dearer to us. All worldly good is most valued, at least by carnal hearts, at a distance; they promise themselves more contentment in it, than it hath to pay them; their possession is their disappointment. While they lusted, they idolized, they adored; but when they have tasted and eaten, it comes out at their nostrils. Or else they sit down with the shame of the disappointed; they are either surfeited, or hungry still. Is this all? all you can do for me? all the pleasure, and comfort, I shall have of you? is all my expectation of delight and satisfaction come to no more than this? Miserable comforters are you all! possession and fruition is the proof of all things. And vanity proved, is the less loved. But God being an all-sufficient, incomprehensible good; by how much the nearer to us, by how much the more he is ours, by so much the more we prize and love, because now we find (when we have him, we enjoy him) that before, the one half was not told us.

Now in Christ, we have not only a propriety in
God, but in some degree a present possession. " He
that hath the Son, hath the Father also." We see
his light, we feel his love, we taste of his goodness,
we enjoy his presence, we have God with us, we
have God in us, we have fellowship with him, he
dwelleth in us and we in him, and hence we love,
and herein we rejoice.

3. In all the things of God; in his word, ordinances, sabbaths, saints, in graces, duties, in all his
ways, the saints love God, and love his word; it is
God in the word they love; they love God, and they
love ordinances, and sabbaths, and saints : it is God
in all these they love; they love the ways, and works,
and all the dispensations of God, and it is God in
them all they love, they see God in every thing,
and they love God wherever they see him. They
look on all these things with another eye, and
therefore embrace them with another heart than
other men.

The saints' love to the things of God, is their love
to God : for it is God in them, as was said, that they
love; their love to them is founded either on their
participation of God, or relation to God.

Or else you may say they love the things of God,
because they are, 1. The offspring; 2. The images;
3. The chariots of God.

(1.) The things of God are the offspring of God;
as the saints are born from above, so all the things
of God come down from above, and therefore may
also be called, as the apostle styles them, things
above; " If ye be risen with Christ, seek those
things that are above, set your affection on things
above," Col. iii. 1, 2. Things above, and the things
of God, come all to one ; whatsoever is from God,

and belongs to his heavenly kingdom, is divine and heavenly ; and he that loveth him that begets, therefore loveth those which are begotten, and whatsoever proceedeth from him.

(2.) The word and the saints are the images of God, the character and impression of God are upon them, the grace in the saints, and the holy truths in the word, are the very face of Christ, who is full of grace and truth, and this is their rule, love God, and love his image.

(3.) The things of God are the chariots of God. He that makes the clouds his chariots, makes also his word, and his ordinances, and his ministers his chariots, wherein he rides down into those lower parts to give the world a meeting.   When ministers come, and the word comes down, God comes down in them to visit his people ; as it was said of Paul, so it is true of Apollos, and Cephas, and all the dispensers of the gospel, they are chosen vessels to bear his name, before the sons of men ; and as they are the chariots in which God comes down, so are they also the wagons which he hath sent them, to fetch them up to himself.   The saints send up their hearts in their duties, their hearts in their prayers, in their praises unto God.   Old Israel's heart leaped when he saw the wagons which Joseph had sent. Oh what love doth the psalmist express to the house and court of the Lord ! " Oh how amiable are thy tabernacles ! I was glad when they said unto me, Let us go up into the house of the Lord."   He was glad to go thither, because thence he hoped to be carried higher, from the mountain to the mansion ; from mount Zion here below, to Jerusalem, which is above.

It is the duty and the delight of the saints to be

ascending heavenwards; they are dead with Christ,
they are risen with Christ; and it is not as they
would with them, but when they are ascending up
with Christ; they are dead with Christ, by repentance and humiliation; they are risen with Christ, by
faith and sanctification; and they ascend with Christ
by love and holy affection: this is their chariot of
fire, a chariot within a chariot, that through duties
and ordinances rides up in its own flames to the
God of love.

Or, if you will, the ordinances of God are our
Jacob's ladder reaching from heaven to earth; by
which angels descend, and souls ascend. God comes
down and hearts go up, praises go up and blessings
come down. Thou hast not proved what an
ordinance is, what prayer means, or preaching means,
or sacraments mean, who hast not seen God coming
down, nor felt thine heart ascending by them; he
that hath felt this will say, Here let me dwell, let
others be where they will, amongst their flocks,
amongst their herds, upon their beds, or at their
cups, their pleasures, or in their houses; "It is good
for me to be here."

No wonder, christians, that carnal hearts are such
strangers to the word, can so well set out at duties,
and can want ordinances; preaching, and praying,
and sabbaths, they can spare, and not feel their want;
what wonder? What is heaven to earth? What is
God to flesh? These chariots would carry them
away from their gods, carry them out of their own
country, into a strange land, where they have neither
possession nor acquaintance. But oh! what a sad
wonder is it, that saints should go up so often into
the chariots, and yet get no nearer home; that
they should be still so much on the earth, that have

been so often mounted for heaven; that those hearts should still be on the dunghills, whose feet are so often on the mountain of the Lord; that the wagons should be so often sent down, and go up empty; scarce a heart sent up in them; yea, that they should be so far from God, when God is among them. Where is your love, christians? how is it that it is still below? what have you here? your city is above, your home is above, your God, your Jesus, your treasure is above. Oh how is it, that where your treasure is, your hearts are not also? hear from God, and not God with the messenger? send up to heaven your eyes, your hands, your prayers, your complaints, your promises, and still leave your hearts below? send up hearts to heaven, and let them return again down to this earth? remain earth, and flesh, and filth, and vanity, after so much converse or pretence to it, with the holy God of spirits? Lovest thou God, when thou canst so often go where he is, and not care to see him? or if thou meet him, canst let him go without a blessing? or if he bless thee, canst go presently and exchange thy Father's blessing for a mess of pottage? canst lose a duty in a dinner, the comforts and revivings of a sermon, of a sacrament, of a sabbath, in an hour's carnal converse in the world? Did we love our God more, certainly we should be more with him, and to better purpose. His meetings would be more precious, and the fruits of them more lasting. We should neither go away without his blessing, nor throw it away when we had got it.

Thus much for the object of love.

II. Its act. Love is a natural affection. The love of God is the soul's clasping or closing with the

Lord. It is the expansion or going out of the heart, in its strength, after God, the uniting or knitting of the soul with God, with a complacency and acquiescence in him.

There are three things included in this love.

1. The strength of the heart making out after God. This is that which is commonly called our love of desire, the breathing, or thirsting, or panting of the heart after God, Psa. xlii. 1. The heart's working Godwards with its might; loving him above all things; desiring him above all things, and that both intensive with the greatest vigour and intention, and adequate as its complete and adequate object. God is its all. " Whom have I in heaven but thee, and there is none upon earth that I desire besides thee."

2. The uniting of the soul with God. Our cleaving to him. By love heart cleaves to heart, soul cleaves to soul. It is said of Shechem, Gen. xxxiv. 3. that his heart clave unto Dinah. He loved her with his heart, she was gotten into his heart, and there his heart holds her. Barnabas exhorts the church, that with purpose of heart they would cleave unto the Lord, Acts xi. 23. It is the knitting of the soul with God. It is said, 1 Sam. xviii. 1. That the soul of Jonathan was knit with the soul of David, and Jonathan loved him as his own soul. And of Jacob, Gen. xliv 30. to express his tender love to Benjamin, it is said, his life was bound up in the lad's life. Of the multitude of believers we read, Acts iv. 32. that they were all of one heart, and of one soul. Their love had knit them up all into one. By love we are one with God, and he with us. It is the soul's willing of God, as I may so speak. Willing of God to itself, and willing

itself and all to God. All praises, all honour, all
blessedness to him. Be thou mine, Lord; nothing
less, nothing else. Be thou mine, I need no less,
I desire no more. Let me be thine, be to thee, be
for thee, thy servant, thy sacrifice, or what thou
wilt; and let all mine be thine; my heart, and
my hand, and my tongue, and my time, and my
interest. Let all thine be to thee; thy heavens and
thy earth, with every person, with every creature in
them. Let every heart, every mouth, every limb,
every creature, be a praise to the Lord. Let the
Lord live, and blessed be my rock; let the God of
my salvation be exalted. Let every knee bow, let
every tongue confess unto God. This is our love
of union, as it is called. And it is the heart, the
very essence of saving love, wherein are included
both our accepting God, and our surrender or re-
signation of ourselves unto God: and our wishing
and willing all glory, dominion, and blessedness to
him. And so here also is our love of benevolence.
All these may be included in that opening of the
heart mentioned Acts xvi. 14. It is there said, that
the Lord opened Lydia's heart. The heart is then
savingly opened, when it freely lets out itself upon
God, all its streams run in to the Lord; and when
it takes in, and takes down God into the depth of
the soul. The heart thus opened to the Lord, when
God is come in, will close upon him. Abide with
me; thou hast entered upon thy habitation. O let
this be thy dwelling for ever. Only this must be
further added, that with God it takes in all things of
God; his word, his ordinances, his ways, and all his
dispensations. With his love, his laws; with his comforts, his counsels; with his counsels, his corrections
with thee, I accept of all that is thine; both thy

yoke and thy cross, thyself, Lord, thy love, Lord, and what thou wilt with thee.

3. The soul's taking pleasure, and taking up its rest in him. This is called our love of complacency Where we love, there will be a delightful stay of the mind upon God. The object dwells in the eye; we are still looking where we love. When I awake, I am still with thee; there his thoughts are, of him is his meditation all the day long.

My meditation of him shall be sweet. He that loves, dwelleth in God; "I will dwell in the house of the Lord for ever." And why there? why there his God dwells, and therefore there his soul takes up its dwelling. There is also an acquiescence of the heart in him. "Return unto thy rest, O my soul." But this is not felt, till love hath obtained, till the soul feels itself to love, and to have what it loves; to love, and to be beloved; to accept, and to be accepted of God. When it comes to this, then I have enough. "I am my beloved's, and my beloved is mine." And here is the sweetness of religion, the marrow and fatness of godliness, the pleasure of love. When I love, I can rest; when I can rest, I can rejoice; when I feel myself to love, I know I am beloved; and then what is there wanting? Where love is a stranger, joy is not known; we can never take comfort in anything, but in that which we love. When take we pleasure in eating, but when we have meat that we love? What is a friend, or a wife, or a child, when we love them not? What is society or communion, where love hath not first made a union? Can two walk together except they be agreed? with little comfort sure; they would be better pleased, were they parted asunder. It is love that is the pleasure of our lives. It is love

that makes heaven sweet, there we shall have our
fill of joy, because there we have our fill of love.
Heaven would be no heaven, God himself could not
be the joy, if he were not the love of his saints.
What bitter draughts will love sweeten! Sin, and
lusts, and all the filth of the flesh, are sweet morsels
to carnal hearts; it is meat they love; God is
nothing, Christ is nothing to them. What is thy
beloved more than other beloveds? religion is a
bondage to them, holiness a weariness; not the
labours only, but the joys of the saints are empty
and unsavoury things; there are no feasts but love-
feasts. Love is both the best dish, and the only
sauce to every dish; it is the best dish; he that
feeds on divine love will never complain of a short
meal: and it is the only sauce for every dish; it is
but unsavoury meat that is not seasoned with love;
we may a little change the proverb, Love is the
best sauce. Be the meat ever so excellent, it will
not relish if it be not loved. Love will make any
thing relish. When it puts such a sweetness into
sin, that even death and hell will go down with
carnal hearts for its sake, oh what a feast will love
make of holiness and glory! Get love to Christ,
love to religion, and you will never demand, Where
is the blessedness? where is the sweetness?

Love will sweeten both the comforts and the exercises of religion; it will make duties sweet, yea,
and sufferings sweet: there are two things that are
naturally sweet to love,—To please—To praise.

(1.) He that loves, will please; and observe
whom he loves: how careful are such to watch themselves, that they grieve not their friend! what study
does love put them upon, to find out what is grateful and acceptable! acceptable looks, acceptable

language, acceptable entertainment; what wilt thou, Lord? what wilt thou have me to be? a servant? a door-keeper? a servant of servants for thee? I will be nothing but what thou wilt, anything that thou wilt have me. What wilt thou have me to do, Lord? let me know thy will, appoint me my work. O that my ways were so directed, that I might keep thy statutes. What wilt thou have of me? wilt thou have mine idols, mine ease, or my honour, or my pleasure, or my house, or my estate? wilt thou have mine Isaacs? is there anything dearer to me than another, that might be an offering to the Lord? wilt thou have my liberty or my life? Behold all is at thy feet; I can keep back nothing thou callest for.

Hence love is said to be the fulfilling of the law; there is in this good will, radically every good work. It would walk worthy of the Lord unto all pleasing, being fruitful in every good work. Love is generous, it would do great things, noble things; what shall I do for him whom my soul honours? O for a gift that might be worthy of him! but I have nothing, my goodness extendeth not to thee; it would give more than it owes; but where it cannot do so, where it cannot be generous, yet it would be just; it would level all accounts, and pay all debts; love would have nothing but love owing. It would give to all their due; it would not die in the debt of a servant, of a stranger, much less (could it help it) would it take away from the God of glory. That is the daily charge of love, Pay what thou owest. Its receipts and returns are a pleasure to it; anything that comes down from heaven, and every present it has to send thither, is a joy to love. This is the message that both speak, Happy soul, thou lovest, and art beloved. It catches at all opportunities to send up messages of love, and knoweth no fitter messenger to send by, than by the hand of duty every duty is dispatched with this superscription, The tribute of love.

Love is the spring that sets all our wheels a going, the womb in which all our works are formed; the fire in the heart, that vents itself in our words and ways. "The fire kindled, then spake I with my tongue." Love is to a saint what malice is to Satan; that which gives force to all his actings. Satan's temptations are called fiery darts, and this, not only because they are headed and barbed with fire; as poisoned arrows, they burn where they hit; they set sin on fire, they set the soul on fire, burning with lust and wickedness; but because they are winged with fire, and forced with fire; the bullet is fired out of the gun, and thence it flies so fiercely. It is the malice of Satan's heart, that fires out all his darts. What malice doth with Satan, that doth love with saints. It sets the heart in a flame of holy zeal and activity for God; "Thy word was in me as fire, (it hath kindled a fire there,) I was weary with forbearing," Jer. xx. 9. A heart of love is weary, not of action, but of idleness: weary with forbearing, not with doing; never weary of doing much, ever weary of doing nothing. "O God, my heart is fixed, my heart is fixed," saith the psalmist, "I will sing and give thanks." Love will add, O God, my heart is fixed, my heart is fixed; there is a flame kindled; my heart burneth in holy desires and zeal for thee; and where love hath set the heart a burning, the heart will set the hand a working, and the feet a running.

(2.) He that loves, will praise him whom he loves. Praise is comely, and praise is a pleasure to the upright in heart. It is the delight of love, to be speaking of the perfections, of the virtues, of the beauties, of the excellences of her beloved. The spouse in the book of Canticles, whose whole language is all love, her heart is so full, that her lips overflow with the mention of the excellences of Christ: "My beloved is white and ruddy, the chiefest among ten thousand." His head is fine gold, his eyes dove's eyes, his cheeks a bed of spices, his lips are lilies, his hands are gold rings, his legs pillars of marble, his countenance excellent, his mouth sweet; yea, he is altogether lovely; this is my beloved, and this is my friend, O daughters of Jerusalem, Cant. v. "Who is a God like unto thee, glorious in holiness, fearful in praises, doing wonders? Great is the Lord, and greatly to be praised, in the city of our God. Thy mercy, O Lord, is in the heavens, thy faithfulness reacheth into the clouds. Thy righteousness is like the great mountains, thy judgments are a great deep. How excellent is thy loving kindness, O Lord! therefore the sons of men put their trust under the shadow of thy wings. I will speak of the glorious honour of thy majesty, and of thy wondrous works. The Lord is gracious, full of compassion, slow to anger, and of great mercy. The Lord is good to all, and his tender mercies are over all his works. Let all thy works praise thee, O Lord; let the saints bless thee; let them speak of the glory of thy kingdom, and talk of thy power; let them abundantly utter the memory of thy goodness, and sing of thy righteousness." O my God, thou art all love, all goodness, all grace, all glory. O let thy servant be all praise! Let this heart be an altar, and every service a sacrifice; let this mouth be a trumpet, and every word a psalm; let my breath be as incense, and every member a censer. Let all that is within me, my soul, with all its powers; let all that is without me, my body, with all its members, shout for joy, and sing forth the high praises of God. This is the voice of love.

And now you have another excellency of the new heart laid open to your view; love: a heart to love.

Christians, prize this precious grace, prize it, and you will write down this word also, among the great and precious promises; and if you would prize it aright, take your estimate of it from its worth, and its want; as we use to prize jewels from their excellency and rarity.

[1.] Prize it according to its worth and excellency. Why, what is the worth? " If a man would give all the substance of his house for love, it would be contemned," Cant. viii. 7. The whole world is not of that value, to be a price for love; no, it must come by gift, it is not to be bought for money; love is worth as much as a soul, and that is more than all the world. " What shall it profit a man to win the whole world, and lose his own soul?" Love is as much worth as all religion; it is the soul and the substance of all religion; all the graces, the duties and exercises of it, are only valued according to the love that is in them. What is knowledge, faith, hope, patience, without love? what is prayer, fasting, alms, without charity? They are worth nothing, shall I say? nay, they are nothing; if I had all knowledge, and all faith, and were all prayer, and all labour, and all suffering, and had not charity, I were nothing. Love is worth as much as heaven is worth, as Christ, as God is worth to us. God is love, and God is not, if love be not in us. Dost thou prize thy substance? Is thy house, or thy money, or thy lands, any thing to thee? Dost thou value thy soul? Is religion, is heaven, is Christ, is

God himself, of any account to thee? Then prize
the love of God. Without love, God is no God to
thee, Christ is no Christ to thee, heaven is no heaven for thee; better thou hadst no soul, no being,
than no love. O prize the love of God, prize and
seek, prize and pray; pray as for thy life, as for thy
soul, as for thine everlasting kingdom; Lord, let me
love thee. Get love, and get all; love, and thou wilt
be holy; love, and thou wilt be humble; love, and
thou wilt be fruitful; love, and thou wilt please,
praise, and enjoy thy God; love, and thou wilt
fear, serve, suffer and die for him; love, and thou
shalt live. Prize love, prize it according to its
worth. And,

[2.] Prize it according to its rarity. Things
excellent are rated something the more for their
scarcity; scarcity raises the market; the word of
God was precious in those days, 1 Sam. iii. 1. that
is, when there was a famine of the word, when there
was no open vision. O were the love of God as precious as it is rare! What a spiritless carcass is the
religion of many professors! what has become of the
soul of it? Oh! we freeze in our duties, we freeze in
our devotions, we are almost frozen out of them all; if
we have a sacrifice left, what fire is there to offer it up?
" The God that answereth by fire, let him be God,"
saith Elijah; the heart that asketh by fire, that ascendeth in fire, let that be the heart for God: " Behold the
wood and the fire, but where is the lamb for the sacrifice?" We may say, Behold the wood and the sacrifice,
but where is the fire to offer it up? our spirits have
taken a cold, the chill of them appears in all our
duties: Rabbi, where dwellest thou? Love, where
dwellest thou? Zeal of God, where is thy abode?
how many houses must we search! how many hearts

must we walk through, ere we we find thy habitation! The apostle tells the Romans, "That they have a zeal of God, but not according to knowledge," Rom. x. 2. We have the knowledge of God, but, oh ! where is the zeal ? "The zeal of thine house," saith the psalmist, "hath eaten me up;" but is not that eater eaten ? The house hath burnt up the fire, or if there be any fire left, is it not strange fire ? not the fire of love, but of lust, of pride, or covetousness, or that wild-fire of envy and contention that heats our spirits ? Jehu was also on fire against the house of Ahab; "Come, see my zeal for the Lord of hosts." That fire was fury, not love ; or if it was love, it was self-love; not the love of God that made all that flame; such hearts are like the evil tongue, "Set on fire of hell," Jam. iii. 6. Such heats are not from above, but are earthly, sensual, devilish; we freeze still, while we thus fry; our preternatural heats have extinguished the supernatural.

Oh ! how little kindly warmth do we find in our spirits ! do we feel our hearts working upwards, ascending in our flames ? We all pretend to love, but consider, are our hearts making out in their strength after God ? We wish well to his name and interest, we wish he were ours ; we wish ourselves his : O ! if wishing were loving, what christians should we be ! But doth the kingdom of God suffer violence ? Who are they that so run, as if they would take God by force, take heaven by force ? The kingdom of heaven may offer violence if it will, and take us by force ; but how little violence doth it suffer ! We say, we love God; but is there not something else we love more ? We desire to be holy, but is there not something else we desire more ?

Oh how few hearty friends hath Christ in the

world ! and how little love from these few ! so little,
that we cannot tell ourselves whether it be any thing
or nothing ; how hard are we put to it !   What
a narrow search must we make! how many argu
ments must we consult! how many marks must we
consider, ere we can prove we love him ! and yet at
last are still in doubt whether we love him or not.

When we love our carnal friends, our wives, our
children, we can feel that we love them ; when we
love our ease, or our estates, or our liberties, we can
feel that we love them ; but our God, we cannot tell
whether we love him or not. How few of us can
boldly make our appeal to him ; " Lord, thou knowest that I love thee !"

Oh how many wounds doth Christ receive in the
house of his friends ! how many slights must he put
up with ! how often when he hath sat down in his own
(in the highest) room, have we said to him, Give this
man place, give this friend, or this business place,
and so made him take the lower room !

How hath he, when he hath come to our doors,
(his love hath often brought him thither,) how often
hath he stood, and knocked, and called ; " Open
to me, my love, my sister ;" and there been made to
stand and wait, when strangers have been gotten in,
and taken up all the rooms ! The world can never
come out of season, but Christ is fain to wait his seasons, when he can find us at leisure ; if there be any
other guest with us, our Lord must wait ; " Go thy
way for this time, when I have a convenient season
I will send for thee." How often have we agreed
and appointed to meet the Lord at such an hour, in
our chamber, in our closet, to have converse and
communion with him in duty, and if any thing come
in to carry us another way, then presently, " I pray

thee have me excused!" or, if we do keep our time, and shut in ourselves with the Lord, and sit down to duty, what a multitude of thoughts presently fall a knocking at our doors! and away our hearts go presently with them to the ends of the earth, and leave nothing but our carcasses behind with the Lord. O were our love stronger, our cries would be louder, and would drown the noise of these knockings, that they would not be heard nor heeded, it would command silence to every impertinent thought. I charge you, O daughters, that you stir not, that you disturb not my beloved, and my soul; more love would command their attendance upon the work of the Lord, would gird up the loins of the mind, and gather in all its scattered messengers. Come, all ye powers of my soul, come and do your homage, come and help in the service of my God.

Oh! at what distance are we content to live from the Lord, sometimes for many days together! Our souls and our God are grown strange, and yet we can be merry and quiet; we can be without the presence of God, and yet never miss it; not a smile from his face, nor a look of love from us to him, and yet no trouble follows. The sun may be eclipsed, or under a cloud, and yet no darkness upon our spirits; we do not walk in darkness when we have no light; sorrow and sadness is as far from us, as God is from us; we can warm ourselves at our own fires, and rejoice in the light of our own sparks, as if these were the sun. We can do as well in a mist, as in the sunshine; day and night are both alike to us. The children of the bride chamber do not fast, but can feast and make merry when the bridegroom is taken from them; their carnal contentments they can make a shift with, to supply the room of their Lord.

Can we not sometimes go where our Lord feeds, and never find him? Go to pray, or go to hear, or go to a sacrament, and the Lord never meet us there, and yet can return well enough satisfied? When we thus want communion with God, and can want it; where is our love? what love is that which can so well bear the absence of her beloved? Call me no moro Naomi, pleasant, but call me Marah, bitter; "I went out full, but I return empty:" Full of grace, full of joy, because full of the Lord, but behold all is gone, my husband is lost, my God is departed from me. Call me no more Naomi, but call me Marah, for the Almighty hath dealt bitterly with me, hath hid his face from me; for these things I weep; mine eyes, mine eyes run down with tears, because the Comforter that should relieve my soul is far from me; such are the tears of love for her absent Lord.

Oh how little conscience is there made of bestowing that on the Lord, which we have bestowed on him! We give and take; we pretend to have given all to God, but are we not often taking away what we have given, and bestowing it elsewhere? Love would have all we have, running into God, and would have nothing run besides; but, oh, what waste is there made of our time, of our parts, and other talents, which, were they well husbanded, would come to much, and be given to the Lord! When so many days and hours run out, and no account taken of them, on what, or on whom they are consumed; when our eyes, and our ears, and hands, and tongues, which were made for God, the devil and lust must so often have the using of them; when back, and belly, and friends, and companions, must carry away what should be spent on God and souls; when what should be allowed for religion, and charity to

have the spending of, must be at the disposal of
pride, prodigality, and gluttony ; when our prayers,
our fasting, our preaching and hearing, all our
duties, must become sacrifices to our lust, our idols
are suffered to devour the sacrifices of the Lord ;
when our pride and fleshly ends must have the offering, and eating of our sacrifices, this must make our
prayers, and preach our sermons, and keep our fasts,
and give our alms, and wear the credit and honour
of them as its own crown ; when God is thus
robbed, and we let the thief run away with all, and
is never pursued or questioned : oh ! where is our
love ?

Oh ! how little pleasure do we take in the Lord !
What a weariness is it to us to wait upon him ! how
glad are we when we come back from the house of
the Lord ! When we come off our knees, come
out of our closets ! When the sabbaths are gone,
and the new moons are over, and we make our
returns from heaven to earth ! how much work have
we to keep our hearts near the Lord ! how do they
slink away ere we are aware ! and whilst we are in
his presence, how seldom do we rejoice in his presence ! What hungry meals, what jejune feasts do
we make before the Lord ! We relish not his dainties ; his wine is but lees, his marrow and his fat
things are but leanness to our souls ; a little love
would sweeten every drop, would season every morsel
that comes from his table ; would make our very fasts
to be pleasant bread. We feed upon the dish or the
trencher, and not the meat ; on the bone, and not
the marrow ; ordinances, and the external exercises
of religion, are but the bone, or the shell, or the dish,
it is God that is the kernel, the marrow, and fatness.
How little communion have we with the Lord, in

our approaches to him ! and how little sweetness do
we find in the little we have ! Communion is the
pleasure of love, and love is the sweetness of communion. Now I am where I would be. Oh ! how
amiable are thy tabernacles ! Very pleasant art thou
to me, O Lord ; that is the voice of love. Had we
more love, we should be more spiritual ; and spiritual things would be more grateful to spiritual hearts.
Divine love is like the fire, it rarifies and changes
hearts into its own likeness, and then there is sweetness. Oh, we are carnal, and that is enough to evidence that there is little of the love of God abiding
in us.

Consider these things, and you will see that love
is a rarity, there is but little true love in the world.
O prize the love of God, let its want make it prized ;
shall it be so rare, and yet so cheap ? prize it, and
press on after it.

What do these hearts below ? are they not still
below ? so cold, such clods of clay, and yet above ?
so carnal, so sensual, and yet in heaven ? so hungry, and so greedy in sucking the juice of this earth,
in taking in its pleasures ; so busy in digging out
the wealth of the earth, and searching for its treasures, hearts so busy this way, and yet not here ?
how canst thou say, I am walking with the God of
glory, when thou art still worshipping the gods of the
earth ? How canst thou say, This heart is risen, it
is not here ; when it may be said to thee, " Behold
the place where it lies ?" it is still in the field, in the
ridges and furrows thereof ; it is still in the mines,
in the heart of the earth ; see the place where it lies.
We sow our hearts with our seed ; we send them
down to dig in the heart of the earth.

But what do these hearts below ? Get you up,

get you up; leave nothing but the mantle here, your
carcasses; earth to earth, dust to dust. Come, heave
these souls heavenward; let them take the wing and
be gone. O that I had the wings of a dove, that I
might fly up, and be at rest; be lower than ever by
humility, but let love be on high.

Behold those cords of love, that are let down in
every ordinance, in every providence; there is a
cord let down to gather up hearts; hearken to those
calls of love, come up hither, come up hither.
We come, Lord, thou bidst us come, O lend us thy
hand, and lift us up.

Come on, christians; come, let us be happy; if we
love, we are happy: come, let us rejoice, if we love
we joy: come, let us live; we die, we die, while we
linger on this earth; if we love we live; let us live,
and let our life be love; let our works be labours of love,
our sufferings seals of love, our sorrows the sorrows
of love, our wounds love's scars, our prayers the cries
of love, our praises love songs to our Lord and God.
Let every duty, every exercise, let every member,
every power, let our bodies, let our souls be love's
sacrifices; as we see in all his, so let the Lord see
love in all our ways.

Canst thou not love? look till thou canst; look
up to thy God, send up thy thoughts thither; let thy
meditations be of him; these will not be long before
the throne ere they fetch up thy heart. Look on
thy Jesus, behold his hands and his feet, come and
put thy finger into the print of the nails, and thrust
thy heart into his side, and there let it lie till thou
feel it warm. Look up to thy Jesus, lift up a prayer,
Lord let me love thee; if thou lovest, let me love
thee; I will seek, till I can see; let me see, till I can
love. What have I here, Lord? My all is with

thee, my help, my hope, my treasure, my life is hid with Christ in God. And yet behold, this all is nothing to me, while my heart is no more with thee; take it, Lord, take it up; where my treasure is, there let my heart be also.

Doubting christian, who because thou lovest so little, fearest thou lovest not at all; cry for more, but be thankful for what thou hast; be ashamed thou lovest no more, but be not dismayed; thou complainest thou canst not love God, but dost thou love his image, his saints, his word, his works, his ways? Whilst thou sayest thou lovest not God, dost thou love godliness? If thou canst not love, canst thou grieve, canst thou lament after him? Hast thou chosen? dost thou hang upon, trust in the Lord? If thou canst not love, canst thou fear and follow the Lord? If he be not sensibly in thy affection, is he in thy thoughts, in thy mouth, in thine eye? Is he thine aim and thy scope? Doth thy course bend towards him? Comfort thy heart in these things; thou mayest see, though thou canst not feel thou lovest.

Chapter XIV —*A Heart to fear the Lord*

" I will put my fear in their hearts, that they shall not depart from me," Jer. xxxii. 40. I shall proceed to the opening of this by these steps; I shall show, I. That the Lord God is a dreadful God. II. That the Lord hath put the dread of himself upon the hearts of all the earth. III. That yet by sin the heart of man is much hardened from the fear of the Lord. IV. That God will recover his honour, and again put his fear into the hearts of his people. V. What this fear of the Lord is, that he will put into them.

I. The Lord God is a dreadful God; he is dreadful in the excellency and glory of his majesty. " Shall not his excellency make you afraid, and his dread fall upon you?" Job xiii. 11.   His power is dreadful; "Fear ye not me, saith the Lord? Will ye not tremble at my presence, which have placed the sand for the bound of the sea, by a perpetual decree, that it cannot pass it, and though the waves thereof toss themselves, yet they cannot prevail; though they roar, yet can they not pass over it?" Fear ye not me, saith the Lord? He that did this, what can he not do? His wrath is a dreadful wrath; "At his wrath the earth shall tremble, and the nations shall not be able to abide his indignation," Jer. x. 10. Yea, his holiness, his truth, his righteousness, and all his name. "That thou mayest fear this glorious and fearful name, the Lord thy God," Deut. xxviii. 58.   The Lord God is a dreadful God.

II. The Lord God hath put the dread of himself upon the hearts of all the earth. Not the best only, but the worst of the sons of men. "I am a great king, saith the Lord, and my name is dreadful among the heathen." This dread of the Lord breaks forth upon them.

1. From the impress of God upon the natures of all men. As the law, so the being of God is written in their hearts; he hath his witness in their consciences. If the atheists of the earth could answer all the arguments from without, proving that there is a God; yet they can never confute their own consciences. If the works of God do not, their reins shall instruct them; if they will not see, whether they will or not, they shall feel that there is a God; and wherever God is felt, he is feared; even when their mouth speaketh proud things, their heart shall meditate terror; and when nothing else is, they shall be a terror to themselves.

2. It is increased by the great works of God, his wonders that he doth in the world ; his thunder and his hail, his wind and his waves, his earthquakes, make an earthquake in hearts.

3. It is further heightened by his judgments, which he executeth on the earth. The judgments of God, are God revealing himself from heaven, against the ungodliness and unrighteousness of men, and do then strike most terror, 1. When he smites suddenly, and makes quick work with sinners : as when Herod was smote by an angel of God, Nadab and Abihu consumed by fire from God, immediately upon their sin. Sudden strokes shake secure hearts. 2. When he executes strange judgments, makes a new thing, as in the case of Korah and his company, he made the earth to open her mouth upon them, and swallow them up ; so he made the flies, and the frogs, and the lice, &c. to be the executioners of his wrath on Pharaoh. 3. When he executes great wrath for little sins, as men account them ; as in the case of Uzzah, whom he struck dead, for but touching the ark when it shook. 4. When he exercises great severity on his own, on those that are near him. If he spareth not his sons, what will he do with his enemies ! "If these things be done on the green tree, what shall be done on the dry !"

4. Yet further ; by their conscience of guilt, and their binding over to the judgment to come. The sin of Judah is written with a pen of iron, with the point of a diamond it is graven upon the tables of their heart. The sin of Judah is written ; yea, and the sin of the Gentiles also. "Their conscience also bearing witness, and their thoughts the mean while accusing," Rom. ii. 15. And where their sin is

written, there their judgment is written, which even
nature itself will teach, doth inevitably follow upon
sin; and this is the great dread that is upon them.
The very mention of judgment to come, made a
Felix tremble at the face of a poor prisoner. This
is the terror of the Lord mentioned by the apostle,
" We must all appear before the judgment seat.
Knowing, therefore, the terror of the Lord we
persuade men," 2 Cor. v. 10, 11. Death is said to
be the king of terrors; and this is the terror of
death, after that the judgment. All these, the impress of God upon their hearts, the wonders of God
in the world, the vengeance of God executed on sin,
the sense of guilt, and of a judgment to come; do
preach to the consciences of sinners, that " it is a
fearful thing to fall into the hands of the living
God."

III. Yet by sin the heart of man is much hardened from the fear of the Lord. Sin blinds the eye
and hardens the heart, brings into danger and puts
out of fear. Who in such danger, and yet who so
bold as the blind sinner? When the understanding
is darkened, the next word we read is, " Past feeling," Eph. iv. 19. There is included in the very nature
of sin a slighting of God; and by once slighting we
learn to slight him more. Slight the command, and
you will quickly slight the curse. Laugh at duty,
and it will not be long ere you laugh at fear. And
when sin hath thus hardened, God will also harden,
lets the sinner alone, suspends his judgments, smites
the sinner with judicial blindness, and gives him up
to a reprobate mind, Rom. i. 28. And when once
they come to this, then hell is broke loose: for what
follows? " Being filled with all unrighteousness,
fornication, wickedness, covetousness, malicious-

ness, and what not," Rom. i. 29. " The transgression of the wicked saith within my heart, there
is no fear of God before his eyes," Psa. xxxvi. 1.
When Abraham had such a thought, " Surely the fear
of God is not in this place," Gen.xx.11. what thought
he was there then? Murder, adultery, and all
manner of villany. " What sawest thou amongst
us that thou hast done this thing?" What hurt,
what evil, didst thou see amongst us? What evil!
Evil enough to make me afraid: I thought the fear
of God was not here, and there needs no more to
make me afraid. Say of any person, The fear of
God is not in this man, and you therein say, The
devil is in him: here dwells sin, and all manner of
wickedness. Say of any place, The fear of God is not
in this place; and if you find it an Egypt or Sodom
for abominations, you will not wonder. " The fear
of the Lord is clean," Psa. xix. 9. that is, not only
formally but effectively it cleanseth. Where this is
not, every unclean thing may dwell. The reason
why this world is such a world as it is, such a
wicked world, such a treacherous, deceitful, ungodly
world, why there is so little faith, or truth, or mercy,
or charity, or sobriety, is, because there is so little
of the fear of God. Sin hath cast out fear, and this
hath brought forth sin in abundance. The law is
nothing, threatenings are nothing, conscience is
nothing, God is nothing to men, because he is not
their fear. Wickedness is as righteousness; villany
as honesty; prodigality, debauchery, as temperance
and sobriety; yea, and hath gotten the start of it:
it faceth the sun, it lifts up the head, it wears the
garland; it paints itself virtue, generosity, gallantry,
the beauty and ornament of the world, where the
fear of God is departed.

God may promise, threaten, command, " Hearken to my voice, turn at my reproofs, cast away your transgressions." Awake from your wine, be chaste, sober, be humble; let your merriment be turned into mourning, your jollity into heaviness. Remember your Creator, remember your souls, why will you die? turn and live. God may speak thus once, and twice, and ten times, but is not regarded; his words have no weight, his counsels have no credit, his warnings are of no value with hardened, fearless hearts. If the devil speak but once, he is heard; if lust speak but once, it is obeyed; if a proud companion speak but once, he is followed; whilst the word of the God of glory is made a reproach, and a scorn. Oh the intolerable contempt that is poured out upon the Most High, by men that fear not God! Make thy promises, and give thy gifts to whom thou wilt; give grace, and give glory where thou pleasest; the world for me; my pleasures, my honours, my liberty for me, this world for me, look after the other who will. Let the Lord threaten, let the day of the Lord come; let it hasten that we may see it; let the Almighty do his worst, I will not hearken nor turn. This is the blasphemy of hardened, fearless hearts.

IV. God will recover his honour in the hearts of his people. He will put his fear in their hearts; whilst others are hardened, they shall tremble; whilst others kick, they shall stoop; whoever despise me, of these will I be had in honour.

V. What this fear of the Lord is that he will put into their hearts. The fear of God is taken in scripture sometimes more largely, as it comprehends all religion. Job was said, chap. i. to be a man fearing God; that is, a godly man: but in this sense I shall not here speak of it. Sometimes more strictly, as a distinct grace, as distinguished from faith, love, hope, and other graces of the Spirit. And being taken in this sense there are these two things included in it:

1. A reverence of God.

2. An abhorrence of evil for God's sake.

1. A reverence of God. To fear God is to have the awe of God abiding upon the heart, to be under a sense of the majesty and glory of the Lord, shining forth in all his attributes, especially in his holiness and omniscience ; the glory of his holiness, and the sense of such a holy eye upon the soul strikes it with dread and consternation. This is expressed in scripture by sanctifying the Lord in the heart. " I will be sanctified in them that draw nigh me," Lev. x. 3. " Sanctify the Lord of hosts himself, and let him be your fear, and let him be your dread," Isa. viii. 13. There is mention in scripture of a sanctifying of God, and a justifying of God. As God doth justify and sanctify his people, so they are to justify and sanctify God. These two, the justifying and sanctifying of God, though they be much the same, yet there is some difference betwixt them. To sanctify God is to reverence him in our hearts, and to represent him in the glory of his holiness before men. To justify God, supposeth a sinful judging, and foolish charging of God in the hearts of men, and is our vindicating him from such charges. Is God righteous ? How is it then that he is so partial in his dealings with the righteous and unrighteous ? that he deals worse with those who fear him, than with those who fear him not ? Is God good ? How is it then that he is so hard, not only in imposing, but inflicting such hard things upon his own ? Is

God true ? How is it then that he fails his people
so often when he hath said, I will never fail them
nor forsake them ? Our flesh hath failed, yea, and
our heart hath failed, yea, and our God hath often
failed us too ; we have often called, and have had
no answer ; we have often trusted, and have had no
deliverer. Yet God is righteous, yet God is good,
yet God is true ; he hath not been unrighteous, ne
hath not been a hard master, he hath not failed no.
forsaken ; this is to justify God.

Our justifying God, hath some kinds of re-
semblance with God's justifying us. God's justification of us stands in his not imputing sin to us,
and accepting us as righteous ; and our justifying
of God stands in our not imputing evil to him, and
our acknowledging him to be true, just, and good.
God hath justified me from my sins, and that is
enough to proclaim him good and faithful whatever his other dealings be. Let him afflict me, let
him chastise me, since he will not judge me, nor
condemn me with the world. God hath justified
himself in my conscience. I have found that the
Lord is gracious, I have found that God is faithful ;
he hath said he will not, and I must say he hath not
forsaken. He hath not failed when he hath most
failed me ; when he hath been farthest off from my
help, he hath even then been a present help in trouble. He hath answered when he hath been most
silent ; he hath been most good when he hath been
most hard. I have never found more sweet than in
his bitter cup. I must judge myself, not my God :
I have sinned, I have sinned against him, and therefore I must justify him when he speaketh, and clear
him when he judgeth. Hold thy peace, querulous
heart, be silent all the earth before the Lord, for

truly God is good to Israel, and to them that are of a clean heart. There are few among the worst of sinners, but, if conscience might be suffered to speak, it would justify God. It is lust that quarrels, not conscience. It is vain to serve the Lord, and what profit is there to keep his ordinances. His ways are unequal and hard; his promise fails, take one time with another, oftener than it is made good. Who is it that plagues, and disappoints, and crosseth, and vexeth us? This evil is of the Lord; why should I wait on the Lord any longer? Nay, whom doth he punish more than those that are nearest him? Who have sorrow, who have trouble in the flesh? who are reproached, scorned, hunted up and down the world but these? This they may thank God for, and their following him. It is better being the servant of sin than the servant of Christ. Thus lust blasphemes. But speak conscience; Is God unrighteous? Is God false to his word? Are the pleasures of sin better than the gain of godliness? Have the children of this world made a wiser choice than the children of light? Speak sinner, let thy conscience speak whether it be thus or not. God hath not left himself without witness in the hearts of sinners, much more with his saints, when they do speak their hearts, speak good of his name. But this by the way.

To return to the matter in hand. To sanctify God is especially to reverence him in the heart; to have such a high, and holy, and honourable esteem of him as commands an awe upon the heart; and that,

(1.) At all times: " My son, be thou in the fear of the Lord all the day long." " My son;" it is not only for slaves but for sons to fear. " Be thou in the

fear of the Lord ;" it is not only, Let the fear of
the Lord be in thee, habitually in thy heart; but
actuate and stir up this holy fear, keep up a holy
awe, a deep sense of God always upon thee ; let the
fear of the Lord be before thine eyes ; be possessed
and swallowed up of this fear " all the day long ;"
wherever thou art, with whomsoever thou hast to
do, remember thou hast still to do with God. A
christian should stand always as before the tribunal;
every day should be as the last day, the day of judgment to him. " So speak ye, and so do as those
that shall be judged," Jam. ii. 12. The judge stands
at the door, yea, and thou mayest see him through
every window, yea, through every wall ; every wall
is a window, through which God may see and be
seen. A christian, when he is as he should be,
cannot wink God out of sight : can look nowhere,
but he sees that eye which strikes an awe upon his
spirit.

This abiding reverence of God, what an influence
will it have upon the whole course ! we shall then
serve God acceptably ; when we fear, we shall
please God. " That we may serve God acceptably
with reverence and godly fear." We shall then serve
God universally, in every thing. When we fear
we shall watch unto every duty, against every
sin. " This do and live, for I fear God," Gen. xlii.
18. said Joseph to his brethren ; as if he should
have said, Do not you fear to find falsehood or any
evil-dealing from me, for I fear God. I dare not
be false to you ; you may trust me, you may take
my word, for I fear God. We shall then walk
before the Lord steadily. When we fear we shall
fix, and hold in an even frame and course. Fear
will be our ballast; whilst love fills our sails, fear

will ballast our vessel. How are slight and frothy
spirits tossed up and down! whither do they wander.
How many hearts, and faces, and frames have they
every day! What contradictions are they to themselves! The reverence of God upon them, would fix
them, and hold them in a more even and equal
poise. We should then serve the Lord more ho-
nourably. When we fear, we shall show forth the
virtues of God before the world; so much of the
reverence, so much of the holiness of God upon us.
The presence of a christian walking in the fear of
the Lord, is as the presence of God; the reverence
of God upon his heart, casts a beam of divine majesty into his face, and oftentimes begets an awe
and reverence of him in the hearts of the worst of
sinners; they reverence, even whilst they revile and
persecute him.

Of John Baptist, who was a man of a just, holy
and austere life, it is said, that Herod feared him
and observed him, Mark vi. 20. The austerity and
holiness of his life, commanded a respect from a
Herod's heart. Such christians, their ways are a
conviction, and their very countenances are a rebuke
to the wanton world; they speak with authority,
they exhort with authority, they reprove with authority; and sin often hides itself from them, even as
from the face of God.

(2.) Especially in our drawing nigh to God:
" God is greatly to be feared in the assembly of the
saints, and to be had in reverence of all them that
are about him," Psa. lxxxix. 7. "I will be sanctified
in them that draw nigh me," Lev. x. 3. He that
fears God trembles at the word of God; and God loves
he should. "To this man will I look—that trembles
at my word." Isa. lxvi. 2. That which makes him

tremble, is, that he sees the word carrying upon it the holiness and the authority of God.

He reads the word as the epistle of God sent down to the world; his epistle commendatory; that sets forth the excellency and the glory of God, and his letters mandatory that charge subjection and obedience upon him; he takes every word as coming from the mouth of the Holy One of Israel; he lies prostrate before the Lord; his soul bows the knee, his heart falls down at the feet of the Almighty. The word, by how much the more it is considered as the word of God, by so much the more awe it works upon him. Every look he casts upon his bible, is a looking into heaven. He that fears God, fears when he comes to worship, reve-- rences his sanctuary; " In thy fear will I worship," Psa. v. 7. That which works this fear is, that he looks upon the duties and ordinances of worship, as the institutions of God and his application unto God.

This is that which the Lord hath sanctified; be- hold his image and superscription; here he hath appointed me to wait for him; here he hath ap- pointed to meet my soul; now I am going up to the mount of God, the mount of God is every where, where the worship of God is. My soul, where art thou? I am before the Lord of the whole earth. " Put off thy shoes from off thy feet, the place whereon thou standest is holy ground." I am before the high and Holy One, the God of all the earth; and upon transactions of eternal consequence, to do my homage to the everlasting King, to kneel before the Lord my Maker, to kiss the golden sceptre, to beg my life at his hands, to behold his goings in his sanctuary, his wisdom, and his mercy, and his goodness are all passing before me.   How dreadful is this place!   " This is none other but the house of God, and the gate of heaven," Gen. xxviii. 17.   How dreadful is this word !   This is none other but the word of God.   How dreadful is this ordinance!   This is none other but the door of glory.   Tremble thou heart at the presence of the Lord, at the presence of the God of Jacob.

2. Abhorrence of evil for the Lord's sake.   Here we shall consider, 1. Its object; 2. Its ground.

(1.) The object of this abhorrence in general, is evil, " Abhor that which is evil, cleave to that which is good," Rom. xii. 9.   Good is the object of love, evil of fear.   Evil is twofold, present, or to come.   The former is the object of grief, the latter of fear.   Particularly, the object of this abhorrence is, 1. The wrong of God ; 2. The loss of God.

[1.] The wrong of God.   The great and only wrong of God, is sin.   Sin is the turning away of the heart from God.   The great thing in all the world which God respects and requires as his own, is the heart.   " My son give me thine heart.   Keep thine heart with all diligence," Prov. iv. 23.   Keep thy heart, that is, keep it for me ; keep it clean for God, and keep it safe for God ; see that it be not defiled nor carried away.   When the heart is gone, all is gone with it.   If the world hath gotten hearts, if Satan hath gotten hearts, let them take all, saith God ; let me have either a heart, or nothing ; and all they are like to have, that have the heart. The heart, wherever it goes, carries all with it. Where we bestow our hearts, we bestow all that we have.   Sin is the turning away of the heart.   This is the very nature of sin, the heart's departing from the living God, Heb. iii. 12.   And therefore this is the great wrong of God. There is but one thing in the world that God respects, and this sin steals away.

Sin is the insurrection and rebellion of the heart against God; it turns from him, and turns against him; it runs over to the camp of the enemy, and there takes up arms against God. Sin is a running from God, and a fighting against God, it would spoil the Lord of all the jewels of his crown. It opposeth the sovereignty of God. A sinful heart would set up itself in God's throne, it would be king in his stead, and have the command of all. Sinners would be their own gods; our tongues are our own, who is Lord over us? God shall not be God where sin is risen up as Lord. It assaults the wisdom of God. Vain man would be wise, wiser than his Maker. It charges the Lord with folly, and proclaims itself the only wise. Sinners pretend to know how to choose for themselves, and order themselves to their advantage, better than God. If God would let me alone to myself, to be at my own finding, at my own ordering, it should quickly be better with me. If every thing might be with me, as I would have it, my case would be well mended from what it is now, that every thing must go as God will have it. All our quarrellings at Providence, all our murmurings and discontents at our lot, are our hearts charging the Lord with folly. It casts dirt on the holiness of God, it disparages the goodness of God; it abuseth mercy, violates his justice, despises his power. In sum, it disgraces the throne of his glory, and lays his honour in the dust; sets the Almighty below the lowest of his creatures.

Every companion shall be respected more than

God; every pleasure shall be loved more than God; the devil shall be feared more than God. Where is his love? Where is his fear? Where is his honour? Nay, where were the Lord, might sin carry it? Sin is the wrong of God, and this wrong is the especial object of this abhorrence. A gracious heart would do no wrong, he would not wrong his neighbour, he would not wrong his servant, his enemy, no not his beast that he possesses. But oh! should I wrong my God? Hath he ever done me any wrong? Hath he not been just to me? Yea, hath he not been ever good to me? Kind, pitiful, patient, bountiful? Who hath fed me, clothed me, kept me, succoured me, comforted me? What friend have I in all the world? What father, what portion, what hope, but the Lord? What were I, what had I, but vanity, but woe and misery, had I not a God? I cannot wrong my God, but I wrong myself. "He that sinneth against me, wrongeth his own soul," Prov. viii. 36. But if I did not, if my arrows would not recoil, could I go out with all this injury, and suffer nothing by it: yet, he is God whom I wrong; he is holy, he is righteous, he is good, he is glorious, he is excellent; he only is God, and shall I be injurious to him? He is worthy, he is worthy of all that I have, of all the service I can do, of all the respect I can give, of all the praise I can offer up. If I had a thousand tongues, if I had a thousand hands, if I had a thousand lives, if I had a thousand souls, if I had all the earth for an offering to the Lord, all would be nothing to show forth the praise that is due unto his name, as he is God, and I his creature. And when I owe so much, and have nothing to pay, shall I steal from him? shall I rise up against him? "Wast thou not afraid to lift up

thy hand against the Lord's anointed?" 2 Sam. i.
14. Shall I not be afraid to lift up my hand against
the Lord himself? to kick against God? Oh the
Lord forbid! What art thou, O my soul? What
servest thou for? if thou canst not tremble, if
thou dost not turn within me, if thou dost not start
back at the very thought of such great wickedness?

[2.] The loss of God. As was said before, "He
that sinneth against God, wrongeth his own soul."
His loss is thy loss, and more thine than his; though
(no thanks to thee) the Lord will be no loser at last;
when sinners have done their worst, he can get up
his honour out of dishonour, he can recover his
spoils out of the ashes; if he had lost all the world,
he had lost nothing he is all things in himself.
When earth and hell have spent all their malice,
God will be God, holy, wise, glorious, blessed for
ever. Though such be the malignity of sin, that it
would not give over, till God ceaseth to be God;
yet God is above, too high for sin to reach; its
darts fall short of its mark. God cannot, God will
not sit down a loser by all that sin can do.

But what dost thou suffer, what dost thou lose
who sinnest against God? The carnal world understand not what, nor would make much reckoning of
it, did they understand it. The loss of two pence
goes often nearer them, than the loss of God. But
now a christian knows no other fear, fears no other
loss; let God be secure, and all is well. Sin will
be the wrong of God, and the loss of God; it may
be a total and eternal loss for aught he knows, at
least if not assured; God lost, is the soul lost, the
kingdom lost; this is hell, the loss of God. Better
have no being; better be a dog, or toad, than a
man without a God; or if he be not utterly lost,

yet to his present sense, it will be all one as if
he had no God; his peace is lost, his comfort is
lost, and his soul is often given for lost, from whom
God is departed, though but for a season; he can
take pleasure in nothing, he can find rest nowhere,
whose God is out of sight. He knows not what a
God means, who can spare him till death or judgment. A christian cannot live a day without him;
it is night, it is all dark, he knows no day while the
sun is set upon him. How grievous do they find this
loss, who have proved what it is? "What wilt thou
do for me, whilst I go childless?" What can be done
for me, whilst I go fatherless? here is my house,
here are my friends and my lands, but where is my
God? " My God, my God, why hast thou forsaken
me?" Now I see what this earth is without a
heaven; now I see what ease, pleasure, and carnal
friends are, and how little they can do for me! Yea,
what is prayer? what are sabbaths? what are sermons, sacraments, promises, whilst God looks not
down? Oh I was wont to meet with God here!
these glasses were my windows into heaven; and
then how pleasant were they to me! Sabbaths were
a delight, the word was a treasure, sacraments were
the clusters of Canaan. But now, now all is dark
and dry; ordinances are wells without water; promises are breasts without milk; ministers are stars
without light; oh the stars are but clods, whilst the
sun is a cloud to me; woe is me, I had a God.
I am pained, I am pained, my head is sick, my
heart is faint, my bowels are turned, my liver is
poured out, the light of mine eyes is gone from me.
I am weary of my groaning, I am full of tossings
and turnings, there is no soundness in my flesh, no
rest in my bones, while my soul says daily to me,

Where is thy God? And if the sense of this loss worketh such grief, what wonder if the hazard of it worketh fear? Now sin divides, breaks the peace, makes God and the soul two; sin alienates, produces a distance and estrangement betwixt God and the soul. That soul can either not see him at all, or not as a friend, whom sin hath drawn away. Sin will either cloud the face of God, or clothe him with fury; will cause him either to turn his back upon the soul, or set his face against it. He who knows what it is to enjoy God will dread his loss; he who hath seen his face will fear to see his back; he loves, and therefore would not lose.

(2.) The ground and reason of this abhorrence, that is twofold. 1. God's jealousy; 2. His people's ingenuousness.

[1.] God's jealousy. " The Lord thy God is a jealous God," Exod. xx. 5. The same arguments which the Lord useth to keep up and enforce his authority upon the consciences of his people, the same arguments they do, and ought to make use of, to press it upon themselves. " I am a jealous God," saith the Lord; It is true, saith conscience, the Lord is jealous; and therefore take heed to thyself, soul, how thou fallest into his hands. " It is a fearful thing to fall into the hands of the living God."

The jealousy of the Lord includes in it his tenderness of his honour, and terribleness in case of dishonour.

His tenderness of his honour. The honour of God is very tender to him, he will not lose a tittle of it; " My glory will I not give to another, nor my praise to graven images," Isa. xlii. 8. I will not, and look you to it, that you do not give away

my glory. What was the reason that God dealt so
severely with Eli and with Herod? What was Eli's
sin? Why, that he gave away the honour of God
to his sons. "Thou honourest thy sons above me,"
1 Sam. ii. 29. He was so tender to his sons, that
though they were become sons of Belial, and dealt
so wickedly before the Lord, yet they must be dealt
gently with; "Nay, my sons, it is no good thing
that I hear of you." Such a slight reproof must
serve in so dreadful a case; he was afraid to displease his sons by a sharper reproof; this the Lord
interprets an honouring of his sons above him. Indulgent parents, stand and tremble, you that can
see your children sin, and let them go out with a
"Nay, my sons, it is not good," a slight or cold
reproof; this is no other but your honouring your
sons above your God. What was Herod's sin?
Acts xii. 22, 23. that he gave not God the glory.
He made an eloquent oration, and the people thereupon made him a god: "The voice of God and not
of man," and he accepted of the applause; and
thereupon the angel of the Lord smote him, that he
died. Eli sinned in giving the honour of God to
his sons, and Herod in taking it to himself; but God
taught them both how dear his glory is to him.

The jealousy of the Lord also includes his terribleness in case of his dishonour. The mentioned
instances speak him both tender and terrible; "The
Lord thy God is a consuming fire, even a jealous
God," Deut. iv. 24. The jealousy of a man is the
rage of a man, Prov. vi. 34. And the jealousy of
God is the rage and fury of a God. "Our God is
a consuming fire," that is, the fire of his jealousy.
The wrath of a king is as the roaring of a lion;
when the lion roareth, the beasts of the field tremble;

what then are the terrors of the Lord? The threatenings of the Lord are terrible, " Consider this, ye
that forget God, lest he tear you in pieces and there
be none to deliver," Psa. l. 22. " I, even I, will
tear and go away," Hos. v. 14. Tearing, and tearing in pieces, the very expectation of it is enough to
tear the heart in pieces. I will tear them, saith
God; I myself will do it; I, even I, will tear. It
is terrible to be torn of men or of wild beasts; but
take heed of God's tearing. I will tear in pieces;
I will not tear off their hair, or their garments, or
their ornaments; I will tear their flesh from their
bones, limb from limb, yea, soul from body; I will
tear them in pieces. I will tear them and go away,
tear them, and leave them; wound, and not heal.
I will tear them, and deliver them who can; yea,
I will tear them, and trample upon them; " I will
tread them in mine anger, and trample them in my
fury," Isa. lxiii. 3. Trampling denotes contempt and
indignation. I will make them as the dirt in the
streets; the mark of my scorn and fury.

His judgments are terrible, he doth terrible things
in righteousness. Go to Jerusalem and mount Sion,
and behold the monuments of his fury there. " Go
to Shiloh," saith God, " and see what I did to it,"
Jer. vii. 12. But if you go down to Sodom, or
look down to Tophet, and behold the terrors of the
Lord there; or if you look on particular persons,
let Nadab and Abihu, Korah, Dathan and Abiram,
Uzzah, Uzziah, Ananias and Sapphira, Herod, &c.
be for instances of his dreadfulness and severity.
This jealous God, this terrible God, is the God whom
his people fear; and they, therefore, fear him, because he is such a jealous God. Who would not
fear thee, thou King of nations? Who can stand

before thee when thou art angry? My flesh trembles for fear of thee, and I am afraid of thy judgments.

Christians, let none say, this fear is not the fear of his children; this be to his enemies and slaves, not his children: fear ye not their fear. But are not all these things written for our learning? Is this written only for their sakes? Or saith he not also for our sakes? For our sakes no doubt this is written, saith the apostle in another case. Consider that full scripture to this purpose, "Now these things were our examples, to the intent we should not lust after evil things, as they also lusted; neither be ye idolaters, as were some of them, as it is written, The people sat down to eat and drink, and rose up to play. Neither let us commit fornication, as some of them committed, and fell in one day three and twenty thousand. Neither let us tempt Christ, as some of them also tempted, and were destroyed of serpents. Neither murmur ye, as some of them also murmured, and were destroyed of the destroyer. Now all these things happened unto them for ensamples, and they are written for our admonition upon whom the ends of the world are come. Wherefore let him that thinketh he standeth, take heed lest he fall," 1 Cor. x. 6—12.

Mark, these things are our examples. Are they examples to us, and not warnings too? Are they warnings to us, and must we not by them learn to fear and beware? "Let him that thinketh he standeth, take heed lest he fall." My soul standeth in a sure place, my mountain is so strong, that I shall never be moved; I am safe enough; I am in Christ, and shall not come into condemnation. But whatever thou thinkest, as sure as thou thinkest thou standest take heed, take heed lest thou fall; that is, not only into the same sins, but into the same condemnation; that is the sense of the place. "Because of unbelief they are broken off; thou standest by faith. Be not high-minded, but fear," Rom. xi. 20.

No need of fear! No need of threatenings! What! may we burn half our bibles? Can we spare so great a part of what is written? Have we out-grown the use of judgment, as soon as ever we are partakers of mercy? Have we out-grown the use of the scourge, as soon as ever we are entered into Christ's school? Do we find all too little, mercies, threatenings, judgments, to keep our hearts in order? and yet is it more than needful? There are two parties in us; we are flesh as well as spirit, and must not the flesh be frighted? Will love prevail with lust? This slave sure, this son of the bond-woman, must be kept in awe. Hath God no disobedient children, no rebellious children? and must these have no other discipline but strokings and dandlings?

Believe it, christians, God will not have his terrors lost, nor lost to you; God will sometimes make his children feel that he is a terrible God. He is terrible out of his holy place. Beware you be not presumptuous children. There is a threefold presumption. 1. A presumption upon temptation, in confidence of strength. 2. Upon sin, in confidence of mercy. 3. Upon sin, in contempt of mercy and justice. 1. A presumption upon temptation, in confidence of strength. Some unwary souls, not knowing what spirit they are of, supposing themselves too hard for the devil, will be venturing within his reach; as if they would dare him to try his skill and power; who, having forgotten this prayer "Lead us not into

temptation," put themselves into the tempter's hand:
the falls of such will teach them to understand their
folly. 2. Presumption on sin, in confidence of mercy.
And that either in confidence of mercy already
obtained—I am in Christ, and my sin shall not
separate me from him ; whatever I do, I have a pardon in my hand : or in hope of mercy at last—I
have to do with a merciful God, and therefore may
venture on a little further ; hereafter I will repent,
and then I need not doubt of remission. 3. Presumption on sin, in contempt of mercy and justice
—I will have my sin, though I never find mercy ;
I will have my will and my way, and run the
hazard of what follows ; I will take my course, and
come on me what will.

This last sort, who presume to sin in contempt of
mercy and judgment ; who are so drunken with their
sensual delights, and given over to the hardness of
their hearts, that they neither value mercy, nor fear
wrath :—What do you talk to me of mercy and
judgment to come ? Give me my pleasures, and
my liberties, and my mirth, and my money : think
not to make me such a fool, to let go the pleasure
and comfort of my life, for, I know not what, uncertain fears or hopes. Such as these have one foot
already in hell. If it be not yet thus with thee, thou
darest not contemn either mercy or judgment ,
also beware thou be not presumptuous in the former sense. Be not bold upon temptations ; think
not that thou art strong to overcome a temptation,
when thou art so weak as not to fear it ; he that
fears not a temptation, understands not it, or himself. But especially beware thou presume not upon
sin, in consequence of mercy. Grow not over bold
upon love or patience. God loves me, therefore I

may be bold to take the more liberty, the less care, the less watchfulness, the less fear, because so much love! Spit in thy Father's face, because he weeps over thy neck! Smite him on the face, because thou hopest he will not strike again! Tear his bowels, because they are so tender towards thee! Be froward, stubborn, wanton, and idle, because thou hast found him so indulgent!

Christians, consider whether such wickedness hath not sometimes been found in some of our hearts. But take heed; you will find, though he be a tender, yet he will not be a fond* father; where he loves, he will be feared. Some as bold and as confident as you, have felt to their cost, what it is to abuse patience and kindness; his arrows in their hearts, his terrors in their souls, have made them to know that the God of love is a terrible God. And look to it if thou yet wilt adventure, wilt be a wanton still, froward, or idle, or heedless still, he will either lash thee into better manners, or cast thee out as no child of his, but a bastard and rebel. If thou wilt not take warning by others, take heed lest he make thee a warning to them which shall come after.

Christians know, that though God be tender of his saints, yet he is jealous for his name; he tenders them as the apple of his eye, but not above the least tittle of his honour. As God will have us love our neighbour, so he will love his child, but as himself: first himself, and then his child. He will not abate an iota of his glory, to save a world. As little offences done to his little ones, so little sins allowed by them, are as mill-stones about the neck. If they allow it in themselves, yet heaven and earth shall pass away, and fall to nothing, ere he allow it in

* Injudiciously indulgent, foolish.

them. God will not, and therefore his children dare not indulge themselves in little sins. They therefore fear, because he whom they serve is a jealous God.

[2.] Their own ingenuousness. This fear is from love and good nature, and is most properly the fear of children. Children fear, because God is jealous, and so do slaves ; but only children because God is good. Children fear, because they love ; slaves fear, although they hate. Children fear to be unworthy ; slaves only to be unhappy and miserable. There is nothing more contrary to an ingenuous nature, than to abuse goodness and kindness ; to abuse goodness hath as black an aspect with him, as to provoke wrath. " They shall fear the Lord and his goodness in the latter days," Hos. iii. 5. But how can goodness be the object of fear ? We fear evil and not good. The meaning is, they shall fear to wrong or abuse goodness. They shall fear to wrong the Lord, because he is good, " in the latter days." These latter days that this promise refers to, shall be days of more grace ; wherein there shall be not only a more clear revelation of the goodness of God, (they shall know the Lord and his goodness,) but a more plentiful communication and diffusion of the goodness of God : they shall love the Lord and his goodness. They shall see themselves both more obliged by goodness, and shall feel themselves more seasoned with goodness. By grace they shall be better natured. Religion doth not make morose, but more generous, free, and ingenuous. There is nothing more abhorrent to an ingenuous spirit, than to be base and unworthy. Abuse of goodness is an unworthiness, which an ingenuous nature abhors as death to be guilty of ; it is its destruction, it is disingenuousness. The abuse of the goodness of God is great unthankfulness; and unthankfulness is great disingenuousness.

Call me unthankful, and you call me all that is bad. Call me any thing else but unthankful. Indeed, were I all thanks, I should still be unthankful; I should still be behindhand with the goodness of the Lord; my debt is greater than I can pay, yea, greater than I can acknowledge; but shall I return evil for good? If I cannot pay, should I deny my debt? He that is unthankful, whatever God requires of him, says wickedly, This is more than I owe to thee. God, I owe thee nothing, I care not for thee. Oh this is dreadful to a gracious heart.

If this be in sin, (for all sin is unthankfulness,) if this be sin, if this be the signification of all my neglects of God, and my duty to him; then the Lord forbid, whatever I suffer, that I should yield to sin. How shall I do this wickedness? How shall I neglect this duty, and sin against God? How shall I look my God, or my own soul in the face, should I be so unworthy? For thy sake, Lord, let me not sin against thee; thou art good, thou art kind, thou art gracious, thou art holy; O let me not be a devil; what heart, where a devil is not, but such goodness will charm it into love? Shall I sin? shall I rebel? For thy sake, Lord, I will not do it; I will not for my own sake; for where then shall I appear? In sinning against God, I sin against my own soul; I dare not for my life; sin and death, sin and hell are linked together; but were it not so, might I sin and escape, sin and not die, yet for thy sake, Lord, I will not do it. Thou art good, good in thyself, good to me: thou art my God, thou art my Father; love, care, tenderness, compassion, kindness, is all

that is in thy heart towards me ; what I am, what
I have, what I hope for, that I breathe, that I live,
all is thy goodness, thy bounty to me.   Oh let me
not rise up against the womb that bare me, and the
paps that gave me suck.   I would not to my child,
to my servant, to my friend ; but oh let me never to
my Father, to my God, return "evil for good, and
hatred for his good will."   Let not this evil which
I fear, ever come upon me ; put thy fear into my
heart, O Lord, that I may not sin against thee.

Chapter XV —*Obedience in the Covenant*

" I will put my Spirit within you, and cause you to
walk in my statutes ; and ye shall keep my judgments,
and do them," Ezek. xxxvi. 27.   Obedience is of
the heart, or of the life.   In this scripture, God
undertakes for both.

I. For the obedience of the heart, he undertakes
in the former words, I will put my Spirit in your
heart.   Where the Spirit dwells, he rules ; where
Satan dwells, he rules ; and where the Spirit of the
Lord dwells, there God rules.   The Spirit in the heart,
is the law of the heart.   Those two promises, " I will
put my Spirit in your hearts," and " I will write my
law in your hearts," signify the same thing.   The
law in the heart, is the will of man melted into the
will of God.   The law of God may be in the mouth,
and the heart a rebel ; its reception into the heart,
notes the heart's subjection to it.

The obedience of the heart includes two things
1. The opening of the heart to the word ; 2. The
resolution of the heart for the work of the Lord.

1. The opening of the heart to the word.   What
wilt thou have me to do, Lord ?   That is the voice
of an obedient heart.   Speak Lord, command Lord,

what wilt thou? And when he speaks, whatever it be, the word is embraced and accepted of the heart. " Let my counsel be acceptable to thee," Dan. iv. 27. The acceptance of the word in the heart, is signified by its hearkening to it. To hearken, is more than to hear; though they sometimes denote the same thing, yet ordinarily, hearing is of the ear, hearkening of the heart. " Israel would not hearken, my people would none of me," Psa. lxxxi. 11. They heard what the Lord spake, but they would not hearken; that is, as it is there interpreted, they would none of the Lord. They rejected the word of the Lord which he spake unto them. When the word is let come in with authority, suffered to rule in the soul; when the heart gives up itself unto it, then it is accepted; there is its hearkening to it.

2. The resolution of the heart for the work of the Lord. " I have sworn, and I will perform it, that I will keep thy righteous judgments," Psa. cxix. 106. I have vowed and I will perform; I have covenanted, and I am determined to keep thy statutes. The word which thou hast spoken to us in the name of the Lord, we will not do; that is the rebellious: Whatsoever the Lord shall speak, we will do; that is the obedient heart.

Where the heart is thus resolved to obey, this is that obedience which shall be accepted unto salvation. Where this resolution is, as there is opportunity there will be practice; and where there is not opportunity in God's account, this is it. This is praying, this is hearing, this is giving, and feeding, and clothing, and visiting; this is walking circumspectly, working righteousness, showing mercy, exercising faith, and patience, and repentance; this is outkeeping the commandments of God, and walk ing in his statutes. A heart to obey, is our obeying ; a heart to do, is our doing ; a heart to suffer in God's account, is our suffering for his name.

But here it must be carefully noted, that though sincere resolution for obedience, be obedience ; yet every resolution is not that resolution. Resolution for obedience is then sincere, where,

(1.) It flows from an inward and rooted inclination.

(2.) It is founded on a firm belief of scripture revelation.

(3.) It is built on the highest and weightiest reasons.

(4.) It is the result of the most mature and deep deliberation.

(1.) A sincere resolution flows from an inward rooted inclination ; " I have inclined mine heart to perform thy statutes," Psa. cxix. 112. Our new purpose is from our new nature. It is not produced by some sudden fright, or sense of danger ; or merely by a present force of argument ; but by a divine power working the heart to a suitableness to the will and ways of God, and a habitual propension and inclination thereto. Resolution for holiness, without a holy inclination, is a blade without a root ; as fresh and as green as it looks, it will wither and come to nothing ; no root, no fruit, nor lasting. The heart is the root of action, and grace is the life of the root. When our resolutions are the blade, sprouting forth of this living root, then they will abide, and bring forth the ear and a harvest.

(2.) A sincere resolution is founded on a firm assent to the truth of scripture revelation. A christian resolves for godliness, because he believes God that he is as he hath said, the rewarder of them that

diligently seek him.   He is. built on the scriptures ,
as his hopes, so his purposes have the foundation of
the prophets and apostles, on which they stand.
Whatever resolution hath not this foundation is but
as a house upon the sands.

(3.) A sincere resolution is founded on the highest reason.   Where we resolve without reason we
will quickly find a reason to change.   Where we
resolve we know not why, we shall change we know
not how soon.   To resolve we know not why, and
to resolve on we know not what, will be alike unstable.   Though there be reason for religion, yet
religion may be taken up without reason.   Whatever reason there be for it, yet if it be not understood, or considered, it is all one as if there were no
reason at all.   And if there seem some reason for it,
yet if it be not the highest reason, when a stronger
than it comes, we quickly change our purpose.

The reasons we have for our serving and following God are the highest of all reasons, and that
whether we respect it as our duty or our happiness.
For,

[1.] There is none can lay such claims to us as
God.   Whose am I ?   Who hath made me ?   Who
hath bought me ?   " Glorify God in your bodies
and in your spirits, which are his," 1 Cor. vi. 20.
" Serve the Lord with gladness; for the Lord he is
God ; it is he that hath made us, not we ourselves,
we are his people, and the sheep of his pasture,"
Psa. c. 2, 3.   What reason have you to serve men,
or to serve sin, or the world ?   Men think they have
reason for it, but what reason ?   Are any of these
gods ?   Are men your gods ? is sin or the world
God ? do you owe yourselves to them ?   It is he that
hath made us, and his we are.   As the apostle saith

concerning obedience to parents, much more may it be said here; Children obey your God, for this is right. This is his due, and your duty; if any one can lay as good a claim to you, let him carry you away for servants.

[2.] There is none can be better to us than God. None can requite, none can reward our obedience as he. Where can you be better than with God? He will require no more, than that you serve him till you can find a better master. He that saith, It is best to serve sin and the world, is a fool, and hath said in his heart, There is no God. If God be God, he is the chief, yea, the only good. If any thing in the world, upon what account soever, be thought better than the Lord, that is set up for a god in his room.

[3.] Whomsoever we serve, it is God must pay us our wages at last. God is judge, he is the rewarder both of the evil and the good; both of those who serve him and those who serve him not. If you serve the Lord, he will be your reward; if you serve him not, he will reward you: but what reward have you? "Those, mine enemies, which will not have me reign over them, bring them, and slay them before me;" there is their reward. Sin hath its rewards, but what are they but vanity and vexation? Or if they were better, how long will they last? But when sin hath paid the most it can, oh what a reward is there behind that God hath to pay you! "This shall ye have of mine hand, ye shall lie down in sorrow."

[4.] The wages which God will give shall certainly be blessed or dreadful, according to our obedience or disobedience. The reward that God hath to give is an eternal reward: eternal salvation to

them that obey him ; everlasting destruction to him
that serveth him not.

I have a soul ; this carcass is the least part of me ;
there is another world, a world to come ; a few
years is the most I have to spend in this ; I must
abide eternally, eternally in the other world.

Of how little consequence is it, what I have here,
whether little or more, better or worse ? in a short
time that will come all to one. But oh my eternity !
what is that like to be ? Why it is God that must
determine it, and he will certainly reward every man
according to his works. " Who will render to every
man according to his deeds. To them who, by
patient continuance in well doing, seek for glory and
honour and immortality, eternal life. But to them
that are contentious, and do not obey the truth, tribulation, and anguish," &c. Rom. ii. 6—10. There
is glory and shame, mercy and wrath, life and death,
set before me ; there is no third state, one of the
two must be my lot ; and this is it that doth determine, which, if I obey, I live ; if I disobey, I die
for ever.

Now, when my resolution is founded on such reasons as these, than which none can be imagined
higher and more weighty ; till eternity become of
less regard than time ; and an immortal soul be set
below a perishing body, and when the question being put, Shall I follow God or not ? God or the
world ? God or my lust ? Speak, soul, give in thy
answer : when this is the answer it gives ; Why,
there is none can lay such claim to me as God ;
there is none can be as good to me as God ; whomsoever I serve, it is God must be my rewarder ; my
everlasting blessedness, or eternal ruin, depends on
him, and must be infallibly determined, according

to my obedience or disobedience. This is the plain case, obey and live; obey, or die for ever. And therefore what can I say less or more, but that I am the Lord's, and will be his servant. Let others choose whom they will serve; as for me, O my soul, serve thou the Lord. This resolution, thus founded, is like to stand.

(4.) A sincere resolution is the fruit of mature deliberation. Deliberation gives reason its full weight, makes the strength of it appear; it lays all things in the balance; it is the comparing of reasons for and against, the weighing of arguments and objections, encouragements **and** discouragements; casting the cost, as well as the gain, particularly. In this deliberation there must be a considering, 1. What there is in this obedience, 2. What it is attended with, that may encourage.

There must be a considering what there is in this obedience; or otherwise we resolve upon we know not what. Now there are five things in this obedience: 1. Subjection; 2. Activity and industry; 3. Integrity; 4. Circumspection; 5. Spirituality.

1. Subjection. Servants must be subject, must not be at their own wills, but at the will of another. The heart of man naturally affects dominion; that is the great controversy of sinners with God. "Who shall be Lord? "We are lords," we would be at least, "we will come no more unto thee," Jer. ii. 31. Obedience yields that God should be Lord; yea, and all others also whom he hath made lords over us. The servants of Christ must not be, and yet must be, the servants of men; they must not serve the lusts, but must be subject to their righteous laws and commands. God must be obeyed, and magistrates, ministers, masters, parents must be obeyed in

the Lord, and for the Lord; yea, and they must be, when God will have it so, the servant of servants.

While they must not serve the humours of the greatest, they must serve the necessities of the meanest, must stoop to the lowest of offices, even to the washing of the feet of the least disciple. All this the Lord expects of them, and they must be subject. They must not dispute, but do his will; only it must be considered that there is a double disputing the will of God. There is a disputing whether that which is pretended to be the will of God be so or not; this ought to be done. And there is a disputing or questioning that which is granted to be the will of God, whether it be fit to be done, or safe to be done. Is it not better to let it alone? What advantage is there in it? What reason is there for it? No, they must not thus dispute; this is reason enough, God will have it so. God's will is ever reason, and it must be our reason. It is enough for thee to say, This is that which the Lord hath commanded, and I must be subject. This is one thing that must be considered, I will obey, and must be subject to God.

2. Activity and industry. The servants of the Lord must be active and industrious. Whom he sends into the vineyard he sends to work, and not to sleep. The life of a christian is laborious; whilst others are in their beds, he must be on his knees; whilst others take their pleasure, he must take pains; whilst others take their times, now a little, and then a little, he must sit to it, be ever about his Master's business. An active spirit is an excellent spirit, and it is necessary in a christian.

An active spirit is an excellent spirit; sluggards are the refuse of the earth.

But here it must be considered that there is a double activity, gracious and natural. 1. Natural, which arises from an innate vigour and vivacity of some men's spirits. There needs not industry in such to bring forth action; it is but leaving nature to its course, and that will fly high enough of itself. It requires more industry to regulate, and sometimes to restrain, than to put forth into action. It is more labour for them to rest than to be doing. 2. Gracious; which is either natural activity, managed and improved for God, turned into a right course, running in a right channel; or a naturally inactive spirit, raised and quickened by grace and religious industry. This gracious, this holy activity, this is the excellency; it is the extract of the spirits and life of all our parts and graces, and will go further, and do more high honour, and more abundant service to God and his gospel, than is done by a thousand others.

An active sinner is by accident the worst of men: how much service for the devil will he despatch in a little time? An active sinner is life and death met together He is all life, and yet dead; and the more he hath of death, because so much of life; like poison in wine, he destroys the more effectually. Yet the evil is not in his activity, but in the matter wherein he is employed; the good metal, as keenness of a weapon, is its excellency: but in a madman's hand, better a wooden than an iron sword. An active spirit is so excellent, that it is pity that ever sin should have the using of it; it were well for religion if the devil were a drone, and had no other servants but the sluggards of the earth. But activity, when set right, is of great price in the sight of God, because it sets a great price upon God.

Slothfulness puts a slight upon God; when the scriptures have set forth the great things, and the deep things of God; when the Lord Jesus is evidently set forth as crucified before our eyes, as the propitiation for sin; when the preciousness of his blood, the tenderness of his compassion, the riches of his grace, the sufficiency of his righteousness, his satisfaction and pardons, are all held forth in open sight; when the beauties of holiness, the joys of the Spirit, that peace which passeth all understanding, are laid forth to view; when the most glorious things are spoken of the city of God, Jerusalem, which is above; when God in his word calls to us, Awake sleepers, arise sluggards, see what is before you; all this may be yours if you will; slothfulness puts this slight upon all, Tush! all this is not worth the breaking my sleep for; it is not all worth my labour to seek after; my ease and my quiet is better to me than God and all his glory.

We may best understand the value we put on things, by the pains and the cost we are content to be at to purchase them. When sinners bestow themselves so upon the world, will bear such labour and travail, are so constantly, so indefatigably industrious in the pursuit of it; and withal, run such hazards and dangers for it, they make it evident enough what rate they put upon it. He whose time and strength, whose days and nights, yea, whose soul and hopes, must all be laid out in a purchase, must all go for a piece of a land, or a little money or pleasure; we need no other proof, what a bargain he thinks this world to be. I care not much for this world: it is a vanity, a shadow, the fashion of it passeth away; I hope it is far enough off my heart, however I am charged

with greediness after it. But what then mean all
the expenses of thy time, of thy strength, of thy
spirits, that thou daily layest out upon it? What
means so much hunting after, and heaping it up for
thyself? What! hast thou been hunting all this
while after shadows, heaping up vanities? No, no,
thou mistakest thyself, these shadows are thy substance; these vanities are the god whom thou
adorest; if thou didst not prize thou wouldst not
venture so deeply for them.

And so on the other side, when so little is done
for God; when anything must suffice to be spent
on souls or eternity; what cheap things do we
count them! I love God above all, with all my
heart, with all my soul; he is all my hope, and all
my desire. What a miserable creature were I, if it
were not for my hope in God! What would all the
world be to me, should I lose my soul! But dost
thou speak in earnest? Dost thou think what thou
speakest? What! and such a very drone in seeking
God! What! and so indifferent, so cold, and so
spiritless in thy inquiries after him, in thy motions
towards him! so sparing of thy labour, so negligent
of duty, so seldom at it, so soon weary, so many
delays, so many excuses! How many times hath
God called thee after him, and all thine answer hath
been an excuse! an excuse instead of an ordinance,
an excuse instead of a prayer, an excuse instead of
action, an excuse instead of alms, an excuse instead
of an admonition or a reproof; if he will be served
with excuses, he shall have service enough, but
little besides. I am weary, or it is too late, or it is
cold, and so a short and hasty prayer must serve,
or none at all. I have much business upon me, a
family, a farm, and the cares and troubles of it, that

I cannot have so much time nor freedom to attend upon God as others have, and so a sermon lost, a sacrament lost. I live amongst ill neighbours, if I should be so forward and so active for God, so zealous, and so spiritual in my discourse, in my way, I should be but a scoff and a reproach, and it may be a prey to evil men. I want ability to speak to the edification of others, I have not the boldness as others have, to reprove or admonish ; I pray thee have me excused. Wise men indeed, an excuse instead of a duty ! It is all one, as if when the Lord calls to thee, Come to me and be saved, thy answer should be, I pray thee excuse me, I must to the devil and be damned.

But is this thy love ? is this thy zeal ? is this thy valuing of God above all ?

Tremble, sluggard ; whatever excuses thou findest out, to substitute in the room of duty, this is that thou canst never excuse nor acquit thyself of, a slighting of God. Thy very excuses will accuse thee for a slothful servant, and this for a slighter of God ; whilst the apostle says, " I reckon that the sufferings of this life are not worthy to be compared with the glory that shall be revealed." But I reckon, sayest thou, that all the glory to come, is not worthy to be compared with the present labour.

But now activity and industry puts a great price upon God ; this is written upon all our labours, He is worthy for whom I do all this. Some of the most humble, watchful, laborious christians, do sometimes complain, Oh, I fear I love not God ; his favour, his honour, is little set by of me ; but whence then is thy care to please God ? Whence are all thy labours of love ? Dost thou watch, and pray, and work, and run ? Canst thou spend and be spent for

God, and yet not love him? Dost thou live to God,
canst thou die for God, and yet not prize him?
What greater proof canst thou give of love, than
such labour?

Activity is also necessary. It is vain to think
of making any thing of religion without it; the
work of it is too great to be done by lying still;
the comforts of it lie too deep to be gotten out by a
wish. There is many a poor man in this world,
that would be the richest man in the country, if
riches may be gotten by a wish; he may as
soon wish himself into wealth, as thou into grace
and comfort. This one thing, men's not being
able to bear the labour of religion, is a rock at
which many a soul hath split, and suffered an eternal
wreck.

He that hath some love to holiness, and yet not
so much as to carry him through the work of holiness, is short of sincerity; and short of sincerity,
short of salvation. He that sticks not at labour,
will not stick at suffering: he that slugs at doing,
will shrink back from suffering. Say not, There is
a lion in the streets; overcome the lion, and you
will not fear the bear. Get over difficulties and
there is but one stile more, distress, betwixt thee
and glory. Pass the first, and thou wilt be the
more bold to venture the latter. Holy activity will
be a witness to thy sincerity; carry this witness
in thy heart, and then which way ever the world
does go, and what storms soever may fall, thou wilt
have this to uphold thee—Integrity and uprightness shall preserve me, and eternity reward me.
Where sincerity is the root, and holy activity the
blossom, an eternal weight of glory shall be the
fruit. Lie idle, and all will be lost. Take heed

of " Soul take thine ease," lest the next word
thou hear be, " This night shall thy soul be required of thee."

Well, this is the second thing included in obedience, activity ; and this also must be considered ere
thou resolvest. I will obey ; but can I labour ?

[3.] Integrity. The obedience which God expects
must be entire obedience, not only the obedience of
the whole man, but to the whole will of God. " Then
shall I not be ashamed, when I have respect to
all thy commandments," Psa. cxix. 6. " As obedient children, be ye holy in all manner of conversation," 1 Pet. i. 14, 15. " Teaching them to observe all things, whatsoever I have commanded you,"
Matt. xxviii. 20. But of this having spoken more
largely elsewhere, it shall suffice to give some short
hints of one comprehensive duty, wherein all the
rest are included, and on which they depend ; and
that is—the holding up and maintaining God's authority in the soul. As God hath set up his authority over the soul, his word, which is to have the
government of it ; so hath he set up an authority in
the soul, the understanding and the conscience.
These powers, as they are under authority, under
the authority of the word ; so they are set in authority over the subordinate and inferior faculties, the
will, and the passions or affections. But sin now
hath made a mutiny and insurrection ; the will rises
against reason, and will not be guided ; the passions
rebel against conscience, and will not be governed ;
nay, they do not only resist, but take upon them to
command and impose upon conscience. What the
will would have, conscience must say it is reason it
should have , must be put upon it, to find out arguments to prove will to be reason, and to determine

that what the will would have done, ought to be done. We easily bring our opinion to our affection; bring ourselves to believe that to be right, which we are unreasonably willing to have to be right. But if it cannot prevail thus far, to gain conscience to say that is right, which it would have to be right, then it will put hard for it to carry it, whether it be right or wrong. And this rebellion of the will, and so of the passions against the reason, is the great reason of the soul's rebellion against God.

When conscience hath lost its authority, God's authority is gone. Whilst the understanding and the conscience are maintained in their due authority, where the will and affections are held in their due subjection, there the Lord reigneth. While conscience rightly informed hath its due, God shall have his due: where the will and the passions have no more than their due, he shall have his own. God shall be willed the more, where nothing else is willed too much. God shall be loved the more, and feared the more, where nothing else is loved and feared too much. The more anger, the more hatred, the more grief will be spent upon sin, if it be not inordinately spent elsewhere. Oh how much service might be done, and how much quiet would be enjoyed in the heart, were this authority and subjection maintained and held up!

We may say of our affections, as men say of fire and water, They are the worst masters, but the best servants. How much should the Lord have of us, were these only the executioners of his will! If conscience be commanded by the word, and the will and affections would be commanded by conscience, what would there then be wanting! We should then not only be abundantly serviceable, but all would be serene, and sweet, and comfortable within us. If nothing were willed, but what should be willed, we should ever have our will. If nothing were desired, but what should be desired, and no more than it should be loved or desired, we should ever have what we love. If we were not angry, or grieved, or afraid, but where we ought, and no more than we ought, what a calm would there be upon our spirits, even in such cases wherein the spirits of others are like a troubled sea, that cannot be at rest, whose waters cast forth mire and dirt. But where there is such disorder, such rebellion of the inferior against the superior faculties, there we are at a perpetual loss, both in point of duty and comfort. This therefore is necessary, if we will be obedient ; and those who have proved what there is in it, do understand that this is hard work.

I shall instance some few particular duties that are harder than others. He that will be entirely obedient, must stick at nothing that God will have. There is scarcely any thing that God requires, but lust will be quarrelling at, as too hard ; but there are some duties harder than others. It shall suffice only to name them : The denial of ourselves ; disobliging our nearest friends ; loving our enemies ; disobeying all the world in their unrighteous commands ; obeying God rather than men ; returning good for evil ; reproving men for sin, especially if they be superiors, or such on whom we have dependency ; and the sacrificing our Isaac, yea, parting with all that we have.

Well, this also must be considered, ere you resolve ; you will obey, but are you for any thing, for every thing the Lord requires ?

[4.] Circumspection and care ; " See that ye walk

circumspectly," Eph. v. 15. A little labour will go
far with care, but will be nothing without it. It is
not he that is hot, and busy, and active at all adven-
tures ; he that keeps to his line, and his rule, he is
the obedient christian. It is not so much action as
regular action, wherein the life of christianity lies.
He that lives by rule, peace be on him, and mercy.
Activity without care is extravagance, it is care that
keeps within compass. He that is all action, has
the more need of caution. A christian must have
his eyes in his head as well as a soul in his body.
He that resolves well in generals, and comes not off
in particulars, does but build castles in the air. What
we ordinarily are in particulars will best prove what
we are. He that is for any thing but this, any time
but now, is for nothing.

Circumspection notes two things ; taking notice
and taking heed. He that will be circumspect, must
eye and observe what is before him ; must have his
eye upon his end, his rule, and his goings ; must
eye duty and sin, opportunities and temptations,
his times and seasons ; he must take heed, as well
as take notice ; must keep a strict eye on himself,
and hold a strict hand on himself, that he leap not
over a duty, nor turn aside to inquiry ; must set a
guard upon himself, upon his tongue, upon his
eyes, upon his appetite, upon his company, upon
his habit, upon his thoughts, upon his passions, upon
all the motions of his soul, and the actions of his
body.

This will require something. What! not a word
but must be weighed! Not a look but must be
looked to! Not a thought but must be examined!
Not a sin to be allowed! Not a duty to be abated!
Not a circumstance to be neglected! Must all be in

weight and in measure, by line and by rule, and
this always too ! If *something* might serve, if *sometimes* might suffice, it might be borne ; but to keep
the engagement in every point, and that every day,
this is a hard saying indeed.   But thus it must, be
to live as a christian, and to walk exactly, accurately,
precisely, is the same thing.   Duty and sin, though
they be as far distant as heaven and hell, yet there
is but a hair betwixt them.   The least latitude is a
transgression, either all this, (that is, as to the purpose of the heart,) either all this, or nothing.

Well, all this must be considered ; you will be
obedient, but will you be circumspect ?

5. Spiritually. This must be the obedience of
faith, Rom. xvi. 26. It is the very life of Jesus
made manifest in our mortal flesh : " I live, yet not
I, but Christ liveth in me ; and the life which I now
live in the flesh, I live by the faith of the Son of
God."   Christians' obedience is their walking in
Christ, Col. ii. 6. all the acts of it are exercised
and performed in the strength of Christ.   I
will go in the strength of the Lord : without him
they can do nothing, but can do all things through
Christ which strengtheneth them.   " I live, yet not
I, but Christ liveth in me."   I work, I wrestle, I run,
yet not I, but Christ in me ; as the apostle speaks
of his sins, " It is no more I that do it, but sin that
dwelleth in me."   It is sin that sins ; so may it be
said of duty.   It is no more I that do it, but Christ
that dwelleth in me.   Though both be the act of
the person, both the sin and the duty ; yet the principle of the one is lust, the power of the other is of
Christ.   Christians cannot go through, and they
dare not set upon duty, without looking up to Christ,
and leaning upon him for assistance.   They cannot go

through, and therefore they will not set forth, but in the strength of the Lord. All their acts of obedience are exhibited, and offered up in the name of Christ. Their services are their sacrifices to God, and Christ is their altar. What is a sacrifice without an altar? Christ is our altar, which sanctifies our gift; God looks on all, and so do they as nothing worth without Christ; God will not accept, and therefore they will not offer other than the Lamb for their sacrifice. All their acts of obedience are acknowledged to the praise of Christ. It is no more I that do it, but the grace of God which was with me. Grace does the work, and grace shall carry away the praise. Christ is all in the race, and therefore on his head the crown is set. "Not unto us, Lord, not unto us, but to thy name be the praise." Not of us, and therefore not unto us; of him, and therefore unto him. If I am anything, what others are not; if I have done anything more than others, no thanks to me, and therefore no praise. To him be all, who is all in all to me. The obedience of christians is their walking in Christ.

The obedience of christians is their walking in the Spirit. They have received the Spirit, and they walk in the Spirit, Gal. v. 16. They have not received the spirit of this world, their spirit is not flesh, but the Spirit which is of God, 1 Cor. ii. 12. They are dead to things carnal, the spirit of the world is departed, they have given up this : it is the Spirit of the living God who lives in them, and in this they live and walk. They walk in the light of the Spirit, in the power of the Spirit ; the Spirit of the Lord steers their course and fills their sails ; is their pilot, and their star, and their wind that carries them on. When they pray, they pray in the Spirit ;

when they hear, they hear in the Spirit; through the Spirit they mortify the flesh, are crucified to the world; they obey, they suffer, they fight, they overcome, through the Spirit of the living God that is in them. They live in fellowship with the Spirit, and by him with the Father and the Son. They dwell in the invisible world, their acquaintance and converse is in heaven, thither they have access; and there they have acceptance; thither they have their recourse, and thence they have their returns. Duties and comforts are the tokens that are passing betwixt heaven and earth. Their life is love, and joy, and praise; these are the most noble acts of their obedience, and these give wings to their hearts, carry them on more swiftly and more sweetly through all their course.

Oh how heavily do we drive on, how slowly do our wheels move, when the Spirit of the living God is not in the wheels! Oh how dead are our duties, how lame are our walkings! what low and poor spirited creatures are we! How weak are our hearts, how unripe our fruits, we do but half, do what we do, there is no heart in our life, we are as bodies without souls, whilst our soul is without a spirit. Oh how sad it is with many of us, upon this account! By our estrangement from God, we have even lost ourselves; we are not what we are, because no more where he is. By our distances from heaven, we are even choked with the damps of the earth. We are fit for little, we prosper in nothing, God takes no pleasure, and we take no comfort in any thing we do; our spirits are so chilled and benumbed within us that we neither make no speed in our work, nor riddance of our way. And what are we in our societies! To how little profit do we meet! How little heat do we get; yea, how much do we lose at our brethren's fires. We serve often but to damp and cool each other's spirits; as if it might be no longer said, Woe to him that is alone; but, Woe be to him that is in company: alone he is more warm.

Christians, I solemnly profess, I am ashamed of myself, and my heart is pained within me, to observe how insipid, how spiritless, how carnal our converses are. How often may we meet! How long may we sit, christian with christian, ere any thing that savours of the spirit of a christian comes from us! Oh how hard must we strain for a few gracious words! How little does come! How heartless when it comes! How very few of us are there, whose ordinary converse speaks us to be men of another world, whose business, and whose delight lies above, and are in good earnest pressing on towards heaven! How seldom and how short-breathed are our spiritual discourses! How little must suffice! How quickly are we diverted to things carnal and sensual! Sure it is our little communion with God, that has thus debased the communion of saints.

Oh let us live more in the fellowship of the Spirit, and we shall have fellowship one with another to better purpose. Let us warm ourselves at the sun, let us dwell more in his beams, and we shall get and give more light and heat. Thus must it be considered ere we resolve what there is in this obedience.

Further: It must be considered what it is like to be attended withal from without. What suffering it may cost us, what scorn, and contempt, and reproaches, and persecutions of all sorts; it is like to set earth and hell upon our backs; if carnal counsels and fleshly policies, if all the powers of darkness, if might and malice can do it; this way will be made too hot and too hard for thee; tribulation, great tribulation thou must expect, and canst not escape; and the more strict and circumspect, the hotter must thou look thine assaults will be.

Professors of religion who are of the largest size, who are not so strict to their rule, but they can dispense with duty; nor so forward in point of zeal and activity, but they can remit and abate, as occasion serves, may escape this persecuting world the better; but he that will be faithful, whoever escape, is sure to be made a prey. This also must be well considered, I will follow Christ, but can I drink of the cup that he drank of? Can I be baptized with the baptism, the baptism of blood, that he was baptized with?

There are persons who sometimes take up the profession of religion, and resolve all on a sudden they will follow Christ, not understanding what there is in it, or what christianity may stand them in; who, by the time they have looked a little further, and find it another manner of difficulty than at first they imagined; and withal, find the armies of the aliens to fall on, the dogs to tear, the wolves to worry, the eagles, and the vultures, and all the birds of prey, to pitch upon them; and begin in earnest to feel the smart of religion, in those persecutions that are raised upon them for it, presently make their retreat, and go back; Where am I? What have I chosen? Is this to be a christian? Doth Christ look for all this from his followers, and will he leave them to such violence and rapine, as the reward of their faithfulness to his name? I never thought it had been such hot service, and if I cannot be a saint at a cheaper rate than this, follow Christ who will for me; let those who have nothing to lose, or can bear so much labour, and pains, and violence, take it up if they please ; for my part, I must look to myself, I must not be undone.

Master, I will follow thee whithersoever thou goest, said the scribe, Matt. viii.19. Man thou understandest not what thou sayest. Dost thou know whither I am going, where my dwelling, where my lodging is ? "The foxes have holes, and the birds of the air have nests, but the Son of man hath not where to lay his head." And behold, there is an end of the scribe's christianity, we hear not one word more about it.

But now, he who both knows what it is to be a disciple, who hath looked through religion, through the length and breadth of it, hath duly weighed all that can be said for or against his taking it up, hath examined the grounds and reasons he hath for it, what weight there is in them, hath considered the objections, hath cast up the cost and charges of it, and as the issue and result of the most serious debate, stands settled in his judgment, that, all things considered, it is indisputably the best, and wisest, and safest course he can take—It is beyond all controversy, without all dispute, incomparably better for me to hearken to the Lord in all that he shall require, and to run all hazards with him, and that presently, from this day forward, to the end of my life. He that stands thus settled in his judgment, and thereupon feels his soul fixing itself in this peremptory resolution : Well, through the grace of God, I will be his servant, I give up myself to the government of his will, to follow him in righteousness and holiness all my days. I am sensible it is no light thing to be a christian ; I see I must be subject, I see I must be circumspect, I see I must be active, I must stick at nothing that God will have ; I see this flesh will be pained and put hard to it, will fling and groan under so severe a yoke. I see the devil and this evil world will be upon me, laying on more load, to make my bargain as dear as they can. But be there in it what there will, let it cost me ever so dear, I am at a point ; I will venture all upon it, the Lord is my God, and him will I follow in all things that he shall speak ; I put myself into the everlasting arms ; I trust upon everlasting strength, I will go forth in the name of the Lord, and now speak, Lord, for I will hear.

This sincere resolution, this will hold out ; when our holy inclinations are so rooted and strong, that they bear down all fleshly inclinations ; when our assent to scripture is so firm, that it overbalances all objections against it ; when our reasons for religion are so high and weighty, that they weigh down the highest pretences against it; when we have thoroughly considered what there is in it, and compared all that can be said for or against our following the Lord, and upon the whole matter we judge it our best course, and accordingly resolve for it—this is sincere resolution, this is the obedience of the heart.

II. Obedience of the life. This is the decree bringing forth, or holy inclination and resolution springing up into action, and is a necessary proof of the soundness of the resolution.

Though sincere resolution be obedience in God's account; yet that resolution which (supposing there be time and opportunity) does not break forth into act, is undoubtedly unsound and deceitful. There are two things infallibly included in spiritual life ; a will, and a power. Grace is the disposing, and the enabling the heart for a holy life ; and where there is

both a will and a power, performance will certainly
follow. This sincerity of actual obedience, is that
which the prayer of the psalmist looks to, " Let my
heart be sound in thy statutes, that I be not ashamed."
Psa. cxix. 80.

There is a soundness in the faith, and a soundness
in the statutes of the Lord. Faith denotes in scripture, either the doctrine of faith, or the grace of faith.
And accordingly, soundness in the faith, signifies
both the receiving and entertaining sound doctrine ;
and the sound or sincere embracing that doctrine.
Soundness in the statutes of the Lord notes especially the practice, the living or walking uprightly
under the power of that doctrine, under the government and obedience of the statutes of the Lord.
What this obedience of life is, it is easy to gather
out of what hath been spoken touching the obedience
of the heart ; I shall only add, that this obedience is
then sound and sincere, when,

1. In general, the whole course of life is the issue
of the mentioned sincere resolution ; when the life
is the birth of the purpose, the fruit growing up out
of that holy root. There may be actions materially
good and holy, that yet are not gracious actions,
because they arise not from a right spring. When
the soul hath devoted itself to God in Christ, and
believingly, understandingly, and deliberately decreed,
and determined in his strength to keep his word ;
and this decree or determination, goes into the performances of the life, and is the root and soul of that
holy course we walk in ; there is sincerity.

Some persons may be found, who have taken up
the profession, and go far in the practice of godliness, abstaining from gross sins, yea, and making
attempts upon the mortification of inward lusts ;

applying themselves to the duties of religion, praying, hearing, reading, meditating, discoursing of God, and the things of God, exercising themselves in the works of righteousness and mercy, being meek, temperate, patient ; and if all this do arise only from the advantages of a good nature, good education, good society or acquaintance, a powerful ministry, or the workings of natural conscience, as possibly it may, and doth not spring forth from such a fixed well-founded resolution, it is short of sincerity. Whatever the blades be, they have no root, and will certainly wither away.

2. In particular actions, when they are done in simplicity and singleness of heart unto the Lord ; when whatever sinful mixtures there may sometimes be of carnal respects, that may have an influence upon the exerting and bringing them forth ; yet the great poise that moves the wheels, the swaying motive that brings us on, is God, and our respect to his will and honour.

Now for this also the Lord undertakes, promising not only assistance, but success ; sufficient grace, and efficacious grace : " I will cause them to walk in my statutes, and they SHALL keep my judgments, and do them." I will not only teach them my statutes ; I will not only incline their hearts to my testimonies ; I will not only strengthen them for my work ; but I will cause them to walk in my statutes. The event shall be sure, they shall keep my judgments, and do them ; my word shall fail, my promises shall be of none effect ; let me be accounted unfaithful, if I do not make them faithful to me.

Chap. XVI — *Perseverance in the Covenant*

" I will make an everlasting covenant with them, that I will not turn away from them, to do them good; but I will put my fear in their hearts, that they shall not depart from me," Jer. xxxii. 40.

The perseverance of the saints is founded on the election of God, and the immutability of his counsel; The foundation of the Lord standeth sure. " Whom he did predestinate, them he also called; and whom he called, them he also justified; and whom he justified, them he also glorified," Rom. viii. 30. This golden chain will hold, not a link of it shall be broken; on whomsoever the first link, election, hath taken hold, it will infallibly bring him up to the last, glory. God is not a man, that he should repent. But not to wade further into the deep; our business lies in the promise of God.

There are two sorts of promises concerning perseverance. There are promises to perseverance, and of perseverance. 1. The promise of eternal life is made to perseverance. Hold out to the end, and be saved. Overcome and reign. "Be faithful to the death, and I will give thee a crown of life," Rev. ii. 10. " If thou forsake him, he will cast thee off for ever," 1 Chron. xxviii. 9. " If any man draw back, my soul shall have no pleasure in him," Heb. x. 38. Christians, beware of apostacy, beware of presumption; pass the time of your sojourning here in fear. Let it not be said of you, Ye did run well. He runs well, that gives not off, that sits not down on this side the goal. " So run that ye may obtain." 2. There are promises of perseverance. The covenant of God is an everlasting covenant. He hath commanded his covenant for ever, Psa. cxi. 9.

There are two things in the fore-mentioned scripture, Jer. xxxii. 40. secured to believers, which secure their perseverance.

I. God will not depart from them.

II. They shall not depart from him.

I. God will not depart from them.   " I will not turn away from them." God is with me, but I fear I shall provoke him away : I shall weary him out by my sins, and drive him from me. No, saith the Lord, I will not turn away from them, to do them good. I will never fail thee, nor forsake thee.

II. They shall not depart from him.   It is true, the Lord will be with me, but it is only while I am with him; if I depart, he will depart; if I forsake him, he will cast me off for ever.   Here is my great fear, that I shall turn away from him ; there is in me an evil heart of unbelief, that is ever departing from the living God.   Oh this false and fickle heart, I dare not trust it for an hour ! I doubt it will be gone ere I am aware; my corruptions are strong, my temptations are many, every day brings its temptations; and I am in great fear, that by one means or other, one day or other, I shall fall before them, and depart from the living God ! No, says God, fear not, thou shalt not depart; " I will put my fear in their hearts, that they shall not depart from me. They shall be kept by my Almighty power, through faith unto salvation." My grace shall be with them, and my grace shall be sufficient for them, and shall preserve them to my heavenly kingdom.

And here is the saints' security : the Lord God will not turn away from them, nor ever suffer them to run away from him. If the promise fail, then may their faith also fail. It is true there may be gradual declinings and departures of the saints from

Christ for a season, but total or final there shall not be. They shall not be of them that draw back unto perdition, but of them that believe to the saving of the soul. Though they fall, they shall rise again; they may turn, but they shall return. As hypocrites will not stay with Christ always, so neither will saints always stay from him. And there is a like reason of both: sinners sometimes will step aside and salute religion, and take some turns with Christ, but, after a while, away they must again: and there is a double reason of it.

1. There is that within them that will fetch them back.

2. There is one without them that will fetch them back.

1. There is that within them that will fetch them back. Corrupt nature, the power of unmortified lust, this is it that bears the sway in their hearts; and however, for the time, the stream may be somewhat turned out of its course, or bayed up; however by the impetus of some external motives or arguments, or the impulses of an awakened conscience, or some sudden heat of affection, they are carried on after, and in some fair compliance with the Lord Jesus; yet when the bay is removed, when the external force is spent, conscience laid to sleep, the heat of affection allayed, which is often almost as soon out as in, their very natures will reduce, and bring them back to their old course. What is it that pulls a stone, or a lump of clay down again, that is thrown into the air? Why, when the power by which they were forced up is spent, their natures, their innate gravities, will bring them down to their place. Sinners need no other weights to pull them down to this earth than their earthly hearts.

2. There is one without them that will fetch them off. Satan, the god of this world, whose they are, and whom they serve, who, though he indulge them with so much liberty for their religion, as is consistent with their captive state, and may possibly secure them the more under his dominion, (hypocrites are often the faster to Satan for being so near to Christ,) the very religion they have is but the devil's snare, by which he holds them back from religion; yet, lest by venturing them too far, they should be lost to him at last, he that first tempted them so near to Christ, (hypocrites are often beholden to the devil for the religion they have,) will quickly tempt them back again.

And so on the other side, there are the like reasons why saints cannot always wander, or stay away from Christ.

(1.) There is that within them which will bring them back. The grace of God within them will bring them home. The grace of God is now their nature. Sinners whilst walking with Christ, and saints whilst wandering from Christ, are both under a force, they are carried against the stream; when the winds are down that carried them on, they will return to their course. The grace of God is the seed of God, " He that is born of God sinneth not ;" that is, not unto death; " the seed of God remaineth in him." The seed of God is immortal seed; it may languish, and be ready to die, but it shall not die, it shall recover.

(2.) There is one above them who will bring them back, though he suffer them for a time to wander from the way. " Of those whom thou hast given me I have lost none." He hath lost none, and he will lose none. He sends a word of commandment after them. "Return O backsliding children, for I am married to you," Jer. iii. 14. Whither are you running? Whom are you following after? Come back from your lovers, return to your husband. I am married to you, and we may not part.

After the word of command, he sends a word of promise; "I will heal your backslidings," Jer. iii. 22. Return from your backslidings, and I will heal them. I will forgive your backslidings, and I will cure you of your backsliding heart. All the breaches they have made shall be made up; I will pass by all that you have done, and be reconciled to you. If you will turn, return and I will receive you. And this word of promise is a word of power. I will bring you to Zion: "then shall she say, I will go and return to my first husband," Hos. ii. 7. " Behold we come unto thee, for thou art the Lord our God," Jer. iii. 22. He that will not leave his Israel after the flesh, with their idols, much less will he leave his Israel after the Spirit. " Being confident of this very thing, that he which hath begun a good work, will perform it until the day of Jesus Christ," Phil. i. 6.

A good work may be said to be begun in a double sense.

[1.] When there is some good thing doing: or when something is done towards it. When the Lord hath been ploughing upon the fallow ground, making his batteries against the strong hold, shaking secure hearts, breaking false hopes, awakening consciences, convincing sinners, spreading sin, and death, and hell before them, entering upon a treaty with them, and persuading them over to Christ, to make an escape: there may be hopes in this; the pains of travail give hopes of a birth. But this may

go back, and after the highest hopes prove an abor
tion.   Sinners, awakened sinners, beware you make
not a stand at the threshold; beware that your
ploughed ground be not left to lie fallow.   Beware
that the womb prove not the grave of all your hopes.
Mistake not conviction for conversion; make on,
let not your God, nor your souls, lose the things
which have been wrought.

[2.] When there is some good thing done.
When the rubbish is removed, and the first stone is
laid; when the plough hath been going, and the
good seed is sown; when the new creature hath
passed the birth; when Christ is formed, and the
light of life is newly sprung up in the soul. If there
be but a grain of mustard-seed, the least and lowest
degree of saving grace broken forth in the heart, the
question is not whether it be much or little; if it be
grace, there is the immortal seed, there is the good
work begun, which shall be carried on till the day of
Jesus Christ.   Grace is a security for glory.   Yet
beware, christians, let not this security make you
secure; though there be a harvest in the seed, yet
the seed must be cherished, watched, and well looked
to, that it may grow up to the harvest. He that lets
it die for want of looking to, proves that it was dead
whilst alive.   Let not your falling short of glory
prove that your grace was not grace.

Christians, lay hold on the promise, and lift up
your heads, you are under fears; however it be with
you for the present, you are in doubt how it may
be; your way is long and dangerous, yet your hearts
are deceitful and unstable; you are going on at present, but doubt how you shall hold out: I may meet
with lions in the way, which may fright me back;
I may lose my way, and never recover; I may be

weary, and faint in the way, and lie down and give off. My Lord and my soul have been often upon the parting point ; I have been almost gone, and I tremble to think what may yet become of me. Yet remember who it is that hath said, " I will not turn from you to do you good ; I will put my fear in your hearts, and you shall not depart from me." Rise soul, take care for to-day, and take no thought for to-morrow. Mind the present duty, go on thy way, though weeping and trembling, and hard bestead : go on thy way, and then commit thy way and thyself to him, by whose mighty power thou shalt be kept through faith unto salvation. Faithful is he that hath called you, and will do it.

And now you have all. Let us hear the conclusion of the whole matter. God hath made a covenant with his people, hath given himself for their portion, his Son for their price, his Spirit for their guide in the way, his earth for their accommodation by the way, his angels for their guard, the powers of darkness and death for their spoils, everlasting glory for their crown. And because their way is difficult and their work is contrary to them, he hath given them all that grace which is necessary to bring them to glory. In general, a new heart, in all things suited to their way, and thoroughly furnished for every good work. In particular, knowledge to guide ; oneness to fix and intend ; tenderness to submit to, and yield ; love to constrain and bring on ; fear to fence and hold in ; obedience to perform and bring forth ; and perseverance to go through, and hold out to the end ; and there grace and glory meet. This is the covenant of grace ; this is the word which, by the gospel, is preached unto you.

It will be said—But if God hath undertaken all this for us, what is there then left us to do? Here is a doctrine according to sinners' hearts; if this be gospel, then soul take thine ease, take thy liberty, cast away care, make much of thy body, God will take care of the rest.

But is there nothing required of us? Let the scriptures speak. " Yet for all this will I be inquired of," or sought unto, " by the house of Israel," Ezek. xxxvi. 37. otherwise let them look for no such things. He that will not ask in faith, " let not that man think he shall receive any thing of the Lord," Jam. i. 7. And can he think to receive anything who neither believes nor prays? who neither prays in faith, nor prays at all? " It is God works in you both to will and to do," Phil. ii. 12, 13. What then? Therefore sit you still and do nothing? No such matter; therefore " work out your salvation with fear and trembling," saith the apostle. The promise of God was never intended to make the command of God of none effect. God, in promising grace, promises a power for duty; and as he doth not give, so we must not receive that power or grace of God, in vain. Whilst he gives what he requires, he still requires what he gives. That promise of God, " Ye shall be my people," though he undertake to make it good, yet it is also the matter of our stipulation. And in this promise, wherein the Lord assures us what we shall be, is included a precept, wherein we may understand what we ought to be.

In undertaking to give us a new heart, a tender and obedient, a persevering heart, the Lord doth promise, both to make us what we should be, and to help us in what we are bound to do, and give us at once a clear hint, both of our mercy and duty. This is the sense and sum of that promise, The Lord will work all that in us, and will help and cause us to perform all that which is required unto salvation; and so the promise on God's part, doth not make void, but establish the obligation on ours. Do we then make void the law through faith? Nay, we establish the law.

Though it be certain as to the event, that all which is necessary to salvation shall be accomplished in us—God hath undertaken that, yet it is altogether as certain, that God hath made our loving him, fearing him, obeying his whole will, and our sincerity and perseverance herein, so necessary that we cannot otherwise be saved.

Christians, mistake not, nor abuse the grace of the gospel. The Lord never meant your mercy should make void your obligation to duty. Redemption from sin was never intended as a toleration of sin. He gives not his Spirit in favour of the flesh. What he undertakes to work for you was never with a mind to maintain you in idleness. The grace of God that bringeth salvation teacheth us, " that, denying ungodliness and worldly lusts, we should live soberly, righteously, and godly in this present world," Tit. ii. 11, 12.

Though you are saved by grace; yet you are still, in a sense, debtors to the whole law. Perfect obedience to the whole law, even to the utmost iota, is still due from you; and if it be not in your hearts to pay all that you owe, that is, if there be any duty commanded in the whole book of God, that you dispense with, that you will not set your hearts to observe and obey, if there be any one sin that you must be excused in, and will not part with; if there

be any, the highest pitch of holy care, activity, industry, zeal for God and holiness, that you will not be
persuaded to press hard after;—this is an evidence
of such an unsound heart, as hath no part in the
gospel, or the salvation thereof. Perfection is still
due, though sincerity will be accepted. Sincerity
shall be accepted, but what is sincerity less than a
hearty willingness to be perfect, attested by a striving
and pressing on to that mark which is set before us.

O admire and bless the Lord, the Lord for grace!
but do not turn the grace of God into licentiousness.
Shall we continue in sin, because grace hath
abounded? Will ye thus requite the Lord? Will ye
thus deceive yourselves, O foolish people and un-
wise? Will you slight him, because he hath loved
you? kick at him, because he hath cared for you?
shake off his yoke, because he hath secured you the
crown? Will you serve his enemies, because he hath
saved you from them? Will you nourish your
diseases, because he hath said he will cure you?
Will you live and not eat? reap and not plough?
Will you not eat, because he hath given you meat?
Will you not run, because he hath given you legs?
nor work because he hath given you hands? nor
watch because he hath given you eyes? Or will you
tempt the Lord, and call it your trust in him? Awake
from such madness.

Christians, say not, If God will, I shall; whether
I take care or not, believe or not, repent or not, be
obedient or rebellious, whether I awake or sleep,
work or be idle; my unbelief, my disobedience, my
negligence shall not make the faith of God of none
effect. But rather, since God hath said, You shall,
let thine heart answer, I will walk in his statutes;
arise, O my soul, up and be doing; work out thy

salvation, because it is God that worketh in thee to will and to do. Shake off thy sloth, set to thy work, run out thy race, since God hath said, Thou shalt not run, nor labour in vain. And look to it, for however thy idleness, or greatest unfaithfulness, will not make void the covenant of God ; yet will it make manifest, that thou hast no part nor lot in it.

But, to all these glorious things that have been spoken, possibly some will reply ; O, if all this be so, then happy saints indeed ! " Happy are the people that are in such a case ; yea, blessed are the people whose God is the Lord." But will the Lord indeed do all these things for mortals ? Will he take notice of worms ? Shall such dry bones live ? Will he set such vile dust as the apple of his eye ? Is not this too good to be true ? too great to be believed ? Are we not all this while but in a dream, or a fool's paradise ? O that I were sure the one half were as it hath been told me ! Too great to be believed ! As if it must be questioned whether the sun be light because it dazzles our eyes. But what certainty would you have ? Is all this too great for the great and Almighty God to do, who hath said, " As the heavens are higher than the earth, so are my ways higher than your ways, and my thoughts than your thoughts," Isa. lv. 9. Can he not do it, who can do all things ? Will he not do it, when he hath said he will ? Will the Lord mock ? Can God deceive ? Shall his word, yea, and his oath too, those two immutable things, in which it is impossible for God to lie, can these fail ? If you should hear the Lord himself speaking to you from heaven with audible voice, My covenant I make with thee, and it is my intent and purpose to perform every word that is written in it, according to the plain import and meaning thereof; there shall not a tittle fail, neither will I alter the thing that is gone forth of my lips. Heaven and earth shall fail, but my word shall not fail; trust to it, trust everlasting truth, trust to everlasting strength. Fear not, for there shall not fail one word of all that I have spoken by all my servants the prophets.

If you should hear the Lord speaking thus to you from heaven, what would you say? Would not this satisfy you? Why search the scriptures, that "more sure word of prophecy," 2 Pet. i. 19. Read them diligently, understand what thou readest, and then say, if thou dost not there find the Lord speaking fully to thee the following words.

CHAPTER XVII —*God speaking from Mount Gerizim; or the gospel in a Map: being a short view of the exceeding great and precious promises by another hand. By J. A.**

THE VOICE OF THE HERALD

O ALL ye inhabitants of the world, and dwellers on the earth; come see and hear; gather yourselves together unto the proclamation of the great King. Hear, you that are far off, and you that are near. He that hath an ear to hear, let him hear. I am the voice of one crying in the wilderness, Prepare ye the way of the Lord. Let every valley be exalted and every mountain made low, for the glory of the Lord is to be revealed. Go through, go through the gates, prepare the way. Cast up, cast up the high-way; gather out the stones, lift up the standard for the people; for the Lord proclaimeth sal-

---

* Joseph Alleine, the brother of Richard. Chap. 17 and 18, written by him, are sold separately, price sixpence.

vation to the ends of the earth.   Tidings, tidings, O ye captives! Hear all ye that look for salvation in Israel; behold I bring you glad tidings of great joy. which shall be unto all people.   Blessed news! prepare your ears and hearts.   The Lord hath commanded me, saying; Go unto the people and sanctify them, let them wash and be ready, for the Lord is coming down upon mount Sion, in the sight of all the nations.   Not in earthquakes and fire, not in clouds and darkness, not in thunderings and burnings, rending the mountains and breaking the rocks in pieces.   He speaks not to you out of the blackness, and darkness, and tempest; you shall say no more, Let not God speak to us, lest we die; he cometh peaceably, the law of kindness is in his mouth, he preacheth Peace, peace, to him that is far off, and to him that is near.

Behold how he cometh, leaping upon the mountains, he hath passed mount Ebal, no more wrath or cursing; he is come to mount Gerizim, where he standeth to bless the people : as Mordecai to his nation, he writeth the words of truth and peace, seeking the welfare of his people, and speaking peace to all his seed.

Behold how he cometh, clothed with flames of love, with bowels of compassion, plenteous redemption, and multiplied pardons.   Oh how full is his love! Oh the tenderness of his compassions! Oh how full is his heart, even aching till it is eased by supplying his hungry children!

Hearken therefore, O ye children, hearken to me.   To you it is commanded, O people, nations, and languages, that at what time you hear the joyful sound, the trump of jubilee, the tidings of peace in the voice of the everlasting gospel, that you fall

down before the throne, and worship Him that liveth
for ever and ever.

Arise, and come away; prepare, prepare you.
hear not with an uncircumcised ear; you are not
upon a common thing.   Behold the throne is set,
the throne of grace, where majesty and mercy dwell
together; from thence will the Lord meet you, from
thence will he commune with you, from the mercy
seat, from between the cherubims, upon the ark of
the testimony.   Lo, the Lord cometh out of his
pavilion, the mighty God from Sion, Selah.   His
glory covereth the heavens, the earth is full of his
praise.   A fire of love goeth before him, mercy and
truth are round about him, righteousness and peace
are the habitation of his throne; he rideth on his
horses and chariots of salvation, the covenant of
life and peace is in his mouth.

Rejoice ye heavens, make a joyful noise to the
Lord all the earth.   Let the sea roar, the floods
clap their hands, and the multitudes of the isles
rejoice.   Stand forth the host of heaven, prepare
your harps, cast down your crowns, be ready with
your trumps, bring forth your golden vials full of
odours, for our voices will jar, our strings will
break, we cannot reach the note of our Maker's
praise.

Yet let them that dwell in the dust arise and sing.
Bear your part in this glorious service, but consider
and attend.   Call out your souls, and all that is
within you.   Lift up your voices, fix your eyes,
enlarge your hearts, exert all their powers; there
is work for them all.   Be intent and serious, you
cannot strain too high.

Come forth ye graces, beset the way, be all in
readiness.   Stand forth faith and hope: flame O

love, come ye warm desires, and break with longing.
Let fear with all veneration do its obeisance.   Joy
prepare thy songs, call up all the daughters of music
to salute the Lord as he passeth by.   Let the generations of the saints appear, and spread the way
with boughs and garments of salvation, and songs
of deliverance.   Ye stand this day all of you before
the Lord your God, your captains, your elders, your
officers, with all the men of Israel, your little ones,
your wives, and the stranger that is within thy camp,
from the hewer of wood to the drawer of water.
That thou shouldest enter into covenant with the
Lord thy God, and into his oath which the Lord thy
God maketh with thee this day : that he may establish thee to-day for a people unto himself, and that
he may be unto thee a God, as he hath said unto
thee, and as he hath sworn, Deut. xxix. 10—13.

I have done my errand.   The messenger of the
morning disappeareth ; when the orient sun cometh
forth out of his chambers, I vanish.   I put my
mouth in the dust.   The voice of the Lord ! The
soft and still voice ! O my soul, wrap thy face in
thy mantle, and bow thyself to the ground, and put
thee in the cleft of the rock, while Jehovah proclaimeth his name, and maketh all his goodness to
pass before thee.

THE VOICE OF THE LORD

Hear, O ye ends of the earth, the mighty God, the
Lord hath spoken : Gather my saints unto me,
those that have made a covenant with me by sacrifice.[a]   Behold I establish my covenant between
me and you.[b]   By my holiness have I sworn, that
I will be your covenant friend.   I lift up my hand

[a] Psa. l. 1. 5.   [b] Gen. xvii. 7.

to heaven, I swear I live for ever; and because I
live you shall live also.[a] I will be yours :[b] yours
to all intents and purposes : your refuge and
your rest ;[c] your patron and your portion ;[d] your
heritage and your hope ; your God and your
guide.[e] While I have, you shall never want;
and what I am to myself I will be to you.[f] And
you shall be my people, a chosen generation, a
kingdom of priests, a holy nation, a peculiar treasure unto me above all people.[g] I call heaven and
earth to witness this day, that I take you for mine
for ever. My name shall be upon you, and you
shall be pillars in the temple of your God, and shall
go no more out.[h]

My livery shall you wear, and the stamp of my
own face shall you carry :[i] and I will make you my
witness and the epistles of Christ unto the world,[k]
and you shall be chosen vessels, to bear my name
before the sons of men. And that you may see that
I am in earnest with you, lo I make with you an
everlasting covenant, ordered in all things, and
sure ;[l] and do here solemnly deliver it to you as
my act and deed, sealed with sacred blood,[m] and
ratified with the oath of a God ;[n] a God that cannot
lie, that knows no place for repentance.[o] Come,
ye blessed, receive the instrument of your salvation :
take the writings, behold the seals ; here are the
conveyances of the kingdom. Fear not, the donation

---

[a] John xiv. 19.   [b] Jer. xxxii. 38—40.
[c] Jer. l. 6. Psa. xc. 1. Psa. xlvi. 1.
[d] Psa. lxxiii. 26. Isa. xxv. 4, 5.   [e] Psa. xlviii. 14.
[f] Psa. xxxiv. 9. 10.   [g] Exod. xix. 5, 6. 1 Pet. ii. 9.
[h] Rev. iii. 12.   [i] Ezek. xxxvi. 25, 26. with Eph. iv. 24.
[k] 2 Cor. iii. 3   [l] 2 Sam. xxiii. 5.
[m] 1 Cor. xi. 25.   [n] Heb. vi. 17.   [o] Tit. i. 2.

is free and full.   See, it is written in blood, founded on the all-sufficient merits of your Surety,[a] in whom I am well pleased,[b] whose death makes this testament unchangeable for ever ; so that your names can never be put out, nor your inheritance alienated, nor your legacies diminished; nothing may be altered, nothing added, nothing substracted, no not for ever.[c] Happy art thou, O Israel ! Who is like unto thee, O people ![d] Only believe, and know your own blessedness.   Attend, O my children, unto the blessings of your Father ; and hear and know the glorious immunities, and the royal prerogatives that I here confirm upon you.

The blessings of the covenant are, either its glorious liberties and immunities, or its royal privileges and prerogatives.

Here I seal you your pardons.   Though your sins be as many as the sands, and as mighty as the mountains, I will drown them in the deeps of my bottomless mercies.[e] I will be merciful to your unrighteousness ; I will multiply to pardon ;[f] where your sins have abounded, my grace shall superabound ; though they be as scarlet, they shall be as white as snow ; though red like crimson, they shall be as wool.[g] Behold I declare myself satisfied, and pronounce you absolved.[h] The price is paid, your debts are cleared, your bonds are cancelled,[i] Col. ii. 13, 14.

The immunities and liberties of the covenant consisting in, 1. Our general discharge from all our debts.

Whatever the law, or conscience, or the accuser hath to charge upon you, here I exonerate you, I discharge you.   I, even I, am he, that blotteth out your transgressions, for my name's sake.   Who

[a] Heb. ix.   [b] Matt. iii. 17
[d] Deut. xxxiii. 29.
[f] Heb. viii. 12. Isa. lv. 7.
[h] Job xxxiii. 24.

[c] Gal. iii. 15—17
[e] Mic. vii. 19.
[g] Isa. i. 18.
[i] Isa. xliii. 25.

shall lay any thing to your charge, when I acquit
you? Who shall impeach or implead you, when I
proclaim you guiltless?[a] Sons, daughters, be of
good cheer, your sins are forgiven you.[b] I will
sprinkle your consciences, and put the voice of peace
into their mouths,[c] and they shall be your re-
gisters, in which I will record your pardon, and the
voice of guilt, and wrath, and terror shall cease,
Heb. x. 22. Isa. xxvii. 4, 5.

Here I sign your release from the house of
bondage.[d] Come forth ye captives, come forth ye
prisoners of hope; for I have found a ransom:[e] I
proclaim liberty to the captives, and the
opening of the prison to them that are
bound.[f] Behold I have broken your
bonds, and shook the foundations of your prisons,
and opened the iron gates.[g] By the blood of the
covenant have I sent forth the prisoners out of the
pit wherein there is no water.[h] Arise, O redeemed of the Lord, put off the raiment of your
captivities, arise and come away.

2. Our re-ease from the house of bond-age particularly.

The dark and noisome prison of sin shall no longer
detain you.[i] I will loose your fetters,
and knock off your bolts. Sin shall
not have dominion over you.[k]

From the dark and noisome prison of sin.

I will heal your backslidings, I will subdue your
iniquities,[l] I will sanctify you wholly,[m] and will
put my fear in your hearts, that you shall not depart
from me.[n] Though your corruptions be strong

---

a Rom. viii. 33, 34. b 1 John ii. 12. Mark ix. 2.
c Ezek. xxxvi. 25. Heb. ix. 14. Isa. lvii. 19.
d Rom. vi. 17, 18. 1 Cor. vii. 22. e Job xxxiii. 24. 18.
f Isa. lxi. 1. xlii. 7. g Luke iv. 18. h Zech. ix. 11.
i John viii. 34—36. k Rom. vi. 14.
l Mic. vii. 19. Jer. iii. 12. m 1 Thess. v. 23, 24.
n Jer. xxxii. 40.

and many, yet the aids of my Spirit, and cleansing virtue of my word, and physic of my corrections shall so work together with your prayers and endeavours, as that they shall not finally prevail against you, but shall surely fall before you.[a]

From the strong and stinking gaol of the grave do I deliver you. O death, I will be thy plague; O grave, I will be thy destruction,[b] my beloved shall not ever see corruption.[c] I will change your rottenness into glory, and make your dust arise and praise me.[d] What is sown in weakness, I will raise in power; what is sown in corruption, I will raise in incorruption; what is sown a natural body, I will raise a spiritual body.[e] This very flesh of yours, this corruptible flesh, shall put on incorruption; and this mortal shall put on immortality.[f] Death shall be swallowed up in victory, and mortality of life.[g] Fear not, O my children. Come, and I will show you the enemy that you dreaded. See, here lies the king of terrors, like Sisera in the tent, fastened to the ground, with the nail struck through his temples. Behold the grateful present, the head of your enemy in a charger: I bequeath you your conquered adversary, and make over death as your legacy.[h] O death, where is thy sting? where now is thine armour wherein thou trustedst?[i] Come, my people, enter into your chambers:[k] Come to your beds of dust, and lay you down in peace, and let

[a] Ezek. xxxvi. 37. Eph. v. 26. Isa. xxvii. 9.
[b] Hos. xiii. 14.   [c] Psa. xvi. 10.
[d] Dan. xii. 2, 3. Isa. xxvi. 19.   [e] 1 Cor. xv .42—44.
[f] 1 Cor. xv. 53.   [g] 1 Cor. xv. 54   2 Cor. v. 4.
[h] 1 Cor. iii. 22.   [i] 1 Cor. xv. 55.
[k] Isa. xxvi. 20.

your flesh rest in hope ;[a] for even in this flesh shall
you see God.[b]   O ye slain of death, your carcasses,
now as loathsome as the carrion in the ditch, will I
redeem from the power of the grave,[c] and fashion
those vile bodies like unto the glorious body of your
exalted Redeemer.[d]   Look, if you can, on the sun
when shining in his strength; with such dazzling
glory will I clothe you, O ye of little faith.[e]

From the terrible dungeon of eternal darkness
From the dungeon do I hereby free you.   Fear not, you
of eternal darkness. shall not be hurt of the second death ;[f]
you are delivered from the wrath to come, and shall
never come into condemnation.[g]   The flames of
Tophet shall not be able to singe the hairs of your
heads, no, nor the smell of the fire pass upon you.
Stand upon the brink, and look down into the
horrible pit, the infernal prison, from whence I have
freed you.   See you how the smoke of their torments ascendeth for ever ?[h] Hear you the cursings
and ravings, the roarings and blasphemies ?[i] What
think you of those hellish fiends ? would you have
been willing to have had them for your companions
and tormentors ?[k] what think you of those chains
of darkness ? of the river of brimstone, of the instruments of torment for soul and body, of those
weepings, and wailings, and gnashing of teeth.
Can you think of an everlasting banishment, of a
" Go ye cursed ?" could you dwell with everlasting
burnings, could you abide with devouring fire ?[l]
This is the inheritance you were born to.[m]   But I

[a] Isa. lvii. 2.   [b] Psa. xvi. 9. Job xix. 25—27.
[c] Psa. xlix. 15.   [d] Phil. iii. 21.   [e] Matt. xiii. 43.
[f] Rev. xiv. 11. Rom. viii. 1.   [g] 1 Thess. i. 10. John v. 24.
[h] Rev. xiv. 11.   [i] Matt. xxv. 30.   [k] Matt. xxv. 41.
[l] Isa. xxxiii. 14.   [m] Eph. ii. 3.

have cut off the entail, and wrought for you a great salvation. I have not ordained you to wrath,[a] but my thoughts towards you are thoughts of peace.[b]

Here I deliver you your protection. 8. Our protection from all our enemies. From all your enemies will I save you.[c] I grant you a protection from the arrests of the law: your surety hath fully an- From the arrests of the law. swered it;[d] my justice is satisfied, my wrath is pacified, my honour is repaired.[e] Behold, I am near that justify you, who is he that shall condemn you?

From the usurped dominion of the From the powers of darkness. powers of darkness. I will tread Satan shortly under you, and will set your feet in triumph upon the necks of your enemies.[f] Let not your hearts be troubled; though you be to wrestle with principalities and powers, and the rulers of the darkness of this world:[g] for stronger is He that is in you, than he that is in the world.[h] He may bruise your heel, but you shall bruise his head.[i] Behold your Redeemer leading captivity captive, spoiling principalities and powers, and triumphing over them openly in his cross.[k] See how Satan falleth like lightning from heaven,[l] and the Samson of your salvation beareth away the gates of hell, posts and all, upon his shoulders and setteth them up as trophies of his victory: how he pulleth out the throat of the lion, and lifteth up the heart of the traitor upon the top of his spear, and washeth

[a] 1 Thess. v. 9.   [b] Jer. xxix. 11.   [c] 2 Kings xvii. 39.
[d] Gal. iii. 13. Rom. v. 10.   [e] Dan. ii. 24. 2 Cor. v. 19, 20
[f] Rom. xvi. 20.   [g] Eph. vi. 12.   [h] 1 John iv. 4.
[i] Gen. iii. 15.   [k] Col. ii. 15.   [l] Luke x. 18.

his hands, and dyeth his robes in the blood of those your enemies.[a]

From the victory of the world.[b] Neither its frowns *From the victory of the world.* nor its flatteries shall be too hard for your victorious faith. Though it raise up Egypt, and Amalek, and Moab, and all its whole militia against you: yet it shall never keep you out of Canaan. Be of good comfort, your Lord hath overcome the world.[c] Though its temptations be very powerful, yet this, upon my faithfulness, will I promise you, that no such shall come upon you, but what you shall be able to bear. But if I see such trials, which you fear would be too hard for your graces, and overthrow your souls, I will never suffer them to come upon you; nay, I will make your enemy to serve you,[d] and do bequeath the world as part of your dowry to you.[e]

From the curse of the cross.[f] Affliction shall *From the curse of the cross.* prove a wholesome cup to you; your Lord hath drunk the venom into his own body, and what remains for you is but a healthful potion, which I will promise you shall work for your good.[g] Be not afraid to drink, nor desire the cup should pass from you: I bless the cup before I give it unto you.[h] Drink you all of it, and be thankful; you shall find my blessing at the bottom of the cup, to sweeten the sharpest afflictions to you.[i] I will stand by you in all conditions, and be a fast friend to you in every change.[k] In the wilderness I will speak comfortably to you, and

---

[a] Isa. lxiii. 1—3.   [b] 1 John v. 4. Gal. i. 4.
[c] John xvi. 33.   [d] 1 Cor. x. 13.   [e] 1 Cor. iii. 22.
[f] Psa. cxix. 71.   [g] Rom. viii. 28.   [h] Job v. 17, &c.
[i] Jam. i. 12. Psa. xciv. 12.   [k] Isa. xliii. 2.

in the fire, and in the water I will be with you.[a]
I will be a strength to the poor, and a strength to
the needy in his distress ; a refuge from the storm,
and a shadow from the heat, when the blast of terrible ones is as a storm against the wall.[b] Your
sufferings shall not be a cup of wrath, but a grace
cup; not a curse, but a cure; not a cup of trembling, but a cup of blessing to you.[c] They shall not
hurt you, but heal you.[d] My blessing shall attend
you in every condition.[e] I say not only, Blessed
shall you be in your basket, and blessed in your
store ; but blessed shall you be in your poverty,[f]
and blessed shall you be in your straits : not only
blessed shall you be in your cities, and blessed shall
you be in your fields ; but blessed shall you be in
your bonds, and blessed shall you be in your banishment.[g] Blessed shall you be when you are persecuted, and when you are reviled, and your name
is cast out as evil : yea, then doubly blessed.[h]
My choicest blessings, greatest good, and richest
sweets, will I put into your evil things.[i] These
happy immunities, these glorious liberties of the
sons of God, by this immutable charter I do for
ever settle upon you ; and do in, and with my covenant, unalterably, irrevocably, everlastingly convey
unto you, and confirm upon you.

Yea, I will not only free you from your miseries ;
but will confer upon you royal pri-
vileges and prerogatives, and instate   The privileges and
                                        prerogatives of the
you into higher and greater happiness   covenant.

[a] Hos. ii. 14.   [b] Isa. xxv. 4.   [c] Heb. xii. 6—8.
[d] Psa. cxix. 67.   [e] Gen. xxvi. 3.   [f] Gen. xxviii. 15.
[g] Mark x. 29, 30. 1 Pet. iii. 14.   [h] Matt v. 10—12.
[i] 1 Pet. iv. 13, 14. Luke vi. 20—22.

than ever you have fal.en from.   Lo I give myself
to you, and all things with myself.

Behold, O ye sons of men !   Behold and wonder.
Be astonished, O heavens !   Be moved, ye strong
foundations of the earth !   For you shall be my wit-
He gives himself to us for our God. nesses.   This day do I by covenant
bestow myself upon my servants.[a]   I
will be your God, for ever and ever.[b]   Your own
God.[c]   Nothing in the world is so much your own
as I.   The houses that you have built, that you have
bought, are not so much yours, as I am.   Here
you are tenants at will ; but I am your eternal inheritance.[d]   These are loans for a season, but I am
your dwelling-place in all generations.[e]   You have
no where so great a propriety, so sure and unalter-
To be to us instead of all relations. Our Friend. able claim, as you have here.   What do
you count your own ?   Do you count
your bodies your own, your souls your
own ?   Nay these are not your own ; they are bought
with a price.[f]   But you may boldly make your
claim to me ; you may freely challenge an interest
in me.[g]   Come near, and fear not ; where should
you be free, if not with your own ?   where should you
be bold, if not at home ?   You are never in all the
world so much at home, as when you are with me.
You may freely make use of me, or of any of my
attributes, whenever you need.[h]   I will be all to you
that you can wish.   I will be a friend to you.[i]
My secrets shall be with you,[k] and you shall have all

---

[a] Gen. xvii. 7.   [b] Psa. xlviii. 14. Jer. xxxii. 38. Rev. xxi. 3.
[c] Psa. lxvii. 6. xvi. 2.   [d] Psa. xvi. 5. with lxxiii. 26.
[e] Psa. xc. 1.   [f] 1 Cor. vi. 19, 20.
[g] Jer. iii. 19.   Isa. lxiii. 16.
[h] Psa. l. 15.   Jer. xlix. 11.   Psa. cxlv. 18.
[i] Isa. xli. 8.   Jam. ii. 2, 3.   [k] Psa. xxv. 14.   John xv. 15.

freedom of access to me, and liberty to pour out all your hearts into my bosom.[a]

I will be a Physician to you. I will heal your backslidings, and cure all your diseases.[b] Fear not, never did soul miscarry that left itself in my hands, and would but follow my prescriptions. *Our Physician.*

I will be a Shepherd to you.[c] Be not afraid of evil tidings, for I am with you ; my rod and my staff shall comfort you. You *Our Shepherd.* shall not want, for I will feed you; you shall not wander, to be lost, for I will restore you. I will cause you to lie down in green pastures, and lead you beside the still waters.[d] I will gather you with my arm, and carry you in my bosom, and will lead on softly, as the flock and the children are able to endure [e] If officers be careless, I will do the work myself. I will judge between cattle and cattle. I will seek that which was lost, and bring again that which was driven away, and bind up that which was broken, and strengthen that which was sick ; but I will destroy the fat and the strong, and will feed them with judgment.[f] I will watch over my flock by night.[g] Behold, I have appointed my ministers as your watchmen, and overseers that watch for your souls.[h] Yea, mine angels shall be your watchers, and shall keep a constant guard upon my flock.[i] And if peradventure the servants should sleep,[k] mine own eyes shall keep a perpetual watch

---

[a] Eph. iii. 12. Heb. iv. 16.
[b] Hos. xiv. 4. Psa. ciii. 3. [c] Psal. xxiii. 1. lxxx. 1
[d] Psal. xxiii. [e] Isa. xl. 11. Gen. xxxiii. 13, 14.
[f] Ezek. xxxiv. 16, 17. with verses 2—4.
[g] Isa. xxvii. 3. [h] Heb. xiii. 17. Acts xx. 28.
[i] Dan. iii. 17. 23. Psa. xxxiv. 7. [k] Matt. xiii. 25. 27.

over you, by night and by day.[a]   The keeper of
Israel never slumbereth, nor sleepeth,[b] nor with-
draweth his eyes from the righteous.[c]   I will guide
you with mine eye; I will never trust you out of
mine own sight.[d]

I will be a Sovereign to you.   The Lord is your
judge, the Lord is your law-giver, the
Lord is your king.[e]   Fear not the
unrighteousness of men, I will judge your cause, I
will defend your rights.[f]   You shall not stand at
man's bar; you shall not be cast at their vote;[g] let
them curse, I will bless; let them condemn, I will
justify.[h]

Our Sovereign.

When you come upon trial for your lives, to have
your eternal state decided, you shall see your Friend,
your Father, upon the bench.[i]   Into my hands shall
your cause be cast, and you shall surely stand in
judgment, and be found at the right hand among
the sheep, and hear the King say, Come ye blessed,
inherit the kingdom.[k]

I will be a Husband to you.[l]   In loving-kindness,
and in mercies, will I betroth you
unto me for ever.[m]   I will espouse
your interest, and will be as one with you, and you
with me.[n]   You shall be for me, and not for another; and I also will be for you.[o]   Though I found
you as a helpless infant, exposed in its blood, all

Our Husband.

---

[a] Psa. xxxiv. 15. xxxiii. 18.   2 Chron. xvi. 9.
[b] Psa. cxxi. 3—5.   [c] Job xxxvi. 7.
[d] Psa. xxxii. 8.   [e] Isa. xxxiii. 22.
[f] Deut. xxxii. 36. Psa. cxl. 12. ix. 4.
[g] 1 Cor. iv. 3. 5. 2 Cor. x. 18.   [h] Isa. l. 9. Gen. xii. 3.
[i] Psa. lxxx. 9. Eccl. iii. 16, 17.   [k] Matt. xxv. 33, 34.
[l] Isa. liv. 5.   [m] Hos. ii. 19, 20.
[n] Matt. xxv. 40. 45. Acts ix. 4, 5. [o] Hos. iii. 3.

your unworthiness doth not discourage me.   Lo, I have looked upon you, and put my comeliness upon you.   Moreover, I swear unto you, and enter into covenant with you, and you shall be mine.[a]   Behold, I do, as it were, put myself out of my own power, and do here solemnly, in this my marriage covenant, make away myself to you,[b] and with myself all things.[c]   I will be an everlasting portion to you.[d] Lift up now your eyes eastward, and westward, and northward, and southward.   Have you not a worthy portion, a goodly heritage ?   Can you cast up your riches, or count your own happiness ?   Can you fathom immensity, or reach omnipotency, or comprehend eternity ?   All this is yours.   I will set open all my treasures to you, I will keep back nothing from you.

All the attributes in the Godhead, and all the persons in the Godhead, do I hereby make over to you.   I will be yours in all my essential perfections, and in all my personal relations.

He maketh over himself to us in all his essential perfections, and personal relations.

I. In all mine essential perfections.

Mine eternity shall be the date of your happiness.

In all his essential perfections. His eternity as the date of our happiness.

I am the eternal God, and while I am, I will be life and blessedness to you.[e]   I will be a never failing fountain of joy, and peace, and bliss unto you.[f]   I am the first, and last, that was, and is, and is to come, and my eternal power and Godhead shall be bound to you.[g]

I will be your God, your Father, your Friend, while

a Ezek. xvi. 4—10.   b Jer. xxiv. 7. xxx. 21, 22. xxxi. 33, 34
c Rev. xxi. 7.   d Ezek. xliv. 28.   Jer. li. 19.   Psa. cxix. 57.
e Psa. xc. 1, 2. with xlviii. 14.   1 Tim. i. 17. with 1 Pet. v. 10.
f Psa. xxxvi. 7—9 xvi. 11.   Isa. xxxv. 10.   g Jer. xxxii. 40.

I have any being.[a]   I have made my everlasting
choice in pitching upon you.[b]   Fear not, for the
eternal God is your refuge, and underneath are the
everlasting arms.[c]   My durable riches and righteousness shall be yours.[d]   Though all should forsake
you, yet will I not forsake you.[e]   When the world,
and all that is therein shall be burnt up, I will be a
standing portion for you.   When you are forgotten
among the dead, with everlasting loving-kindness
will I remember you.[f]

My unchangeableness shall be the rock of your
rest.[g]   When all the world is like the
tumbling ocean round about you, here
you may fix and settle.   I am your
resting place.[h]

*His unchangeable-
ness as the rock of
our rest.*

The immutability of my nature, and of my counsel, and of my covenant, are sure footing for your
faith, and a firm foundation for your strong and everlasting consolation.[i]   When you are afflicted,
tossed with tempests,[k] and not comforted; put in
to me : I am a haven of hope, I am a harbour of
rest for you; here cast your anchors, and you shall
never be moved.[l]

Mine Omnipotency shall be your guard.   I am
God Almighty, your almighty Pro-
tector, your almighty Benefactor. [m]

*His Omnipotency
for our guard.*

What though your enemies are many? more are

[a] Isa. ix. 6. Jer. x. 10.
[b] Psa. cxxxii. 13, 14. Hos. ii. 19.
[c] Deut. xxxiii. 27.   [d] Prov. viii. 18.
[e] Heb. xiii. 5. Psa. xxvii. 10.   [f] Isa. liv. 10.
[g] Psa. lxii. 6, 7. xcii. 15.
[h] Jer. l. 6.   2 Chron. xiv. 11.
[i] 2 Tim. ii. 19. Heb. vi. 17, 18.   [k] Isa. liv. 11.
[l] Jer. xvii. 13. 17. Psa. xlvi. 1, 2. 5. cxxv. 1.
[m] Gen. xv. 1. xvii. 1.

they that are with you, than they that are against
you ; for I am with you.[a] What though they are
mighty ? they are not almighty. Your Father is
greater than all, and none shall pluck you (pluck
while they will) out of my hands.[b] Who can hinder my power, or obstruct my salvation ? [c] Who
is like unto the God of Jeshurun, who rideth on the
heaven for your help, and in his excellency on the
sky ? I am the sword of your strength, and the
shield of your excellency.[d] I am your rock and
your fortress, your deliverer, your strength, the horn
of your salvation, and your high tower.[e] I will
maintain you against all the power of the enemy.
You shall never sink, if Omnipotency can support
you.[f] The gates of hell shall not prevail against
you.[g] Your enemies shall find hard work of it.
They shall overcome victory, or enervate Omnipotency, or corrupt fidelity, or change immutability,
or else they cannot finally prevail against you ; either
they shall bow or break.[h] Though they should
exalt themselves as the eagle, though they should
set their nest among the stars, even there will I
bring them down, saith the Lord.[i]

My faithfulness shall be your security,[k] my truth,
yea, my oath shall fail if ever you come off losers
by me.[l] I will make you to confess,   His faithfulness
when you see the issue and upshot of   for our security.
all my providences, that I was a God worthy to be
trusted, worthy to be believed, worthy to be rested

[a] 2 Chron. xxxii. 7. 8   2 Kings vi. 16.   [b] John x. 29.
[c] Isa. xliii. 13. Dan. iv. 35.   [d] Deut. xxxiii. 26. 29.
[e] Psa. xviii 2.   [f] 1 Pet i. 5.   [g] Matt. xvi. 18.
[h] Rev. iii. 9. Isa. lxvi. 24.
[i] Obad. 4. Jer. xlix. 16.   [k] Psa. lxxxix. 33—35.
[l] Isa. liv. 9, 10. with Mark x. 29, 30.

in, and relied upon.[a]   If you walk not in my
judgments, you must look for my threats and frowns,
yea, and blows too, and you shall see that I am not
in jest with you, nor will indulge you in your sins.[b]
Nevertheless my loving kindness will I never take
from you, nor suffer my faithfulness to fail.   My
covenant will I not break, nor alter the thing that is
gone out of my lips.

My mercies shall be your store.[c]   I am the Father
His mercies as our store.of mercies, and such a Father I will
be to you.[d]   I am the fountain of
mercies, and this fountain shall be ever open to you.[e]

My mercies are very many, and they shall be
multiplied towards you;[f] very great, and they shall
be magnified upon you;[g] very sure, and they shall
be for ever sure to you;[h] very tender, and they
shall be infinitely tender of you.[i]   Though the fig-
tree do not blossom, nor the vine bear, nor the flock
bring forth; fear not, for my compassions fail not.[k]
Surely goodness and mercy shall follow you all the
days of your lives.[l]   Even to your old age I am he,
and even to hoar hairs will I carry you: I have
made, and I will bear, even I will carry and deliver
you.[m]   I will make an everlasting covenant with
you, that I will not turn away from you to do you
good.[n]   I swear that I will show you the kindness

[a] Psa. xxxiv. 4—6. 8. lxxxiv. 12. cxlvi. 5.   Jer. xvii. 7, 8.
Psa. xxii. 4, 5.
   [b] Psa. lxxxix. 30—32, &c.   Amos iii. 2.   2 Sam. xii.—xv.
1 Pet. iv. 17.   [c] Isa. lxiii. 7.   Psa. cxix. 41.
   [d] 2 Cor. i. 3.   [e] Psa. xxxvi. 9. with Rev. xxi. 6.
   [f] Neh. ix. 17. with Isa. lv. 7.
   [g] 1 Chron. xxi. 13. with Gen. xix. 19.   [h] Isa. lv. 3.
   [i] Psa. cxix. 156. with ciii. 4.   [k] Hab. iii. 17. Lam. iii. 22.
   [l] Psa. xxiii. 6.   [m] Isa. xlvi. 4.   [n] Jer. xxxii. 40.

of God.[a] I can as soon forget to be God, as forget to be gracious.[b] While my name is Jehovah,
merciful, gracious, long-suffering, abundant in goodness and truth, I will never forget to show mercy to
you.[c] All my ways towards you, shall be mercy
and truth.[d] I have sworn that I would not be
wroth with you, nor rebuke you; for the mountains
shall depart, and the hills be removed; but my
kindness shall not depart from you, neither shall the
covenant of my peace be removed, saith the Lord
that hath mercy on you.

Mine Omnisciency shall be your overseer, mine
eyes shall be ever open, observing your wants to
relieve them, and your wrongs to avenge them.[e]
Mine ears shall be ever open to hear   His Omnisciency
the prayers of my poor, the cries of as our overseer.
mine oppressed, the clamours, calumnies, and
reproaches of your enemies.[f] Surely I have seen
your affliction, and know your sorrows. And shall
not God avenge his own elect? I will avenge them
speedily.[g] I see the secret plots, and designs of
your enemies against you,[h] and will disannul their
counsels.[i] I see your secret integrity, and the
uprightness of your hearts towards me, while the
carnal and censorious world condemn you as hypocrites.[k] Your secret prayers, fasts, and tears,
which the world knoweth not of, I observe them,
and record them.[l] Your secret care to please me,

---

[a] 1 Sam. xx. 14, 15. 17.   [b] Psa. lxxvii. 9.
[c] Psa. ciii. 17. with xxxiv. 6, 7.   [d] Psa. xxv. 10.
[-] 1 Pet. iii. 12.   Exod. iii. 7.
[f] Psa. xxxiv. 15.   Exod. ii. 24, 25.   Zeph. ii. 8—10.
[g] Luke xviii. 7, 8.   [h] Jer. xviii. 23.
[i] Isa. viii. 10. with xxix. 14, 15.   Psa. xxxiii. 10.
[k] Job i. 8—11.   2 Chron. xv. 17.
Matt. vi. 6. 18.   Acts x. 4.

your secret pains with your own hearts, your secret
self-searchings and self-denial ; I see them all, and
your Father which seeth in secret, shall reward them
openly.[a]

My wisdom shall be your counsellor. If any want
His wisdom as our   wisdom, let him ask of me, and it shall
counsellor.   be given him.[b] I will be your deliverer.
When you are in darkness, I will be a light to you.
I will make your way plain before you.[d] You are
but short-sighted, but I will be eyes to you.[e] I
will watch over you, to bring upon you all the good
I have promised,[f] and to keep off all the evil you
fear, or to turn it into good.[g] You shall have your
food in its season, and your medicine in its season :
mercies, afflictions, all suitable, and in their season.[h]

I will outwit your enemies, and make their oracles to speak but folly.[i] The old serpent shall not
deceive you. I will acquaint you with his devices.[k]
The deceitful hearts you fear shall not undo you; I
will discover their wiles.

I know how to deliver the godly out of temptation, and to reserve the unjust to the day of judgment to be punished.[l] Trust in me with all your
hearts, and lean not to your own understanding.[m]
I am God that performeth all things for you.[n] I
will forfeit the reputation of my wisdom, if I make
you not to acknowledge, when you see the end of
the Lord,[o] (though at present you wonder, and

[a] Matt. xxv. 34—36. 2 Chron. xxxiv. 27.   [b] Jam. i. 5.
[c] Mic. vii. 8.   [d] Isa. xliii. 19. lvii. 14.
[e] Isa. xlii. 6, 7. xlix. 6.   [f] Jer. xxxi. 28. with xxxii. 24.
[g] Psa. xci. 10. 14. Jer. xxiv. 5.
[h] Psa. xxiii. 2, 3. 1 Pet. i. 6. Isa. xxvii. 7—9.
[i] Isa. xix. 11—15.   [k] 2 Cor. ii. 11.   [l] 2 Pet. ii. 9.
[m] Prov. iii. 5.   [n] Psa. lvii. 2.   [o] Jam. v. 11

reach not the meaning of my proceedings,[a]) that all
my works are in weight, and in number, and in time,
and in order :[b] if I force you not to cry out, Manifold
are thy works, in wisdom hast thou made them all.[c]

My justice shall be your revenger and rewarder.[d]
Fear not to approach ; fury is not in
me.[e] My justice is not only appeased   His justice as our
towards you, but engaged for you. I   avenger and reward-
                                          or.
am so fully satisfied in the sacrifice of my beloved,
that justice itself, which was as a flaming sword drawn
against you, doth now greatly befriend you ; and
that which was an amazing, confounding terror, shall
now become your relief and consolation.[f] Under
all your oppressions, here shall your refuge be.[g]
Let me know your grievances, my justice shall right
your wrongs, and reward your services.[h] You may
conclude upon your pardons, conclude upon your
crowns, conclude upon reparation for all your inju-
ries, and all from the sweet consideration of my justice,[i] the thought of which, to others, is as the
horror of the shadow of death. If you sin, despair
not ; remember, I am just to forgive you. If you
are at any pains or cost for me, do not count it lost ;
for I am not unrighteous to forget you. I am the
righteous Judge, that have laid up for you, and will
set on you the crown of righteousness. Are you
reviled, persecuted, defamed? Forget not that I
am righteous to render tribulation to them that trouble you, and to you that are troubled, rest with me.

[a] Jer. xii. 1.   [b] Eccl. iii. 14.
[c] Psa. xxxiii. 4. civ. 24. cxlv. 10.
[d] 2 Thess. i. 6.   2 Tim. iv. 8.   [e] Isa. xxvii. 4.
[f] Eccl. iii. 16, 17. v. 8. Psa. xcvi. 10—14. xcvii. 1. with xcix. 1.
[g] Psa. vi. 9. ciii. 6.   [h] Psa. cxlvi. 7.   Heb. vi. 10.
[i] 1 John i. 9.   2 Tim. iv. 8.   1 Pet. ii. 23.

Though all your services and sufferings deserve not the least good at my hands; yet as I have freely passed my promise to reward them, so I will as justly keep it.

Mine Omnipresence shall be company for you.[a]

His Omnipresence as company for us.
Surely I will be with you, to bless you.[b] No bolts, nor bars, nor bonds, nor banishment, shall remove you from me, nor keep my presence, and the influences of Heaven from you.[c] I am always with you:[d] in your darkest nights, in your deepest dangers, I am at hand with you, a very present help in the time of trouble.[e] I am not a God afar off, or asleep, or in a journey, when you need my counsel, mine ear, or mine aid: I am always nigh unto them that fear me.

No Patmos, no prison shall hinder the presence of my grace from you.[f] My presence shall perfume the noisomest wards, and lighten the darkest dungeon where you can be thrust.[g]

My holiness shall be a fountain of grace to you.[h]

His holiness as a fountain of grace to us.
I am the God of hope,[i] the God of love,[k] the God of patience,[l] the author and finisher of faith,[m] the God of all grace,[n] and I will give grace to you.[o] My design is to make you partakers of my holiness.[p] I will be a constant spring of spiritual life to you.[q] The water that I shall give you, shall be in you as a well

---

[a] 1 Chron. xxii. 18.   Josh. i. 5. 9.   Isa. xli. 10.
[b] Gen. xxvi. 24.   [c] Gen. xxxix. 21. 23.
[d] Matt. xxviii. 20.   [e] Psa. xlvi. 1. xxxiv. 18.
[f] Rev. i. 9, 10.   Acts xvi. 25, 26.
[g] Acts xii. 7.   Isa. lviii. 10.   [h] John i. 16.   2 Pet. i. 4.
[i] Rom. xv. 13.   [k] 2 Cor. xiii. 11   [l] Rom. xv. 5.
[m] Heb. xii. 2.   [n] 1 Pet. v. 10.   [o] Psa. lxxxiv. 11.
[p] Heb. xii. 10.   [q] Gal. ii. 20. John xiv. viii. 12. x. 10.

of water, springing up into everlasting life.[a]   The seed of life that I shall put into you, shall be so fed, and cherished, and maintained by my power, that it shall be immortal.[b]   The unction that you shall receive from the Holy One, shall abide in you, and teach you all things necessary for you, and as it hath taught you, you shall abide in him.[c]   Keep but the pipes open, and ply the means which I have prescribed, and you shall flourish in the courts of your God.[d]   Yea, I will satisfy your souls in drought, and make fat your bones, and you shall be like a watered garden. Lo, I will be as the dew unto you, and you shall grow as the lily, and cast forth your roots as Lebanon ; and your branches shall spread, and your beauty shall be as the olive tree.[e]   You shall still bring forth fruit in old age, you shall be fat and flourishing.

My sovereignty shall be commanded by you.[f]   You shall be my favourites, men of power, to prevail with me.[g]   All my attributes shall be at the command of your prayers.[h]

His sovereignty to be (as it were) commanded by us.

In sum, my all-sufficiency shall be the lot of your inheritance.[i]   My fulness is your treasure.[k]   My house is your home.[l]   You may come as freely to my store, as to your own cupboard.[m]   You may have your hand as freely in my treasures, as in your own purses. You

His all-sufficiency to be the lot of our inheritance.

---

[a] John iv. 14.   [b] 1 John iii. 9.   1 Pet. i. 23.   Col. ii. 19
[c] John xiv. 16, 17.   1 John ii. 20. 27.
[d] Prov. viii. 34.   Psa. xcii. 13.   [e] Hos. xiv. 5, 6.
[f] Gen. xxxii. 26. 28.   Deut. ix. 14.
[g] Hos. xii. 4.   Jam. v. 17, 18.   [h] Isa. xlv. 11.
[i] Gen. xvii. 1.   Lam. iii. 24.   Psa. xvi. 5, 6.
[k] Num. xviii. 20.   Deut. x. 9   [l] Psa. xci. 1. 9.
[m] Eph. iii. 12.

cannot ask too much, you cannot look for too much from me.[a] I will give you, or be myself to you instead of all comforts.[b] You shall have children, or I will be better to you than ten children.[c] You shall have riches, or I will be more to you than all riches.[d]

You shall have friends, if best for you, or else I will be your comforter in your solitude,[e] your counsellor in your distress.[f] If you leave father, or mother, or houses, or lands for my sake, you shall have a hundred fold in me, even in this time.[g] When your enemies shall remove your comforts, it shall be but as the letting the cistern run, and opening the fountain, or putting out the candles, and letting in the sun. The swelling of the waters shall raise higher the ark of your comfort.[h] I will be the staff of bread to you, your life, and the strength of your days.[i] I will be the house and home to you, you shall dwell with me ; yea, dwell in me and I in you.[k] I will stand and fall with you.[l] I will repair your losses, and relieve your needs.[m] Can you burn out the lamp of heaven, or lave out the boundless ocean with your hands? why, the sun shall be dark, and the sea be dry, before the Father of lights, the Fountain of mercies shall be exhausted. Behold, though the world hath been spending upon the stock of my mercy, ever since I created man upon earth, yet it runs with full stream still. My sun doth diffuse its rays, and disburse its light, and

a Eph. iii. 20.   Matt. vii. 8.
b Gen. xv. 1.   Psa. lxxxiv. 11.   c Isa. lvi. 5.
d 2 Cor. vi. 10.   e Isa. li. 3. John xiv. 26.   2 Cor. i. 3, 4.
f Psa. lxxiii. 24.   g Mark x. 30.
h Rom. v. 3.   Heb. x. 34.   Acts v. 41.
i Deut. xxx. 20.   Isa. xxxiii. 16.
k Deut. xxxiii. 12.   John xiv. 23.   1 John iii. 24.
l Psa. xxxvii. 17. 24. liv. 4.   Isa. xli 10.
m Phil. iv. 19.   Mark viii. 35.   Matt. xix. 27—29.

yet shines as bright as ever: much more can I dispense of my goodness, and fill my creatures brim
full, and running over, and yet have never the less
in myself: and till this all-sufficiency be spent, you
shall never be undone.   I am the God of Abraham,
and of Isaac, and of Jacob, and whatever I was to
them, I will be to you.

Are you in want, you know whither to go.   I am
ever at home, you shall not go away empty from
my door.   Never distract yourselves with cares and
fears, but make known your requests by prayer and
supplication unto me.[a]   I will help when all do fail.[b]
When friends fail, and hearts fail; when your eye-
strings crack, and your heart-strings crack; when
your acquaintance leave you, and your souls leave
you, my bosom shall be open to you.[c]   I will lock
up your dust, I will receive your souls.

And mine infiniteness shall be the extent of your
inheritance.   Can you by searching find out God?
can you find out the Almighty to per-
fection? it is as high as heaven, what   His infiniteness to
can you do? deeper than hell, what can   be the extent of our
inheritance.
you know? [d] This height incomprehensible, this deep
unfathomable, shall be all yours, for ever yours.

I am your inheritance, which no line can measure,
no arithmetic can value, no surveyor can describe.[e]

Lift up now your eyes to the ancient mountains,
and to the utmost bounds of the everlasting hills, all
that you can see is yours: but your short sight cannot ken the moiety of what I give you: and when
you see and know most, you are no less than.

---

[a] Phil. iv. 6.   [b] Psa. lxxiii. 26. Isa. lxiii. 5. Psa. cii. 17.
[c] Psa. xlix. 15.   2 Cor. v. 1.   Luke xvi. 22.
[d] Job xi. 7, 8.
[e] Ezek. xliv. 28.   Eph. iii. 8.   1 Tim. vi. 16.   Psa. cxlv. 3.

infinitely short of the discovery of your own riches, Job xxvi. 14.

In all his personal relations.   Yea, further, I will be yours in all my personal relations.

I am the everlasting Father, and I will be a Father to you.[a] I take you for my sons and daugh-

God the Father to be a Father to us.   ters.[b] Behold I receive you not as servants, but as sons to abide in my house for ever.[c] Whatever love or care children may look for from their father, that may you expect from me ;[d] and so much more as I am wiser, and greater, and better than any earthly parents. If earthly fathers will give good things to their children, much more will I give to you.[e] If such cannot forget their children, much less will I forget you.[f] What would my children have ? Your Father's heart, and your Father's house ;[g] your Father's care, and your Father's ear; your father's bread,[h] and your father's rod ;[i] these shall be all yours.

You shall have my fatherly affection ; my heart I

He promiseth his fatherly affection.   share among you, my tenderest loves I bestow upon you.[k]

My fatherly compassion. As a father pitieth

His fatherly compassion.   his children, so will I pity you.[l] I will consider your frame, and not be extreme to mark what is done amiss by you, but cover all with the mantle of my excusing love.[m]

My fatherly instruction. I will cause you to hear the sweet voice behind you, saying, This is the way.[n]

a John xx. 17.   b 2 Cor. vi. 18.   c John viii. 35, 36.
d Matt. vi. 31,32.   e Luke xi. 13.   f Isa. xlix. 15.
g Job vii. 17.   John xiv. 2.
h 1 Pet. v. 7.   Matt. vii. 9.   i Heb. xii. 7.
k 1 John iii. 1. Jer. xxxi. 3. Isa. liv. 8.   l Psa. ciii. 13, 14.
m Psa. lxxviii. 39.   n Isa. xxx. 21.

I will tender your weakness, and inculcate mine
admonitions, line upon line, and feed His fatherly in-
you with milk when you cannot digest struction.
stronger meat.[a] I will instruct you, and guide you
with mine eye.[b]

My fatherly protection. In my fear is strong
confidence, and my children shall have His fatherly pro-
a place of refuge.[c] My name shall tection.
be your strong tower, to which you may at all times
fly, and be safe.[d] To your strong hold, ye prisoners
of hope.[e] I am an open refuge, a near and invio-
lable refuge for you.[f]

My fatherly provision. Be not afraid His f therly proof want, in your father's house there is vision.
bread enough.[g] I will care for your bodies. Cark
not for what you shall eat, drink, or put on. Let it
suffice you, that your heavenly Father knoweth that
you have need of all things.[h] I will provide
for your souls, meat for them, and mansions for
them, and portions for them.[i]

Behold, I have spread the table of my gospel for
you, with privileges and comforts that no man taketh
from you.[k] I have set before you the bread of life,
and the tree of life, and the water of life.[l] Eat, O
friends; drink abundantly, O beloved.

But all this is but a taste of what I have prepared.
You must have but smiles and hints now, and be
contented with glimpses and glances here; but you

[a] Isa. xxviii. 13.   1 Cor. iii. 2.   [b] Psa. xxxii. 8.
[c] Prov. xiv. 26.   [d] Prov. xviii. 10.   [e] Zec. ix. 12.
[f] Psa. xlviii. 3.   Deut. iv. 7.   John x. 29.
[g] Psa. xxxiv. 9.   Luke xv. 17.
[h] Matt. vi. 25—34.   Luke xii. 22—32.
[i] John vi. 30—59.   Lam. iii. 24.
[k] Isa. xxv. 6.   Matt. xxii. 4.   Prov. ix. 2.
[l] John vi. 48.   Rev. ii. 7. xxii. 17

shall be shortly taken up into your Father's bosom
and live for ever in the fullest views of his glory
1 Thess. iv. 17.

My fatherly probation. I will chasten you
_{His fatherly proba-} because I love you, that you may not
_{tion.} be condemned with the world.[a]

My Son I give unto you, in a marriage covenant
_{God the Son to be} for ever.[b] I make him over to you
_{a Husband to us.} as wisdom, for your illumination;
righteousness, for your justification; sanctification,
for the curing of your corruptions; redemption,
for your deliverance from your enemies.[c] I bestow
him upon you with all his fulness, all his merits,
and all his graces. He shall be yours in all his
offices. I have anointed him for a Prophet. Are
you ignorant, he shall teach you; he shall be eye-
salve to you;[d] I have sent him to preach the gospel
to the poor, and recovering of sight to the blind;
to set at liberty them that are bruised.[e] I have
established him by oath, as a Priest for ever.[f] If
any sin, he shall be your Advocate: he shall expiate
your guilt, and make the atonement.[g] Have you
any sacrifice, any service to offer, bring it unto him,
and you shall receive an answer of peace.[h]

Present your petitions by his hand, him will I
accept.[i] Having such a High Priest over the house
of God,[k] you may come and welcome; come with
boldness. Him have I set up as King upon my
holy hill of Sion. He shall rule you, he shall

---

[a] 1 Cor. xi. 32. Prov. iii. 11, 12.
[b] Isa. ix. 6. xlii. 6. 2 Cor. xi. 2.   [c] 1 Cor. i. 30.
[d] Isa. xlix. 6. xlii. 16. Rev. iii. 18.   [e] Luke iv. 18.
[f] Psa. cx. 4.   [g] 1 John ii. 1, 2. Zec. xiii. 1.
[h] 1 Pet. ii. 5. Heb. xiii. 15.   [i] John xvi. 23, 24.
[k] Heb. x. 19—22.

defend you.[a] He is the King of righteousness, King of peace ; and such a King shall he be to you.[b] I will set up his standard for you :[c] I will set up his throne in you.[d] He shall reign in righteousness, and rule in judgment ; and he shall be a hiding place from the wind, and a covert from the tempest, and the shadow of a great rock in a weary land.[e] He shall hear your causes, judge your enemies,[f] and reign till he hath put all under his feet ;[g] yea, and under your feet ; for they shall be as ashes under you, and you shall tread them, saith the Lord of hosts.[h] Yea, I will undo them that afflict you, and all they that despised you, shall bow themselves down at the soles of your feet.[i] And you shall go forth and behold the carcasses of the men that have trespassed against me, for their worm shall not die, neither shall their fire be quenched ; and they shall be an abhorring to all flesh, Isa. lxvi. 24.

My Spirit do I give unto you, for your Counsellor, and your Comforter.[k] He shall be a constant inmate with you, and shall dwell in you, and abide with you for ever.[l]

God the Spirit to be Counsellor and Comforter to us.

I consecrate you as temples to his holiness.[m] He shall be your guide, he shall lead you into all truth.[n] He shall be your advocate, to indite your

---

[a] Isa. ix. 6, 7.
[b] Heb. vii. 2. Jer. xxiii. 6. Eph. ii. 14.   [c] Isa. xlix. 22.
[d] Psa. cx. 2.   [e] Isa. xxxii. 1, 2.   [f] Isa. xi. 3—5.
[g] Psa. cx. 1. 1 Cor. xv. 25.   [h] Mal. iv. 3.
[i] Isa. lx. 14. Zeph. iii. 19.
[k] John xvi. 7. Rom. viii. 14.
[l] Ezek. xxxvi. 27. John xiv. 16, 17.
[m] 1 Cor. iii. 16, 17. vi. 19.
[n] Gal. v. 18. John xvi. 13.

prayers, and make intercession for you, and shall fill your mouths with the arguments that he knows will prevail with me.[a]   He shall be oil to your wheels, and strength to your ancles, wine to your hearts, and marrow to your bones, and wind to your sails.   He shall witness your adoption.[b]   He shall seal you up to the day of redemption, and be to you the earnest of your inheritance, until the redemption of the purchased possession.[c]

And as I give you myself, so much more all things with myself.[d]   Earth and heaven, life and death, things present and things to come.[e]

He giveth all things with himself both present and to come.

Things present are yours; lo, I give you Caleb's blessing, the upper springs, and the nether springs.   I will bless you with all spiritual blessings in heavenly places in Christ.[f]

Things present ours.

To you pertaineth the adoption, and the glory, and the covenants, and the service of God, and the promises.[g]   To you will I give the white stone, and the new name,[h] access into my presence,[i] the acceptation of your persons,[k] the audience of your prayers.[l]

The upper springs or blessings spiritual, as adoption, access, audience, peace, perseverance, &c.

Peace I leave with you, my peace I give unto you.[m]   I will undertake for your perseverance, and keep you to the end, and then will crown my own gift with eternal life.[n]   I have made you heirs of

---

[a] Rom. viii. 26, 27.   [b] Rom. viii. 16.
[c] Eph. iv. 30. i. 13, 14. 2 Cor. i. 22.   [d] Rom. viii. 32.
[e] 1 Cor. iii. 22.   [f] Eph. i. 3.   [g] Rom. ix. 4.
[h] Rev. ii. 17.   [i] Eph. iii. 12.   [k] Eph. i. 6.
[l] 1 John v. 14, 15.   [m] John xiv. 27.
     Jer. xxxii. 40. John x. 28, 29. 1 Pet. i. 5. Phil. i. 6.

God, and coheirs with your Lord Jesus Christ, and
you shall inherit all things.[a]

I have granted you my angels for your guar-
dians. The courtiers of heaven shall   The protection of
attend upon you ; they shall be all   his angels.
ministering spirits for your good.[b] Behold I have
given them charge over you, upon their fidelity to
look after you, and, as the tender nurses, to bear
you in their arms, and to keep you from coming to
any hurt.[c] These shall be as the careful shepherds,
to watch over my flock by night, and to encamp
round about my fold.[d]

My ministers I give for your   The inspection of
guides.[e] Paul, Apollos, Cephas, all   his ministers.
are yours.[f] I am always with them, and they shall
be always with you, to the end of the world.[g] You
shall have pastors after my own heart,[h] and this
shall be my covenant with you, that my Spirit which
is upon you, and my words which I have put into
your mouth, shall not depart out of your mouth,
nor the mouth of your seed, nor of your seed's seed,
saith the Lord, from henceforth and for ever.[i]

n short, all my officers shall be for the profiting
and perfecting of you.[k] All my ordinances shall
be for edifying and saving you.[l] The very
severities of my house, admonitions, censures, &c.
and the whole discipline of my family,   The rod of his
shall be for preventing your infec-   discipline.
tion, curing corruption, procuring your salvation.[m]

[a] Rom. viii. 17. Rev. xxi. 7   [b] Heb. i. 14.
[c] Psa. xci. 11, 12.   [d] Psa. xxxiv. 7.   [e] Eph. iv. 11.
[f] 1 Cor. iii. 22.   [g] Matt. xxviii. 20. Eph. iv. 13.
[h] Jer. iii. 15. xxiii. 4. [i] Isa. lix. 21.   [k] Eph. iv. 12.
[l] Acts x. 33. Rom. i. 16.
[m] 1 Cor. v. 5—7. Matt. xviii. 15.

My word have I ordained for converting your soul, enlightening your eyes, rejoicing your hearts, cautioning you of dangers, cleansing your defilements, and conforming you to my image.[a]   To you I commit the oracles of God.[b]   Here you shall be furnished against temptations,[c] hence you shall be comforted under distresses and afflictions.[d]   Here you shall find my whole counsel.[e]   This shall instruct you in your way, correct you in your wanderings, direct you into the truths to be believed, detect to you the errors to be rejected.[f]

The light of his word.

My sacraments I give you, as the pledges of my love. You shall freely claim them, they are children's bread. Lo! I have given them as seals, to certify all that I have here promised you;[g] and when these sacred signs are delivered unto you, then know, and remember, and consider in your hearts, that I therein plight you my troth, and set to my hand, and do thereby ratify and confirm every article of these indentures, and do actually deliver into your own hands this glorious charter, with all its immunities and privileges as your own for ever.[h]

The pledges of his sacraments.

And having sowed to you so largely in spiritual blessings, shall you not much more reap the temporal? Be you not of doubtful mind, all these things shall be added unto you.[i]   My creatures I grant for your servants and supplies.[k]   Heaven

The nether springs, or mercies temporal.

The supply of his creatures.

---

[a] Psa. xix. 7—9. 1 . Eph. v. 26. 2 Cor. iii. 18.
[b] Rom. iii. 2.   [c] Matt. iv. 4. 7. Eph. vi. 17.
[d] Psa. cxix. 92, 93.
[e] Acts xx. 27.
[f] 2 Tim. iii. 16. Psa. cxix. 105.
[g] Rom. iv. 11.
[h] 1 Cor. xi. 25. Gen. xvii. 10.
[i] Luke xii. 29. 31.
[k] Psa. viii. 3—9.

and earth shall minister to you.   All the stars in their courses shall serve you, and, if need be, shall fight for you.[a]   And I will make my covenant for you with the beasts of the field, and with the fowls of heaven ; and you shall be in league with the stones of the field, and all shall be at peace with you.[b]   I will undertake for all your necessities. Do I feed the fowls, and clothe the grass, and do you think I will neglect my children ?[c] I hear the young ravens when they cry, shall I not much more fulfil the desires of them that fear me ?[d] Fear not, you shall be sure to want no good thing ;[e] and you would not yourselves desire riches, pleasures, or preferment, to your hurt.   I will give meat to them that fear me : I will be ever mindful of my covenant.[f]

My providences shall co-operate to your good.[g] The cross winds shall blow you the   *The co operation of his providences.* sooner and swifter into your harbour. You shall be preferred, when you seem most debased ; and then be greatest gainers, when you seem to be deepest losers, and most effectually promote your good, when you seem most to deny it.[h]   Things to come are yours, the   *Things to come ours.* perfecting of your souls, the redemption of your bodies, the consummation of your bliss

When you have glorified me for a while on earth, and finished the work I have   *At death in glorification initiate.* given you to do, you shall be caught up

---

[a] Judg. v. 20.   [b] Job v. 23. Hos. ii. 18.
[c] Matt. vi. 25—34.   [d] Psa. cxlv. 19. with cxlvii. 9.
[e] Psa. xxxiv. 10.   [f] Psa. cxi. 5.   [g] Rom. viii. 28
[h] 2 Cor. iv. 17. Mark x. 29. Phil. i. 29.

into paradise, and rest from your labours, and your works shall follow you.[a] I will send *The convoy of angels.* of my own life-guard, to conduct home your departing souls,[b] and receive you among the spirits of just men made perfect.[c] And you shall look back upon Pharaoh, and all his host, and *Redemption from all afflictions and corruptions.* see your enemies dead upon the shore. Then shall be your redemption from all your afflictions, and all your corrup- *The thorn in the flesh taken out.* tions.[d] The thorn in the flesh shall be pulled out, and the hour of tempta- tion shall be over, and the tempter for ever out of work.

The sweat shall be wiped off from your brows, *The sweat wiped off from our brows.* and the day of cooling and refresh- ing shall come, and you shall sit down for ever under my shadow.[e] For the Lamb that is in the midst of the throne shall feed you, and lead you to the living fountains of water, Rev. vii. 17.

The tears shall be wiped away from your eyes, and there shall be no more sorrow nor crying, neither shall there be any more pain ; for the former things are passed away, and behold I make all *The tears wiped away from our eyes.* things new.[f] I will change Marah into Naomi, and the cup of sorrow, into the cup of salvation ; and the bread and water of affliction into the wine of eternal consolation.[g] You shall take down your harps from the willows, and I will turn your tears into pearls, and your penitential psalms into songs of deliverance.   You

---

[a] Rev. xiv. 13. Luke xxiii. 43.   [b] Luke xvi. 22.
[c] Heb. xii. 23.   [d] Luke xxi. 28. Eph. iv. 30.
[e] Acts iii. 19. Heb. iv. 9.   [f] Rev. xxi. 4, 5.
[g] John xvi. 20—22. Luke vi. 21.

shall change your Ichabods into hosannas, and your ejaculations of sorrow into hallelujahs of joy.[a]

The cross shall be taken off from your backs and you shall come out of your great tribulations, and wash your robes, and make them white in the blood of the Lamb, and you shall be before the throne of God, and serve him night and day in his temple, and he that sitteth on the throne shall dwell among you, and you shall hunger no more, and thirst no more, neither shall the sun light upon you, nor any heat.[b]

The cross taken off from our backs.

The load shall be taken off from your consciences. Sins and doubts shall no more defile you or distress you.[c]   I will make an end of sin, and knock off the fetters of your corruptions, and you shall be a glorious church, not having spot or wrinkle, or any such thing ; but holy and without blemish.

The load taken off from our consciences.

Thus shall you be brought to the king all glorious, in raiment of needle-work, and clothing of gold ; with gladness and rejoicing shall you be brought, and enter into the king's palace.[e]   So shall the beloved of the Lord dwell safely by him, and you shall stand continually before him, and behold the beauty of the Lord, and hear his wisdom.[f]   Then will I open in you an everlasting spring of joy, and you shall break forth into singing, and never cease more, nor rest day nor night, saying, Holy, holy, holy.[g]

The soul's admission into the chamber of presence and vision of God.

Thus shall the grand enemy expire with your

[a] Rev. xix. 1. 4. 6.   [b] Rev. vii. 14—16.
[c] Rev. xxii. 17. Heb. xii. 23.
[d] Eph. v. 27. Rev. vii. 9. 13, 14.
[e] Psa. xlv. 9. 13—15.   [f] 1 Cor. xiii. 12.
[g] Rev. iv. 8. Psa. xvi. 11.

breath, and the body of death be put off with your dying body; and the day of your death shall be the birth-day of your glories, Phil. i. 23. Luke xxiii. 43.

Have faith in God, Mark xi. 22. Wait but a little, and sorrow shall cease, and sin be no more.

And then a little longer, and death shall be no more;[a] but your last enemy shall be destroyed, and your victory completed. Yet a little while, and He that shall come, will come, and you also shall appear with him in glory.[b] This same Jesus which is taken from you into heaven, shall so come as he went up into heaven :[c] and when he cometh, he will receive you to himself, that where he is there you may be also.[d] Behold his sign; he cometh in the clouds of heaven with power and great glory; and every eye shall see him, and all the tribes of the earth shall mourn because of him,[e] but you shall lift up your heads, because the day of your redemption draweth nigh.[f] Then shall he sound his trump,[g] and make you to hear his voice in your dust,[h] and shall send his mighty angels to gather you from the four winds of heaven,[i] who shall carry you in the triumphant chariot of the clouds, to meet your Lord ;[k] and you shall be prepared for him, and presented to him, as a bride adorned for her husband.[l] And as you have borne the image

Marginal notes:
At the resurrection, in glorification consummate, redemption complete.

The return of the Redeemer.

The raising of the body.

---

a Rev. xx. 14. xxi. 4.
b Heb. x. 37. Col. iii. 4.
c Acts i. 11.
d John xiv. 3.
e Rev. i. 7. Matt. xxiv. 30.
f Luke xxi. 28.
g 1 Cor. xv. 52. 1 Thess. iv. 16.
h John v. 28.
i Matt. xxiv. 31.
k 1 Thess iv. 17.
l Rev. ii. 2.

of the earthly, so shall you bear the image of the heavenly; and you shall be fully conformed both in body and spirit to your glorious Head.[a] Then shall he confess you before his angels,[b] and you shall receive your open absolution before all flesh, and be owned, approved, and applauded in the public audience of the general assembly.[c] And you shall be, with all royal solemnities, espoused unto the king of glory, in the presence of all his shining courtiers,[d] to the envy, and gnashing, and terror of your adversaries.[e]

Full conformity, both in body and soul, to our glorified Saviour.

Public approbation and absolution.

Solemn espousals.

So shall your Lord, with his own hand, crown you,[f] and set you in thrones,[g] and you shall judge men and angels,[h] and you shall have power over the nations,[i] and you shall set your feet upon the necks of your enemies.[k]

The coronation and enthronement of the saints. Their sitting in judgment upon the world.

Lo, I have set the very day for your instalment,[l] I have provided your crowns,[m] I have prepared the kingdom.[n] Wherefore do you doubt, O ye of little faith? these are the true sayings of God.[o] Are you sure that you are now on earth? so surely shall you be shortly with me in heaven. Are you sure that you shall die? so surely shall you rise again in glory. Lo, I have said it, and who shall

---

[a] Phil. iii. 21. Heb. xii. 2, 3.   [b] Rev. iii. **5.**
[c] Matt. x. 32. xxv. 32. 34, 35, &c.
[d] Rev. xix. 7, 8. 2 Cor. iv. 14. Matt. **xxv.** 31.
[e] Luke xiii. 28.   [f] Rev. ii. 10.
[g] Rev. iii. 21. Matt. xix. 28.   [h] 1 Cor vi. **2, 3.**
   Rev. ii. 26, 27.   [k] Psa. xlix. 14
[l] Acts xvii. 31.   [m] 2 Tim. iv. 8.
[n] Matt. xxv. 34.   [o] Rev. xix. 9.

reverse it ? You shall see me face to face, and be
with me where I am, and behold my glory.[a]   For
I will be glorified in my saints, and admired in all
them that believe ;[b] and all flesh shall know that I
have loved you.[c]   For I will make you the instances
of my grace,[d] in whom the whole world shall see,
how unutterably the Almighty God can advance the
poor worm's-meat, and dust of the ground.   And
the despisers shall behold, and wonder, and perish :[e]
for they shall be witnesses to the riches of my magnificence, and exceeding greatness of my power.[f]
They shall go away into everlasting punishment, but
you into life eternal.[g]

For no sooner shall their doom be past, but the
Our triumphant as-
cension into heaven. bench shall rise,[h] and the Judge shall
return with all his glorious train ;
with sound of trumpet and shouts incredible shall he
ascend, and shall lead you to your Father's house.[i]
Then shall the triumphal arches lift up their heads,
and the everlasting gates stand open, and the heavens shall receive you all, and so shall you be ever
with the Lord.[k]

And now will I rejoice over you with singing,
and rest in my love ; and heaven shall ring with
joys and acclamations, because I have received you
safe and sound, Luke xv. 20. 23. 25. 27.

And in that day you shall know that I am a
rewarder of them that diligently seek me ;[l] and

[a] 1 Cor. xiii. 12. **John** xvii. 24.   [b] 2 Thess. i. 10.
[c] Rev. iii. 9.   [d] Eph. i. 5, 6. ii. 7.
[e] Acts xiii. 41.   [f] Luke xvi. 23.
[g] Matt. xxv. 46.   [h] Matt xxv. 41. 46.
[i] Psa. xlv. 14, 15. Matt. xxv. 23. John xiv. 2. with 2 Cor.
v. 1.
[k] John xii. 26. 1 Thess. iv. 17.   [l] Heb. xi. 6.

that I did record your words,[a] and bottle your tears, and tell your wanderings,[b] and keep an account, even to a cup of cold water, of whatever you said or did for my name.[c] *Blessed eternity.* You shall surely find that nothing is lost;[d] but you shall have full measure, pressed down, and running over, thousands of years in paradise, for the least good thought, and thousand thousands for the least good word; and then the reckoning shall begin again, till all arithmetic be non-plussed.   For you shall be swallowed up in a blessed eternity, and the doors of heaven shall be shut upon you, and there shall be no more going out.[e]

The glorious choir of my holy angels, the goodly fellowship of my blessed prophets, the happy society of triumphant apostles, *Glorious company.* the royal hosts of victorious martyrs, these shall be your companions for ever.[f] And you shall come in white robes, with palms in your hands, every one having the harps of God, and golden vials full of odours, and shall cast your crowns before me, and strike in with the multitude of the heavenly hosts, glorifying God, and saying, Hallelujah! the Lord God omnipotent reigneth.[g]   Blessing, honour, glory, and power be unto Him that sitteth upon the throne, and unto the Lamb for ever and ever.[h]

In short, I will make you equal to the angels[i] of God, and you shall be the everlasting trumpets of my praise.[k]   You shall be abundantly satisfied

[a] Mal. iii. 16.   [b] Psa. lvi. 8.   [c] Matt. x. 42
[d] 1 Cor. xv. 58.   [e] Dan. xii. 2, 3. Rev. iii. 12. Luke xvi. 26.
[f] Matt. viii. 11, 12.   Heb. xii. 22, 23.
[g] Rev. vii. 9—12.   xix 5, 6.   [h] Rev. v. 13.
[i] Luke xx. 36.   [k] Rev. vii. 10—12. 15.

with the fatness of my house, and I will make you drink of the rivers of my pleasures.[a] *Beatifical vision.* You shall be an eternal excellency,[b] and if God can die, and eternity run out, then and not else, shall your joys expire. For you shall see me as I am,[c] and know me as you are known;[d] and shall behold my face in righteousness, and be satisfied with my likeness.[e] And you shall be the vessels of my glory, whose blessed use shall be to receive the overflowings of my goodness, and to have mine infinite love and glory poured out into you brimful, and running over for evermore.[f]

And blessed is he that hath believed, for there shall be a performance of the things that have been told him.[g] The Lord hath spoken it, you shall see my face, and my name shall be written in your foreheads; and you shall no more need the sun, nor the moon, for the Lord God shall give you light, and you shall reign for ever and ever.[h]

And as I give myself to you for your God, and *He taketh us for his people.* all things with myself; so I take you for my covenant people,[i] and you shall be mine in the day when I make up my jewels, saith the Lord of hosts; and I will spare you as a man spareth his own son that serveth him.[k] The Lord shall count, when he writeth up the people, Surely they are my children.[l]

I do not only require you to be mine, if you would have me to be for you; but I do promise to

---

[a] Psa. xxxvi. 8.   [b] Isa. lx. 15.   [c] 1 John iii. 2.
[d] 1 Cor. xiii. 12.   [e] Psa. xvii. 15.
[f] Rom. ix. 23.   2 Tim. ii. 20. Rev. xxii. 1.
[g] Luke i. 45.   [h] Rev. xxii. 3—5.
[i] Heb. viii. 10. Isa. xliii. 1.   [k] Mal. iii. 17.
   Ps. lxxxvii. 6.

make you mine,[a] and to work in you the conditions which I require of you. I will circumcise your
hearts to love me.[b] I will take out the heart of
stone.[c] My laws will I write within you.[d]

Yet you must know that I will be sought unto
for these things,[e] and as ever you expect to partake of the mercies, I charge you to lie at the pool,
and wait for my Spirit, and be diligent in the use of
the means.[f]

I am content to abate the rigour of the old
terms;[g] I shall not stand upon satisfaction.[h] I
have received a ransom, and do only expect your
acceptance.[i] I shall not insist upon perfection.[k]
Walk before me, and be upright, and sincerity shall
carry the crown.[l] Yea, both the faith and obedience that I require of you are my own gifts.[m]

I require you to accept my Son by believing: but
I will give you a hand to take him,[n] and to submit to, and obey him: but I must and will guide
your hand to write after him, and cause you to
walk in my statutes.[o] I will take you by the
arms, and teach you to go:[p] I will order your
steps.[q] Yea, those things will I accept of you as
the conditions of life, which, viewed in the strictness of my justice, would deserve eternal death.[r]
Grace! Grace!

---

[a] Lev. xx. 26. Ezek. xxxvi. 28.   [b] Deut. xxx. 6.
[c] Ezek. xxxvi. 26.   [d] Jer. xxxi. 33.   [e] Ezek. xxxvi. 37.
[f] Prov. ii. 3—5. viii. 34. Luke xi. 13.   [g] Rom. iv. 6.
[h] Luke vii. 42.   [i] Rev. xxii. 17. 1 Tim. ii. 6.
[k] 1 John i. 8, 9.   [l] Prov. xi. 20. Gen. xvii. 1. Psa. xcvii. 11.
[m] Eph. ii. 8.   [n] Phil. i. 29. John vi. 65.
[o] Ezek. xxxvi. 27.   [p] Hos. xi. 3, 4.   [q] Psa. xxxvii. 23. 31.
[r] Eph. iii. 8. with 1 Thess. iii. 10. Heb. v. 5. 9. with Eccles.
vii. 20.

The Voice of the Redeemed

Amen, hallelujah. Be it to thy servants according
to thy word. But who are we, and what is our Father's
house, that thou hast brought us hitherto? And
now, O Lord God, what shall thy servants say unto
thee? for we are silenced with wonder, and must sit
down in astonishment, for we cannot utter the least
tittle of thy praises. What meaneth the height of
this strange love? And whence is this unto us,
that the Lord of heaven and earth should conde-
scend to enter into covenant with his dust, and take
into his bosom the viperous brood, that have so often
spit their venom in his face? We are not worthy
to be as the handmaids, to wash the feet of the ser·
vants of our Lord: how much less to be thy sons
and heirs, and to be made partakers of all these
blessed liberties and privileges which thou hast
settled upon us? But for thy goodness' sake, and
according to thine own heart, hast thou done all
these great things. Even so Father, because so it
seemed good in thy sight.

Wherefore thou art great, O God, for there is
none like thee, neither is there any God besides
thee. And what nation on earth is like thy people,
whom God went to redeem for a people to himself,
and to make him a name, and to do for them great
things and terrible? For thou hast confirmed them
to thyself, to be a people unto thee for ever, and
thou, Lord, art become their God, 2 Sam. vii. 18.
to the end.

Wonder, O heavens, and be moved, O earth, at
this great thing! Rev. xxi. 4. For behold, the
tabernacle of God is with men, and he will dwell

with them, and they shall be his people, and God himself shall be with them, and be their God. Be astonished and ravished with wonder, for the infinite breach is made up; the offender is received, and God and man reconciled, and a covenant of peace entered, and heaven and earth are all agreed upon the terms, and have struck their hands, and sealed the indentures. Oh happy conclusion! Oh blessed conjunction! Shall the stars dwell with the dust? or the wide distant poles be brought to mutual embraces?

But here the distance of the terms is infinitely greater. Rejoice, O angels! shout, O seraphims O, all ye friends of the Bridegroom, prepare an epithalamium,[a] be ready with the marriage-song. Lo, here is the wonder of wonders : for Jehovah hath betrothed himself for ever to his hopeless captives, and owns the marriage before all the world, and is become one with us, and we with him. He hath bequeathed to us the precious things of heaven above, and the precious things of the earth beneath, with the fulness thereof, and hath kept back nothing from us.

And now, O Lord, thou art that God, and thy words are true, and thou hast promised this goodness unto thy servants, and hath left us nothing to ask at thy hands but what thou hast already freely granted. Only the word which thou hast spoken concerning thy servants, establish it for ever, and do as thou hast said, and let thy name be magnified for ever, saying, The Lord of Hosts, he is the God of Israel. Amen. Hallelujah.

[a] Wedding song

Chapter XVIII —*A Soliloquy, representing the believer's triumph in God's covenant; and the various conflicts and glorious conquests of faith over unbelief.**

Yea, hath God said, I will be a God unto thee? Is it true indeed? Will the Lord be mine? Will he lay aside the controversy, and conclude a peace? Will he receive the rebel to mercy, and open his doors to his prodigal? I will surely go unto my Father, I will take unto me words, and bow myself before his footstool, and say, O Lord, I have heard thy words, and do here lay hold on thy covenant, Isa. lvi. 4. I accept the kindness of God, and will adventure myself upon thy fidelity, and trust my whole happiness here and hereafter upon these thy promises.

The soul taketh hold on God's covenant.

Farewell, deceitful world, get thee under my feet. Too long have I feared thy vain threats; too long have I been deluded with thy flattering promises. Canst thou promise me or deny me such things as God hath covenanted to give me? I know thou canst not, and therefore I renounce thee for ever from being the object of my faith or fear. Nor longer will I lean to this rotten reed, no longer will I trust to this broken idol. Avoid, Satan, with thy tempting baits. In vain dost thou dress the harlot in her paint and bravery; and tell me, All this will I give thee, Matt. iv. 8, 9. Canst thou show me such a crown, such a kingdom as God hath

* By Joseph Alleine.

promised to settle upon me? Or that which will balance the loss of an infinite God, who here gives himself unto me? Away deceitful lusts and pleasures, get you hence; I have enough in Christ and his promise to give my soul full content; these have I lodged in my heart, and there is no longer room for such guests as you. Never shall you have quiet entertainment more within these doors.

Thou God of truth, I here take thee at thy word; thou requirest but my acceptance and consent, and here thou hast it. Good is the word of the Lord which he hath spoken, and as my Lord hath said, so will thy servant do. My soul catcheth hold of thy promises. These have I taken as my heritage for ever. Let others carry the preferments and possessions of this world, it shall be enough to me to be an heir of thy promises.

O happy soul, how rich art thou! What a booty have I gotten! It is all mine own. *She maketh her boast in God.* I have the promises of this life, and of that which is to come, 1 Tim. iv. 8. Oh what can I wish more! How full a charter is here! Now my doubting soul may boldly and believingly say with Thomas, My Lord, and my God! What need we any further witness? We have heard his words. He hath sworn by his holiness that his decree may not be changed, and hath signed it with his own signet.

Rejoice ye heavens, strike up ye celestial choirs. Help heaven and earth. Sing unto the Lord, O ye saints of his. Bless the Lord, O my soul. Oh had I the tongues of men and angels, all were too little for my single turn. Had I as many tongues as hairs, the whole were not sufficient to utter my Creator's praises.

My beloved is mine, and I am his, Cant. ii. 16. The grant is clear, and my claim is firm. Who durst deny it, when God himself doth own it? Is it a hard adventure to speak after Christ himself? Why, this is the message that he hath sent me : I ascend to my Father, and your Father ; my God, and your God, John xx. 17. He hath put words into my mouth, and bid me say, Our Father.

I believe; Lord help my unbelief. O my God, and my Father, I accept thee with all humble thankfulness, and am bold to take hold of thee. O my King, and my God, I subject my soul, and all its powers to thee. O my glory, in thee will I boast all the day. O my rock, on thee will I build all my confidence and my hopes. O staff of my life, and strength of my heart; the life of my joys, and joy of my life; I will sit and sing under thy shadow, and glory in thy holy name, Cant. ii. 3.

O my soul, arise and take possession. Inherit thy blessedness, and cast up thy riches. Thine is the kingdom, thine is the glory, and thine is the victory. The whole Trinity is thine. All the persons in the Godhead, all the attributes in the Godhead are thine. And behold here is the evidence, and these are the writings by which all is made sure to thee for ever.

And now, *She quelleth discontents, and reasoneth down unbelief.* Return to thy rest, O my soul, for the Lord hath dealt bountifully with thee, Psa. cxvi. 7. Say if thy lines be not fallen to thee in a pleasant place, and if this be not a goodly heritage! Psa. xvi. 6. O blasphemous discontent! how absurd and unreasonable an evil art thou, whom all the fulness of the Godhead cannot satisfy, because thou art denied in a petty comfort, or crossed in thy vain

expectations from the world? O my unthankful
soul, shall not a Trinity content thee? Shall not
all-sufficiency suffice thee? Silence, you murmuring
thoughts, for ever. I have enough, I abound, and
am full. Infiniteness and eternity is mine, and
what more can I ask?

But methinks I feel some secret damps upon my
joy, and when I would soar aloft, and The assaults of
triumph in the riches of my portion, a unbelief. 1. It questions the truth of
secret diffidence plucks me back, as the promise.
the string doth the bird, and unbelief whispers in
mine ear, Surely this is too good to be true.

But who art thou that disputest against God?
The Lord hath spoken it, and shall not
I believe him? Will he be angry if I The triumph of
faith in the certainty
give my assent, and speak it confi- of God's truth.
dently upon the credit of his words?

O my Lord, suffer me to spread the writing before thee. Hast not thou said, Thy Maker is thy
husband? Isa. liv. 5. I will betroth thee unto me?
Hos. ii. 19. Thou shalt call me, My Father? Jer. iii. 19.
I pray thee, O Lord, was not this thy saying, I am
God, even thy God? Psa. l. 7. I will be a Father
unto you, and ye my sons and daughters? 2 Cor.
vi. 18. Why then should I doubt? Is not the
truth of the living God sure footing for my faith?

Silence then, O quarrelling unbelief. I know in
whom I have believed. Not in friends, though numerous and potent; for they are men, and not God,
Isa. xxxi. 3. Not in riches, for they make themselves wings, Prov. xxiii. 5. Not in princes, for their
breath is in their nostrils, Psa. cxlvi. 3, 4. But let
God be true, and every man a liar. In God have I
put my trust, in his word do I hope. Oh sure
word! Heaven and earth shall pass away, but not

one jot or tittle of this, I have not built upon the sand of mortality. Let the rain descend, and the floods come, and the winds blow, nevertheless the foundation of God standeth sure. His everlasting counsel and everlasting covenant are my stay. I am built upon his promises, and let hell and earth do their worst to blow up this foundation, Matt. vii. 25. 2 Tim. ii. 19.

Now shall my faith triumph, and my heart be glad, and my glory rejoice. I will shout with the exulting multitude. The Lord he is the God, 1 Kings xviii. 39. and he is not ashamed to be called my God, Heb. xi. 16. He is not ashamed of my rags or poverty, of my parentage or pedigree ; and since his infinite condescension will own me, will he take it ill if I own him? Though I have nothing of my own to glory in, 1 Cor. i. 29. 31. (unless I should glory in my shame) yet I will glory in the Lord, and bless myself in him.

For who is like unto the God of Jeshurun ? Deut. xxxiii. 26. Bring forth your gods, O ye nations. Lift up your eyes, and behold who hath created all these things. Can any do for their favourites as the Lord can ? Or if he be angry, who is the god that shall deliver out of his hands ? Will you set Dagon before the ark ? Or shall Mammon contend with the Holy One? O ambitious Haman, where is now thine idol honour ? O rich glutton, that madest a god of pleasure, where is now the god whom thou hast served ? O sensual worldling, that knewest not where nor how to bestow thy goods : Do riches profit thee ? Could Mammon save thee ? Deceived souls ! go now to the gods that you have chosen. Alas, they cannot for ever administer a drop of water to cool your tongues.

But the portion of Jacob is not like them, Jer. x. 16. From everlasting to everlasting he is God Psa. xc. 2. His power is my confidence, his goodness is my maintenance, his truth is my shield and my buckler.

But my clamorous unbelief hath many wiles, and afresh assaults me with the difficulty of the things promised, and labours to non-plus and confound me with their amazing greatness.

2. It confounds the soul with the amazing greatness and difficulty of the things.

But why should I stagger at the promise through unbelief, robbing at once my Master of his glory, and my soul of her comfort? It is my great sin to doubt and dispute, and yet shall I be afraid to believe? O my soul, it is the highest honour thou canst put upon thy Lord, to believe against difficulties, and to look for and reckon upon great things and wonderful, passing all created power and human faith.

The triumph of faith in God's omnipotency and veracity.

Let not the greatness, nor the strangeness of the benefits bequeathed unto thee, put thee to a stand. It is with a God thou hast to do, and therefore thou must not look for little things; that were to darken the glory of his munificence, and the infiniteness of his power and goodness. Knowest thou not, that it is his design to make his name glorious; and to make thee know he is able to do for thee above all thou canst ask or think? Surely they cannot be any small or ordinary things that shall be done for thee, when the Lord shall show in thee what a God can do, and shall carry thee in triumph before the world, and make proclamation before thee, Thus shall it be done to the man whom the Lord delighteth to honour. What wonder if thou canst not comprehend these things?—if they exceed all thy apprehensions and conceptions? This is a good argument for thy faith: for this is that which the Lord hath said, that it hath not entered into the heart of man to conceive what things he hath prepared for them that love him. Now if thou couldst conceive and comprehend them, how should his word be made good? It is enough for thee that the Lord hath spoken it. Is not the word nigh thee? Hath God said, I will receive you? You shall be kings and priests unto God, and inherit all things; and shall sit on thrones, and judge angels, and be ever with the Lord, and shall I dare to say him nay? Unreasonable unbelief! What! never satisfied! still contradicting and blaspheming! False whisperer! no more of thy tales. I believe God that it shall be as he hath told me, Acts xxvii. 25.

And now, thanks be to God, who always causes us to triumph in Christ, 2 Cor. ii. 14. therefore my lips shall praise thee, and my soul which thou hast redeemed, Psa. lxxi. 23. For thou hast made me glad through thy word, and I will triumph in the works of thy hands, Psa. xcii. 4. I will praise the Lord whilst I live. I will sing praises to my God whilst I have any being, Psa. civ. 33.

O my soul, if thou couldst wear out thy fingers upon the harp, and wear thy tongue to the roots, thou couldst yet never sufficiently praise thy Redeemer.

O mine enemies! where is now your confidence, and where is your armour wherein you trusted? I will set Christ alone against all your multitudes, and all the powers, and malice, and policy, wherewith they are armed. The field is already won, and the Captain of our salvation returned, with the spoils of his enemies, having made a show of them openly, triumphing over them in his cross, Col. ii. 15. And thanks be to God, who hath given us the victory, through our Lord Jesus Christ, 1 Cor. xv. 57.

Of whom then should I be afraid ? Behold he is near that justifieth me ; who shall plead with me ?

O ye powers of hell ! you are but chained captives, and we have a sure word, that the gates of hell shall not prevail against us, Matt. xvi. 18. Though the world be in arms against us, and the devil at the head of them as their champion ; yet who is this uncircumcised Philistine, that he should defy the armies of the living God ? 1 Sam. xvii. 45—47. Behold, I am come out to thee, as the stripling against Goliath ; not with sword, and with spear, but in the name of the Lord of hosts, in whose strength I am more than a conqueror.

O grave, where is now thy victory ? Christ is risen, and hath broken up thy prison, and rolled away the stone, so that all thy prisoners have made an escape. Rejoice not against me, O mine enemy ; though I fall, I shall rise again ; though I lie in darkness, the Lord shall be a light unto me, Mic. vii. 8. Enlarge not thy desires, O Tophet, but shut up thy flaming mouth ; for there is now no condemnation to them that are in Christ Jesus, Rom. viii. 1.

O deceitful world, thou art already overcome, John xvi. 33, and the conquered enemy is become my servant, 1 Cor. iii. 22. and I am fed with the honey taken out of the carcass of the slain lion. I fear not thy threats, nor the enchantments of thy syren songs, being kept by the power of God, through a victorious faith, unto salvation, 1 Pet. i. 5. 1 John v. 4.

O my sins; you are already buried, never to have any resurrection, and the remembrance of you shall be no more, Heb. viii. 12. I see my sins nailed to the cross, and their dominion is taken away, though their lives be prolonged yet for a little season. Awake therefore, O my glory; awake psaltery and harp, and meet the deliverer with triumph; for his right hand, and his holy arm, have gotten us the victory, Psa. xcviii. 1, 2. and all the ends of the earth have seen the salvation of our God.

Yet methinks my unworthiness flies in my face, and I hear my cavilling unbelief thus *3. It upbraids the trembling soul with its unworthiness.* upbraiding me, and crying out, O proud presumption! that thou who art conscious to thyself of thy great unworthiness, shouldst pretend a claim to God and glory! Shall daring dust think to share with the Almighty, and say of his endless perfections, They are my right? Bold sinner, stand off, and tremble at thy presumptuous arrogance.

O my God, I lay my hand upon my mouth. I *Faith subscribes the charge, and triumphs in God's free grace.* confess the charge of mine unworthiness. My guilt and shame is such as I cannot cover, but thou canst, and dost. Thou hast cast a mantle upon my nakedness, and hast promised my transgressions shall not be mentioned, and that thou wilt multiply pardons. And shall I take up what thou hast buried, and then affright myself with the ghosts that infidelity hath raised? Is it presumption to take the pardon that thou dost offer? or to receive and claim thee as mine, when it is but what thou hast promised. I durst not have approached thee, but upon thy call; nor have pretended a title, but upon thy grant. I should have thought it diabolical pride, to have pleaded an interest in thee, and claimed kindred to thee, but that thou hast showed me the way.

And thou, my soul, art thou ignorant of God's great design? Knowest thou not, that it is his purpose to glorify free grace? And how should grace appear to be grace indeed, were there any worthiness in the subject? Thine unworthiness is but a foil, to set off the beauty and riches of free grace and mercy.

But I cannot shake off this brier: alas, what a cavilling sophister is unbelief! and will never be answered. Now is it ready to tell me, What if the promise should be a sure foundation! yet thou mayest not build upon another man's ground. What though the grace and mercies of God are infinite! yet dogs may not catch at the children's bread. Thou hast not right nor title to the promise, therefore cease thy pretended claim. *4. It questions the believer's title to God's grace, and interest in the promise.*

But, O my soul, wherefore shouldst thou doubt? Whose image and superscription is this? Dost thou not bear upon thee the marks of the Lord Jesus? I have given up my name to him, and taken hold of his covenant, Isa. lvi. 4. and therefore may claim an interest. *The triumph of faith in the clearness of the believer's evidences.*

I have accepted the matter, and closed with the Mediator, and subscribed to the conditions of the covenant, and therefore cannot question but it is mine.

The Lord hath offered to be my God, and I have taken hold of his offer. I have taken him as God, and given him the supremacy. O my soul, look round about thee, in heaven and in earth; is there any thou dost esteem or value in comparison of God? Psa. lxxiii. 25, 26. Is there any thou dost love like him, or take that content or felicity in,

that thou dost in him ?[a] Are not thy chief desires
and designs to glorify and enjoy him ?[b] Thou canst
not deny, but it is truly thus. I am sure nothing but
God will content me. I am never so well in all the
world, as in his company.[c] My soul seeketh him
above all, and rests in him alone, as my satisfactory
portion.[d] He offereth to take me as one of his people, and I have resigned myself accordingly to him
as his, and have put both my inward and outward
man under his government, and given up all to his
disposal, and am resolved to be content with him, as
my all-sufficient happiness.[e]

Besides, I have taken him in his own way through
Christ, whom he hath tendered to me as my head
and husband, and I have accordingly, solemnly and
deliberately taken him. O my soul, dost not thou
know thy often debates?[f] Hast thou not put
Christ, and all the world, into the balance? Hast
thou not cast up the cost, and reckoned upon the
cross, and willingly put thy neck under Christ's
yoke,[g] and ventured thy salvation upon Christ alone,[h]
and trusted him with all thy happiness, and all thy
hopes?[i] Hast thou not over and over resolved to take
him with what comes, and that he shall be enough,
though in the loss of all things?[k] Thou canst not
but know, that these have been the transactions between Christ and thee, and therefore he is thine, and
all the promises. Yea and amen to thee through him.

And for the terms of the covenant, I love and like

---

[a] Phil. iii. 8.   [b] Phil. i. 20.
[c] Psa. xxvi. 8. lxxxiv. 1—3. xxvii. 4.   [d] Psa. cxix. 57.
[e] Psa. cxix. 38. 2 Cor. v. 8. Acts xxiv. 16. with Rom. vi. 19.
Luke xiv. 33. Psa. xvi. 5, 6. John i. 12.
[f] Luke xiv. 26—35   [g] Matt. xi. 29
[h] Phil. iii. 9.   [i] 2 Tim. i. 12.   [k] 1 Cor. i. 30.

them; my soul embraceth them; neither do I desire
to be saved in any other way, than by repentance
towards God, and faith towards our Lord Jesus
Christ,[a] and sincere obedience to his gospel.[b]

I am willing to go out of my flesh, and do look
unto Jesus for righteousness and strength, and trust
my salvation wholly on this foundation.[c] I am content to deal upon trust, and venture all in hopes of
what is to come, and to tarry till the next world for
my preferment.[d] I am willing to wait till the coming of our Lord Jesus Christ, and have laid up my
happiness on the other side the grave.[e]

And though my sins be many, yet I should belie
my own knowledge, if I should say they were not
my constant trouble and burden,[f] and the enemies
against which I daily watch, and with whom my soul
hath no peace.[g] My own heart knoweth that I hate
them, and desire and endeavour their utter destruction, and do resolve against them all, and am willing
to use all God's means (that I know) to mortify them.[h]
It is too true that I often fall, and fail; yet my conscience beareth me witness, that I confess and bewail
it, and do not ordinarily and deliberately allow myself in any sin whatsoever against my knowledge.[i]
And though my obedience be miserably lame, yet, O
Lord, thou knowest, that I have respect unto all thy
commandments,[k] and do strive to come up to what
thou requirest.[l] The Holy Ghost is witness, and my
conscience also, that I first seek the kingdom of God,

[a] Acts. x. 21.   [b] Rom. ii. 7.
[e] Phil. iii. 3—10.   [d] 2 Cor. v. 7. iv. 18.
[e] 1 Thess. i. 9, 10. Tit. ii. 13. Heb. x. 34. xi. 35.
[f] Rom. vii. 24. Gal. v. 17.   [g] Psa. xxxix. 1. xvii. 3.
[h] Psa. cxix. 101. 104.
[i] Rom. vii. 15, 16, &c. 1 Cor. ix. 26, 27. 1 John i. 9. Rom.
vi. 16.   [k] Psa. cxix. 6.
  Psa. cxix. 5. 30. 173. 2 Cor. v. 9. Psa. xix. 13. cxix. 133.

and the righteousness thereof,[a] and that it is my chief care to please God, and keep from sin.[b] Speak, O my soul, is not holiness thy design? Dost thou not thirst for it, and follow after it? Dost thou not, in thy settled choice, prefer the holy ways of God before all the pleasures and delights of sin? Thou knowest it is thus, and therefore no more disputing; thou hast sincerely taken hold of God's covenant, and without controversy it must be thine.

O my God, I see thou hast been at work with my soul. I find the prints, I see the footsteps. Surely this is the finger of God. I am thy servant, O Lord, truly I am thy servant,[c] and my soul hath said unto the Lord, Thou art my Lord.[d] It must be so. Wouldst thou ever set thy mark upon another's goods? Or shall God disown his own workmanship? My name is written in heaven. Thou hast written thy name upon my heart, and therefore I cannot question but thou hast my name on thy heart. I have chosen thee, O Lord, as my happiness and heritage, and therefore I am sure thou hast chosen me, for I could not have loved thee, except thou hadst loved me first.[e] O my Lord, discern, I pray thee, whose are these, the signet, the bracelets, and the staff? I know thou wilt acknowledge them.

And now blessed be God, and the Father of our Lord Jesus Christ, who, of his abundant mercy, hath begotten me again to a lively hope.

And thou, my soul, believe and wait, look through the window, and cry through the lattice, and rejoice in the hope of the glory of God. The vision is for an appointed time, wait for it. It will come in the end, and will not tarry, Hab. ii. 3. Behold, the husbandman waiteth for the precious fruits of the

[a] Matt. vi. 33. [b] Psal. xix. 33. cxix. 133. [c] Psal. cxvi. 16.
[d] Psal. xvi. 2. [e] 1 John iv. 19. Hab. ii. 3.

earth.[a] Be thou also patient. He hath long patience, and wilt not thou have a little patience? He for the fruits of the earth, but thou for the joys of heaven. He upon mere probabilities, but thou upon infallible certainties. *Faith makes its claim to all the benefits of the covenant, and stirs up the soul to joy and thankfulness.* He for a crop of corn, but thou for a crown of glory. Were he but sure that every corn would bear a crown, how plentifully would he sow, how joyfully would he wait! Why such is thy harvest. As sure as the summer's delights do follow the winter's severities; as sure as the wished-for harvest doth follow the toilsome and costly seed-time, so sure shall thy Lord return, and bring thy reward with him,[b] Therefore, my soul, love and long for the approaching jubilee, and wait all the days of my appointed time, until my change shall come.

Oh blessed state that my Lord hath translated me into! Oh happy change that he hath made! I was a stranger, and he took me in, and made me an heir; and preferred me from the dunghill to the throne, and from a hewer of wood, and drawer of water, to attend his court, and know his counsels, and do his pleasure. Happy am I that ever I was born to partake of this endless dignity.

O my Lord, it is no little thing thou hast given me in hand. I am already come to Mount Zion, and the city of the living God, the heavenly Jerusalem, and to an innumerable company of angels, to the general assembly and church of the first-born, and to God the Judge of all, and unto the spirits of just men made perfect, and unto Jesus the Mediator of the new covenant, and unto the blood of sprinkling,[c] My heart reviveth as Jacob's, when I behold the tokens which thou hast sent me, the spirit of

[a] Jam. v. 7.   [b] Rev. xxii. 12.   [c] Heb. xii. 22—24.

adoption,[a] the pardon of my sins.[b]   My patent for
heaven,[c] the chain of thy graces,[d] the Son of thy
bosom, and the new testament in his blood,[e] and the
letters of his love.[f]   My Lord said, that he will love
me, and manifest himself unto me ; and that the
Father will love me, and both will come unto me,
and make their abode in me.[g] But is it true, indeed ?
Will the Lord dwell on earth ? Or if he will, shall
so foul a stable, so unclean a place, as my heart hath
been, shall this be the place that the Lord of life will
take up his lodging, and keep his court in ? Will
he indeed come with all his train of graces, and live
and walk in me ? how can these things be ? But
he hath said it, and I do, and I will believe it.

Yet all this is but the earnest of what is to come.
Oh how great is thy goodness, laid up for them
that fear thee![h] Yet a little, and my warfare shall
be accomplished, and the heavens must receive me
till the time of the restitution of all things. It is
but for a short term that I shall dwell in this flesh,
in an earthen tabernacle,[i] My Lord hath showed
me, that where he is, there shall his servant be,[k]
Now the living is tied to the dead ; and my soul is a
stage of strife, and a field of war. But it is but a
little moment, and that which is perfect shall come.[l]
Perfect holiness and perfect peace ; eternal serenity
and a serene eternity.

O my sins, I am going where you cannot
come ; where no unclean thing shall enter, nor
any thing that defileth.[m] Methinks I see all my
afflictions and temptations, all my infirmities and

a Gal. iv. 6.   b Luke v. 20.   c Luke xii. 32
d Cant. i. 10.   e 1 Cor. xi. 25.   f John iii. 16.
g John xiv. 21. 23. h Psa. xxxi. 19.   i 2 Pet. i. 14.
k John xii. 26.   l 1 Cor. 13. 10.   m Rev. xxi. 27

corruptions falling off me, as Elijah's mantle at his translation.

O my soul, dost thou not see the chariots of fire, and the horses of fire, come to take thee up? Be thou as poor as Lazarus, Luke xvi. 22. yet God will not disdain to send a party of angels to conduct thee home. How canst thou doubt of ready reception, who hast such a friend in court, who will lead thee with boldness into his Father's presence? If there was joy in Pharaoh's court, when it was said, Joseph's brethren are come, Gen. xlv. 16. surely it will be welcome news in heaven, when it is told, Jesus's brethren are come.

My soul, fear not to enter, though the Lord be clothed with terror and majesty: for thy Redeemer will procure thee favour, and plead thy right. I am sure of welcome, for the Father himself loveth me, John xvi. 27. I have tasted and tried his love; and when I had played the wicked prodigal, Luke xv. yet he despised not my rags, but fell on my neck, and kissed me, and heaven itself rejoiced over me. Much more will he receive me gladly, and let out his loves upon me, when presented to him by his Son, in his perfect likeness, as a fit object for his everlasting delight. Fear not, O my soul, as if thou wert going to a strange place. Why heaven is thy country and thy home: wilt thou doubt of leave, or fear of welcome, when it is thine own home? Why, my soul, thou wast born from above, and here is thy kindred, and thy Father's house, and therefore thou shalt surely be admitted. And then shall I see the glorious preparations of eternal love, and the blissful mansions of the heavenly inhabitants.

Doubtless it will be thus. These are not sick men's dreams, or children's hopes. The living God cannot deceive me : and may not I certainly promise myself, what the Lord hath promised me ?   I will sooner think that all my senses are deluded, and what I see, and feel, and taste, is but a fancy, than think that the living God will deceive me, or that his unchangeable covenant will fail.   Now I am a son of God, but it doth not yet appear what I shall be : But this I know, I shall be like him, and see him as he is, 1 John iii. 2.

I know it shall be thus.   Why, what security should I ask of God ?   He hath given me all the assurance in the word.   And though the word of God be enough, yet he, willing to show more abundantly to the heirs of promise the immutability of his counsel, confirmed it by an oath : that by two immutable things, in which it was impossible for God to lie, I might have strong consolation, Heb. vi. 17.   Oh unreasonable unbelief!   What! shall not the oath of a God put an end to thy strife ?

O my God, I am satisfied : it is enough.   Now I may be bold without presumption, and boast without pride.   And will no more call my duty arrogance, nor my faith a fancy.

O my soul ! there is but a short life betwixt thee and glory, where holy angels, and glorified saints, shall be my associates, and love and praise my only employment.   Methinks I hear already how the morning stars sing together, and all the sons of God shout for joy, Job xxxviii. 7.   O that I could come in for one !   But it was said unto me, I should rest yet for a little season, but I shall stand in the lot at the end of the days, Dan. xii. 13.

It is well, Lord, thy word is enough.   Thy bond is as good as ready payment.   The Holy Ghost tells me, that life and glory abide me ; that look what day I loose from the body, the same day I shall be landed in paradise. Amen, Luke xxiii. 43. It is as I would have it.

But this is not all. When my body hath slept a short nap in the dust, Christ will call to it, Come up hither. Ah true yoke-fellow, it will be a hard parting, but welcome meeting. I could not leave thee, but to live with Christ, Col. iii. 4. But he will raise thee a glorious temple; and when he shall appear, will bring me with himself in glory; and then I shall re-enter thee as a royal mansion, wherein I shall abide with the Lord for ever. For as we have served our Redeemer together, so we must be glorified together with him. And when the Lord hath married us both together again, then will he marry us both unto himself. For I know that my Redeemer liveth, and that he shall stand at the last day over the earth. And though after my skin, worms destroy this body, yet in my flesh I shall see God; whom I shall see for myself, and mine eyes shall behold, and not another, though my reins be consumed within me. My Lord hath already told me how it shall be. He hath set down the time, and showed me the robes of immortality, and the crown of life, that I must put on; and the throne of glory, and the seat of judgment. that I must sit in. He hath told me the manner, in which I shall be presented to him, and espoused by him. He hath told me where he will set me, and what he will say to me, and how he will acknowledge my mean services, and remember what I have forgotten, Matt. xxv. 35. 37. how he will praise the works that I have been ashamed of, and reward me openly, for what I have buried in secresy, Matt. vi. 4. and not forget the poorest alms that I have given for his name.

Then will he confess me before his Father, and before the angels of God. Thus saith the true and faithful witness, and we know that his testimony is true.

Ah, my soul, see that thou make not God a liar, 1 John v. 10.

O my God, I have believed thy report, and do look for all these things, according to thy promise. I know thou intendest me but for a very little while in this lower region. This world is but the house of my pilgrimage, and my soul now is but like a bird in the shell; but when the shell is cracked, then shall she take wings like a dove, and soar aloft to thee, and flee away, and be at rest.

Yet I doubt not thy care for my despicable dust, John vi 39. I know that nothing will be lost; I know not where they will lay me: but thy wakeful eye observeth, and will not be to seek at what door to knock, nor at what grave to call for me. I believe, and am sure that I shall come a glorious piece out of thy hands, fair as the moon, clear as the sun, crowned with honour and glory. And when my absolution is read, and sentence past upon the world, then must I be taken up to dwell with thee.

Let not my Lord be angry, that thy dust and ashes speaketh thus unto thee. Thou Lord hath raised my expectations, and hast made me to look for all these great things from thee. In vain hast thou written all these things unto me, if I should not believe them; and a distrustful diffidence would put a high dishonour upon thy truth.

O Lord, it repenteth me; it repenteth me of my jealousies, and my doubtful thoughts about thee. I know thou lovest an humble confidence, and delightest in nothing more than to see thy children trust thee.   I know the building of my hopes lies not a hair's breadth over the foundation of thy promises, yea, it is sure, my expectations are infinitely short of what I shall find.

O my God, my heart trusteth safely in thee, and I here set to my seal that thou art true, John iii. **33**. Christ is the corner stone on which I build, Eph. ii. 20. and therefore my building will challenge the winds and floods.

And now, O Lord, what wait I for ? my hope is in thee, Psa. xxxix. 7.   O my blessedness, let me enjoy thee.   O my life, let me possess thee.   O desire of mine eyes, let me see thy face and hear thy voice ; for thy voice is sweet, and thy countenance is comely.   I ask but what thou hast promised : for thou hast told me, that I shall see God, and thou wilt speak to me mouth to mouth, Matt. v. 8. even apparently, and not in dark speeches, and the similitude of God shall I behold.

So shall my knowledge be perfected, 1 Cor. xiii. 9, 10. and I shall see the inaccessible light, and my tender eye shall not water, nor my sight dazzle ; but I shall with open face look stedfastly on the Sun of Righteousness, and behold his glory.   Then shall faith be turned into fruition, and hope into possession, and love shall arise like the full moon in her brightness, and never wax nor wane more.

O thou God of my hopes, I look for a new body, and a new soul ; for new heavens, and for a new earth, according to thy promise ; when my whole soul shall be wholly taken up with thee, and all my affections strained to the highest pitch, and all the wheels of my raised powers set in most vigorous and perpetual motion towards thee, still letting in, and still laying out ; and thus shall there be an everlasting communication of joy and glory from thee, and of love and praise from me.

O my soul, thou art rich indeed, and increased in goods. Thou hast no reason to envy the glory or grandeur of the mightiest on earth : for their glory shall not descend after them ; like sheep shall they be laid in their graves, and death shall feed upon them, and there is an eternal end of all their pomp and excellency. But my kingdom is an everlasting kingdom. My robes shall never wear, my crown shall never totter, my throne shall never be vacant, my bread shall never decay, my garland shall never wither, my house shall never moulder, my wine shall never sour, but everlasting joy shall be upon my head, and sorrow and sighing shall fly away.

O my God, how happy hast thou made me ! It is better than I could have wished. Thou hast done all things well. Thou hast settled them for ever. The whole earth cannot show any such heritage or tenure. The world can state out her possessions but for years, nor can she make a good title for that neither. But my inheritance is for ever, and none can put me out of possession. The thing is established in heaven, and in the volume of the book it is written of me. My evidence cannot be lost ; it is recorded in the court above, and enrolled in the sacred leaves of the word, and entered upon the book of my conscience, and herein I do and will rejoice.

Now, my soul, wipe thine eyes, and go away with Hannah, and be no more sad. What though my house be not so with God, so happy, so prosperous as I could wish ? What though they be increased that trouble me, and my temptations and afflictions are like the rolling billows, riding on one another's backs for haste ? Yet shall my soul be as a rock unmoved, and sit down satisfied in the security and amplitude of my portion. For God hath made with me an everlasting covenant, ordered in all things, and sure; and herein is all my salvation, and all my desire.

And now, what remaineth, O Lord, but that I should spend the remainder of my days in loving, praising, and admiring thee? But wherewithal shall I come before the Lord, or bow myself to the most high God? What shall I give thee, to express my thankfulness, though not to requite thy bounty? Alas, my poor little soul! Alas thou art so little! How narrow are thy capacities! How disproportionate are thy powers! Alas that my voice can reach to no higher a note! But shall I do nothing because I cannot do all?

Lord I resign to thee. With the poor widow, I cast my two mites, my soul and body, into thy treasury. All my powers shall love and serve thee. All my members shall be weapons of righteousness for thee. Here is my good will. Behold, my substance is thy stock, mine interest is for thy service. I lay all at thy feet: there thou hast them, they are thine. My children I enter as thy servants. My possessions I resign as thy right. I will call nothing mine but thee. All mine are thine. I can say, My Lord and my God, and that is enough; I thankfully quit my claim to all things else. I will no more say, My house is mine, or my estate mine; I myself am not mine own. Yet it is infinitely better for me to be thine, than if I were mine own. This is my happiness, that I can say, My own God, my own Father. And oh what a blessed exchange hast thou made with me! to give me thyself, who art an infinite sum, for myself, who am but an insignificant cipher.

And now, Lord, do thou accept and own my claim. I am not worthy of any thing of thine, much less of thee. But since I have a deed to show, I bring thy word in my hand, and am bold to take possession. Dost thou not know this hand? wilt thou not own this name? wilt thou not confirm thine own grant? It were infidelity to doubt it. I will not disparage the faithfulness of my Lord, nor be afraid to aver, and stand to what he hath said and sworn. Hast thou said thou art my God, and shall I fear thou art my enemy? Hast thou told me thou art my Father, and shall I stand aloof, as if I were a stranger? I will believe. Lord silence my fears; and as thou hast given me the claim and title of a child, so give me the confidence of a child. Let my heart be daily kept alive by thy promises, and with this staff let me pass over Jordan. May these be my undivided companions and comforters. When I go, let them lead me; when I sleep, let them keep me; when I awake, let them talk with me. And do thou keep these things for ever upon the imaginations of the thoughts of the hearts of thy people, and prepare their hearts unto thee. And let the heart of thy servant be the ark of thy testament, wherein the sacred records of what hath passed between thee and my soul, may for ever be preserved. Amen. Thus far my friend. So be it.

CHAPTER XIX —*An Exhortation to Sinners*

O EARTH, earth, earth, hear the word of the Lord. Ye men of this world, ye spirits that are in prison, held captive to iniquity, under the prince of this world; in a covenant with death, at an agreement with hell, without Christ, aliens from the commonwealth of Israel, strangers from the covenant of pro·

mise, having no hope, without God in the world; who have said, We will not have this man to rule over us; let us break his bonds asunder, and cast his cords from us; who are joined to idols, have chosen you other gods, are following after other lovers; who walk after the course of this world, according to the prince of the power of the air, the spirit that now worketh in the children of disobedience; having your conversation in the lusts of the flesh, fulfilling the desires of the flesh, and of the mind, and being still, as you were by nature, the children of wrath, in the gall of bitterness, and bond of iniquity.

O ye sons of death, ye children of the night and of darkness, hear, and your souls shall live; to you also is the word of this salvation sent; even the strangers, and those who are afar off, that will lay hold on the covenant, and choose the thing that pleaseth God, these also shall have a name in his house, even the glorious name of sons and daughters. The Lord hath sent a word into Jacob, and it shall light upon Edom, and Amalek, and the uncircumcised Philistines, even as many of them as the Lord our God shall call, Acts ii. 39.

Hearken, O people, you that are polluted in your blood, written in the earth, free among the dead; come in, let your covenant with death be made void, and your agreement with hell be disannulled, strike a league with the Almighty, and your names also shall be written amongst the living in Jerusalem.

Stand ye before the Lord, come, let us reason together.

Where are you? What is your portion and inheritance? Ye are cursed with a curse. Fire and brimstone, and a horrible tempest, this shall be the portion of your cup, Psa. xi. 6. What are you seeking? whither are you travelling? After a few years of your vanity are over, where must your dwelling be? Who can dwell with the devouring fire? Who can dwell with everlasting burnings? Look before you, behold that smoking furnace, that burning lake, that bottomless pit which is gaping for you, and which, at your next step, may swallow you up. Escape for your lives; why will ye die? Turn and live.

Do you believe the resurrection from the dead, the judgment to come, and the invisible world? Is it to the spirit of a man, as to the spirit of a beast? Doth it perish with his carcass? Dieth a man as a dog dieth? Dieth a wise man as a fool dieth? Fall all things alike to all, just and unjust, good and bad, after this life as well as in it?

Do you believe the scriptures? Are they but a fable? If you hope they are, are you sure they are? Dare you venture your souls upon it? Whilst the saints venture on the truth, dare you venture your souls on the falsehood of it? Dare you stand forth, and say, If this word be not a lie, let me be damned for ever; I am content that the everlasting worm shall gnaw my heart, that the infernal fire shall burn my flesh, and bones, and soul for ever and ever, if it prove not at last a mere forgery and imposture.

Do you believe the scriptures to be true indeed? if you do, what do they preach to you? Do they speak any thing, if not this, That there is another life and death, besides that which is within the ken of mortal eyes; that the other life, and the other death, are eternal; that upon your being found within or without the covenant of God, hangs your eternal judgment, either for life or death; that whilst you are in a covenant with death, and in a course of iniquity, you are without the covenant of God, and can have no benefit by it; that under sin, and out of covenant; out of covenant, and out of Christ; out of Christ, and under condemnation?

Are there any things, which that word which you profess to believe to be as true, and to stand as sure as heaven and earth; are there any things which this speaks more plainly, than these things, and such like? What, and yet secure in a state of sin! Aliens from God, enemies of all righteousness, and yet in quiet! Are you resolved to sell eternity for time, life for death, a soul for the pleasures of sin? Is this the choice you have made, and are you resolved to stand to it? Let me have this world, my portion here, my good things here, and then let me be damned in the other world: let me sin here, and suffer hereafter: let me laugh here, and lament hereafter: let me flourish, and prosper, and live at ease, and in honour, and in pleasure, and at liberty here; and let my prison, and my pain, and my anguish, and my plagues be beneath; there let me be torn, let me burn, let me roar, let me die, so I may be rich, and be merry, and rejoice a while here; let time be my heaven, and eternity be my hell: speak in earnest, is this your choice? Or that you may not be put to it to make a new choice; will you take upon you to make a new gospel? And, dividing what God hath joined together, will you join what he hath divided? Will you write this for gospel—Holiness and hell, sin and glory, Christ and the curse, the devil and the crown: let the wicked hold on his way, and the unrighteous his thoughts, let him still run away from the Lord, and he shall have mercy; and from his God, and he will abundantly pardon? Strait is the gate, and narrow is the way, that leadeth unto death, and few there be that find it; but broad is the gate, and wide is the way, that leadeth unto life, and the whole world are going in thereat? Blessed are the proud in spirit, for theirs is the kingdom of heaven? Blessed are they that laugh now; blessed are the froward, the merciless, the impatient in heart, the persecutors for righteousness' sake; for great is their reward in heaven? Within shall be the dogs, and the swine, the whoremongers, the sorcerers, the drunkards, the ruffians, the blasphemers, the gallants, the idolaters, and whosoever loveth and maketh a lie? and without shall be the lambs, and the doves, the holy, and the humble, and the meek, and the merciful, and the upright in heart, and the poor in spirit, and peace-makers, the persecuted for righteousness' sake, and whosoever loveth truth, and maketh God his trust: these shall go into everlasting fire, but the ungodly into life eternal?

Are these the articles of your creed? Is this your gospel? If it be, oh! what is your heaven? If it be not, if the old gospel must stand, oh! where are your souls? Are your souls lost, and are they not worth the recovery? Why will ye die? Turn and live; oh! when shall it once be?

As an ambassador for Christ, to whom is committed the word of reconciliation, having hinted to you what is law, so in the name of the eternal God, I publish to you the everlasting gospel.

The Lord God having entered into a covenant of life, with the first Adam, for himself and all mankind in him; this covenant being broken, whereby sin hath entered, and death by sin, and all the world is now become guilty before God; bound over to the vengeance of eternal fire, and under an utter impossibility of recovery, by aught which that covenant can

do, hath out of his abundant grace, made a new covenant, on which whosoever shall lay hold, shall be
delivered out of the state of death and wrath, into a
state of life and blessedness. What the law could not
do, being weak through the flesh, God sent his Son
in the likeness of sinful flesh, Rom. viii. 3. and with
him this gracious grant, that whosoever believeth in
him, shall not perish, but have everlasting life, John
iii. 16. And this is the covenant which hath been
declared unto you.

This new covenant is a marriage covenant; I will
betroth thee unto me.for ever, yea, I will betroth thee
to me in righteousness, and in loving kindness, and in
mercies, Hos. ii. 20. In it the Lord makes offer, and
invites you to accept of a husband and a dower : the
husband is the King's son, the Lord Jesus Christ ;
and with him the lost kingdom, and all that belongs
to the kingdom of God for a dower. Liberty for the
captives, the opening of the prison to them that are
bound ; riches to the poor, eyes to the blind, feet to
the lame, healing to the diseased, and life to the
dead.

And whoever among you all, who are persons
under the law, held by the cords of your sins, whose
souls are fast bound in fetters of iron, who are willing that your covenant with death be made void,
and your agreement with hell be disannulled, and
will join yourselves to the Lord, and be brought
within the bonds of this covenant, all the blessings
of this covenant are made over, and stand sure
unto you.

The grant is made, the deed is drawn and sealed;
the Lord hath set to his seal, come you in, and seal
the counter part; set to your seal, and the match is
made up. Christ, and with him all things are yours,

and you are his.   Accept and live, refuse and die for
ever.

Come on then, sinner, what sayest thou ?   Dost
thou consent ?   Dost thou accept ?   Or, as Laban
to Rebekah, Will thou go with this man ?   Let me
espouse thee to this one Husband ; only let me first
tell thee, the matter is solemn, and thou must be
serious.   It is for life, it is for eternity.

Consider, therefore, and let thy heart, lying prostrate before the Almighty, come in and make
answer to these demands, which from him, and in
his great and dreadful name, I make unto thee.

I. Wilt thou have Jesus for thy Husband ?   Understand before thou answer.   The taking of Christ
for thy Husband, implies—

Intimate union—ingenuous subjection—total
dependence.

1. Intimate union ; by choosing and accepting
him for thine, and resigning and giving up thyself to
him for his own ; to live with him, in the dearest
conjugal affection for ever.

2. Ingenuous subjection ; by a free and cheerful
putting thyself under him, as thy Lord whom thou
wilt obey, and be subject to, in all things.   The wife
must be subject to her husband ; yet not as a slave
by constraint, but freely and by consent.

3. Total dependence ; holding him as thy Head,
expecting nothing, owning nothing, but what descends upon thee from him : depending on him for
all things ; the bearing of thy debts, thy discharge
from thy bonds, and thy whole provision for a livelihood and maintenance.

Consider, then, what sayest thou?   Doth thine
heart choose, and accept, and resign up itself unto
Christ ?   Dost thou choose him as a Husband ?

Thou canst choose him as a Refuge, to hide thee from danger; thou canst choose him as a Friend, to help thee in thy need; but dost thou choose him for thy Husband? Wilt thou cleave to him; love, honour, and obey him? Dost thou understand his manner, the law of his house, his family order and discipline? Dost thou know his commands and expectations; how holy, how spiritual, how strict, and self-denying, how humble and submissive he expects thy whole carriage should be? Wilt thou be at his finding? Wilt thou look unto him, and lean upon him for all thou needest? Shall all thy desire be to him, and thy dependence on him? Thou art a bondman, who shall be thy redemption? Thou art a malefactor, who shall be thy satisfaction? Thou art a leper, whence dost thou look for cleansing? Thou art a beggar, whence dost thou expect an inheritance? Wilt thou lean upon thy Beloved for all? Shall he be thy wisdom, righteousness, sanctification, redemption, and inheritance? Wilt thou do him this honour, to trust him for all this; to cast all thy burdens, thy care, thy fears, thy sins, thy guilt, thy hopes upon him? Canst thou say, O my God, I have sinned, I have sinned, thy law have I broken, thy love have I slighted, I have fallen from thee, and run over to thine enemies; I have fallen under thy displeasure, wrath is provoked, justice hath taken hold of me, my soul is undone? How dreadful is thy controversy with me! And I have nothing to answer but this, My Jesus shall answer for me.

O my Jesus, thou hast wooed and invited sinners unto thee; thou hast sent forth thy messengers, and thy word into the highways and hedges, into the gaols and hospitals of the world: among the poor, the blind, and the bound, and the diseased, and those who are in debt and distress; to take from among them a wife for thy bosom.   Behold, thy word hath found among the captives this wretched adulteress, my poor harlot soul, which hath dealt treacherously with thee, and hath followed after other lovers, hath fallen among thieves and robbers, is bruised, wounded, and undone ; having prodigally spent and wasted all that I had.

But, behold, I come at thy word ; if thou sayest, I have no pleasure in thee, if thou spurn me with thy foot, and trample me in the dirt, or send me back to my prison, and leave me to bear the shame of my sins, I must be silent and speechless.

But wilt thou receive me ? wilt thou take me into thine house ? shall I be called by thy name ? wilt thou love me, and be joined unto me ? wilt thou be surety for thy servant ? wilt thou that my debts be upon thee, my bonds be upon thee, my wants, my sins, my sorrows, my fears, my plagues, my help, my soul be upon thee ?   Wilt thou, Lord, and can I say thee nay ? wilt thou take them, and can I refuse to lay them upon thee ? I consent, Lord, I consent to thee ; be thou my husband, and my helper ; love me, discharge me of this guilt, loose me from these fetters, cleanse me from this filthiness, and then ask what thou wilt, impose upon me whatever thou pleasest : love thee, honour thee, obey thee ? Oh ! what is my love ? what is my obedience, that thou shouldst accept, or I should deny it to thee ?   It is but little that I can do, this heart is so false and so feeble, that I am afraid how I undertake for it, but such as it is, take it to thee, I bestow it wholly upon thee, with this promise, that if thou wilt help me, I will love thee ; if thou wilt help me, I will be subject to thee, and lay up all my hopes and expectations with thee. Now soul, now that thou knowest what it means, now say, wilt thou have Christ for thy Husband?

II. Wilt thou take him for better for worse, for richer for poorer?

Though thy Lord be a King, yet his kingdom is not of this world. He came not to be ministered unto, but minister; he came to serve and to suffer, and all those that will follow him, must suffer with him. He came not to divide lands, and spoils, and crowns, and temporal dignities, and honours amongst his disciples; but crosses, and prisons, and scourges, and wants. Thou wilt join thyself to the Lord, but wilt thou take up thy lot with him? Thou wilt live with him, and abide with him; but dost thou know where he dwells, and what his entertainment is? Sometimes he hath bread, and sometimes he is hungry; sometimes he hath clothes, and sometimes is naked; sometimes he hath a house, and sometimes he hath none; sometimes he hath friends, and sometimes he hath none; he is sometimes used kindly, and sometimes as coarsely; sometimes it is Hosanna, and sometimes Crucify; sometimes he is cried up as a king, sometimes cried out against as a devil; and as it is with the master, so will it be with the scholar; as with the Lord so with the disciple; where he is, thou must be also. Canst thou say, Whither thou goest, I will go with thee; where thou feedest, I will feed with thee; where my Lord dwelleth, if in a tent, if in a cave, if in a dungeon, if in a wilderness, wherever my Lord dwelleth, let me dwell with him? Consider what thou sayest, and be not over hasty. May be thou dost not yet know what hunger, and thirst, and nakedness mean; what the wrath of man, what their reproachings, and spit-tings, and stripes, and bonds mean ; may be thou hast thought, this may be far enough off, and may never come upon me ; or hast taken up a resolution through thoughtlessness, not weighing how sharp and how pinching they may be to thee. But sup-pose thou wert now just come to it; and that thou sawest, that thy first foot Christ-ward would be the parting point betwixt thee and all that is dear unto thee in the world; that thy first step heaven-ward would be into the fire, or the water, or into the camp of the Philistines, whose faces were all filled with fury against thee. Hast thou yet such a far deeper sense of the eternal sufferings, thou art in danger of; such a settled belief, of thy absolute necessity of Christ to thy escaping these; such a high value of the love of Christ, and the everlasting salvation thou expectest by him, as does overbalance and swallow up the sharpest and the quickest sense thou hast or canst have of the greatest things thou shalt suffer by him? Hast thou cast up all afflictions imaginable, and then put thy soul to it? Now re-solve what to do ; either this, or no Christ; either this, or no crown; either this cross, or the curse ; either the wrath of man, or the wrath of God ; scor-pions, and dragons, and devils ; shrieking, and howl-ing, and gnashing of teeth for ever and ever. Confess Christ, and be confessed by him ; suffer with Christ, and reign with him ; weep with Christ, and rejoice with him ; die with Christ, and live for ever; deny Christ, forsake Christ, and perish for ever. Hast thou thus put thyself to it? And after the most solemn debate thou hast had, what is the result? Now tell me, Christ, or no Christ? Wilt thou have Christ for better for worse, how dear soever he cost thee?

III. Wilt thou forsake all others?

Thou hast three husbands that lay claim to thee, sin, the world, and the devil. Wilt thou renounce, and be divorced from all these? There is no compounding betwixt Christ and them, he or they must go.

The renouncing of sin stands,

1. In the disengaging of the heart from it.

2. In the engaging of the heart against it.

1. In the disengaging or loosening of the heart from sin. It is a hearty willingness to let it go; a willingness to part is our parting with sin. A breaking the peace, the cutting off the league betwixt sin and the soul, when a sinner stands so clearly convinced of the worth of Christ, of the value of a soul, of the enmity of sin against Christ and the soul, of the unworthiness of sin, with all its pleasures and advantages, to be laid in the balance with Christ, is willing to be rid of it. What is there in it? what can it do for me? how long will it last me? where will it lead me? O the tail of these locusts, the sting, the sting that I see there! Can I want a Christ? or can I hope that he will dwell with such neighbours? Can I bear the loss of my soul? or can it escape if these escape? I see it is vain to think of keeping both Christ and lusts, it is vain to think of saving both my sins and my soul; it is all one, as to be saved, and to be damned; I may as well bring heaven and hell together. Well, let them go; henceforth hold thy peace, sin, plead no more with me for entertainment, be a stranger for ever to me, henceforth I know thee no more.

2. In the engaging of the heart against sin. When the heart is not only content to let it depart, but

gives it a bill of divorce, and sends it away. When it can want it, and cannot bear it. When it deals with it, as the Egyptians with Israel; at first they have only leave given them to be gone, but at length they thrust them out. They were urgent upon them, " that they might send them out of the land in haste, for they said, We be all but dead men," Exod. xii. 33.

Begone sin, I am but a dead man if thou abidest with me ; and so it will no longer court it as a friend, but curse it as an enemy; fears it, hates it, and is resolved to be its mortal enemy; and to this end is determined to use all God's means, 1. To discover ; 2. To destroy it.

(1.) To use all God's means to discover it ; to bring to light the hidden things of darkness. Sin goes under a disguise ; it is hard to know friends from enemies ; they had need have their senses about them, and well exercised too, that can discern betwixt good and evil, Heb. v. 14. Who can understand his errors ? Psa. xix. 12. Sin lies in the dark. " The heart of man is desperately wicked, who can know it ?" There is too much wickedness, and it lies too deep to be discerned by every eye ; he that means in earnest to cast out must first search out his iniquities. " Let us search and try our ways," Lam. iii. 40. He must search the scriptures which describe these enemies, and mark them out, what they are, and how many, and how you may know them, wherever you find them, and under what disguise soever they appear ; must search the heart, where, if they walk no more openly, they will hide themselves, that they be not discovered or suspected.

Thou art a fool, a self-deceiver, sinner, who

takest thyself to be an adversary to sin, and takest no care to find it out; much more who willingly hidest it out of sight. He takes part with sin who will not take pains to know it. I hate the devil and all his works, I repent, I forsake all my sins; and though I have done iniquity, by the grace of God, I will do so no more. Thus vain men talk, but dost thou know what thou sayest? What is sin? Dost thou know a friend from an enemy, good from evil? What are thy sins? what hast thou done? wherein hast thou transgressed? what are those that have done thee mischief? what are their names? May be thou wilt say their name is Legion, for they are many.

In many things I have transgressed, in many things I have offended; but in what things? Dost thou know thine enemy when thou seest him? or wouldst thou know him if thou couldst? Dost thou make any search or inquiry after him? When thou readest of a proud heart in the scriptures, art thou able to say, There is one of them that have done me mischief? or of a covetous heart, There is another of them? or of an envious, malicious, froward heart, There are more of them? or of a hard and hypocritical, ignorant, unbelieving heart, This is he, this is my great enemy? or if thou canst not tell, dost thou ask, Is not this he? Are not these they? O that I could understand mine errors, Lord, make me to know my transgressions.

Sinners, never make yourselves believe you are enemies to sin till you make narrow and particular inquiry after it; after all sin, the several kinds of it, whether of omission or commission, whether outward or spiritual, open or secret, greater or smaller, sins of ignorance or knowledge, of infirmities or presumption ; your beloved, your most pleasing sins, your most gainful lusts, whatever they be, you can never renounce till you resolve to make a diligent search after them.

(2.) To use all God's means to destroy and over-come them. He that hides his enemy, and he that will spare him when he hath found him, is not an enemy but a friend. He that says, I will destroy, and will not use his weapons, either knows not what he says, or says what he never means. Thou sayest thou wilt renounce and resist all thy sins, but art thou in earnest? What course dost thou mean to take? Wilt thou take God's way? He bids thee hear, believe, pray, fast, mourn, strive, watch, &c. Wilt thou hearken to his counsels? Wilt thou be healed of thy diseases? But wilt thou take the counsel of the Physician? Wilt thou use his medicines? Thou wilt overcome thine enemy, but wilt thou take heed of him? Wilt thou fight against him? Wilt thou take in all the help that is offered thee? Wilt thou not only believe, and lean upon God for his help, but wilt thou pray, and lift up thy heart for his help? Wilt thou not only pray against thy sins, but watch against them? against the occasions, temptations, and beginnings of sin? Wilt thou use all God's means, and against all thy sins? Shall not thine eyes spare any of them? Wilt thou make thorough work with them, root and branch, old and young? Shall there be neither the lowing of the oxen, nor the bleating of the sheep heard with thee? Wilt thou destroy the greater, and dash the little ones also against the stones?

Wilt thou avenge thyself of thine adversaries, and wilt thou never again agree with thine adversaries?

Wilt thou never again say, Is it peace, Jehu? Is it peace, Jezebel? So if thy sins say to thee, Is it peace, soul? wilt thou answer, What have you to do with peace? get you behind me. Wilt thou neither make a truce with sin, nor embrace a parley, nor entertain a treaty for peace with it? Wilt thou not draw back thine hand, nor put up thy weapons, nor give over thy watch, nor go off thy guard, till all thine enemies become thy footstool; all this is included in the renouncing of sin.

Beware you be not mistaken here, this is the damnation of the world, their mistakes about repentance. They easily say, I repent of my sins, I forsake the devil and all his works; and they as easily persuade themselves that they do as they say. But did they understand what there is in this repentance, a searching out their sins, dividing their souls from them; a painful and watchful shunning and resisting them in their whole course; did they know what their particular sins are, how near they are to their hearts, how they have been nursed in their bosoms, and how hard it will be now to part; even this covetousness must go, even this sensuality must go, these dear pleasures, these beloved gains, these pleasant companions, must all be sent away, not one to be spared, not so much as once more; did they understand this, they would then see what wind all their good words be. They as much mean to pluck their eyes out of their heads, to tear their flesh off their bones, as to repent, if this be repentance. Well, now say, wilt thou repent? Wilt thou now renounce sin?

Wilt thou renounce the world also? By the world understand all the substance of the world,

houses, lands, money, and whatsoever worldly possessions; all the shadows of the world, its honours,
pleasures, pomps, with all its glory; the men of
this world, the friendship of the world, all fleshly
relations, fathers, mothers, brothers, sisters, children;
all sinful companions and societies whatsoever is in
and of the world.

These are then renounced, when we are resolved
that they shall neither be our gods or idols—our
devils or tempters. 1. Not our gods. Then we
make the world a god to us, when we make it our
happiness or end. When we bless ourselves in it,
and count that our very life consists in the abundance of the things which we possess. When we
devote ourselves to it, making it as the blessedness, so the great business of our life. He that
can want the world, and yet be blessed; he that
can want, or have the world, and yet not serve it;
he hath renounced it, even whilst he hath it;
though it is his still, yet it is not his god. 2. Not our
devils or tempters. The world tempts in a double
way : by objects and instruments. As objects,
which, by something that is apprehended desirable
in them, entices and invites out the heart after
them; or by something apprehended as formidable
affrights us out of our way. Thus pleasant meats
tempts the glutton, and wine the drunkard, and a
lion in the streets the coward. Also by instruments :
as under-devils, or the devil's instruments, or agi-
tators, by which he betrays and beguiles unstable
souls. In the former sense the things of the world,
in the latter, the men of the world, are temptations
and tempters to us. He renounces the world
that will not be tempted by the world; that takes up
with Christ, and will not be bribed off by worldly

advantages, nor proselyted by worldly companions.

He that is resolved for Christ, though with the
loss of all, and with the displeasure of all the
world ; he that can be poor for Christ, that can be
vile for Christ, that can go hungry and naked with
Christ, that can go alone with Christ, and that even
then, when it is but turning away from Christ, and
he may be rich and honourable, and be clothed, and
be filled, and have company enough, as much as he
desires,—he forsakes the world.

He that can renounce the world, whenever it
comes to be a case, either Christ must be forsaken,
or all things for Christ ; he that can, whose heart
is brought to it, he hath renounced the world. What
sayest thou now soul ?

Thou wilt have Christ, but what if thou must
leave all behind thee ? What if he say to thee, Sell all
that thou hast, and follow me ? Canst thou be poor ?
Canst thou be naked ? Canst thou be hungry for
Christ ? Thou wilt have Christ, but how wilt thou
leave thy companions ? What will all thy carnal
friends say of thee ? He is a fool, he is mad, he is
beside himself. How wilt thou look thy father or
thy mother, or thy wife in the face, who are all
against it ? who will be persuading, beseeching thee,
weeping over thee, hanging upon thy neck ; or it
may be, scoffing and reviling, to discourage and
hold thee back. What sayest thou now ? Art thou
yet for Christ ? Wilt thou forsake them all, cast off
all that stands in thy way ?

Wilt thou forsake the devil also ? But I need not
now ask thee that, that is done already : farewell
devil, when once sin and the world are cast out.
If thou wilt not be tempted to sin ; if the world

ceases to be a temptation, the devil were as good cease to be a tempter. There be many that say, I defy the devil, and yet defy not sin and the world. Wise men! They like not the devil, but yet will follow his will; they hate the devil, and yet are never well longer than they are dancing in his chains. Defy the devil, and yet love sin! Such defiance is his delight. Let sin be defied, let the world be despised, and the devil is conquered.

IV. Wilt thou cleave unto Christ from henceforth unto death?

Thou wilt have Christ, but when? Shall this be the marriage-day? Wilt thou from henceforth be the Lord's, or when shall it be? Must it be to-morrow, or next month, or next year, or some time or other, thou knowest not when? May we not take thy promise as they did the prophecy, "Is it not for many days to come? is it not of the times that are afar off," Ezek. xii. 27. To-morrow thou wilt, hereafter thou wilt; as good as thou hadst said nothing. As good thou hadst said "Never," as "Not yet." Speak, soul, wilt thou give thyself to the Lord? wilt thou presently? if thou wilt, how long wilt thou abide with him? wilt thou not endorse on thy deed of gift a power of revocation? wilt thou not repent, not return again from heaven to earth? wilt thou be chaste, and play the harlot no more? wilt thou be faithful to the death, obedient to the death? Is this thy voice, I have opened my mouth to the Lord, and I cannot go back? As the Lord liveth, nothing but death, no not death itself, shall part thee and me, I am persuaded, I am resolved, "that neither life nor death, angels nor principalities, nor powers, nor things present, nor things to come, nor height, nor depth, nor any other creature, shall separate me from the love of God, or withdraw me from Jesus Christ my Lord."

Now soul, gather up all this together, stand thou before the Lord, the God of all the earth, and this once more say, Wilt thou have Jesus Christ for thy Husband? Dost thou choose him for thy Lord? wilt thou cleave to him in love? wilt thou lean upon him for righteousness and strength? for righteousness to pay thy debts, and for strength to pay thy vows? wilt thou be subject to him? thou knowest the commandments, how holy, how strict they are. Wilt thou obey them in all things? wilt thou exercise thyself to godliness in the strictness of it? wilt thou be a thorough-paced disciple? wilt thou not content thyself with such a cold or luke-warm indifferency in religion, as thy lazy flesh will bear; as thy credit, thy safety, or the temper of the times will bear? Wilt thou follow thy Lord fully? Wilt thou take up thy lot with Christ, be it better or worse? Shall his Father be thy Father, his inheritance, be thy inheritance? yea, and his sufferings thy sufferings? his stripes, his bonds, his poverty be thine? wilt thou espouse not his crown only, but his cross too? wherever he goes, wilt thou go? where he dwells, wilt thou dwell? wilt thou say, Wherever my Lord is, there let his servant be? Wilt thou forsake all others? all thy sins? Wilt thou be made clean? Wilt thou give up thy fleshly lusts to be purged out? Does thy heart stand disengaged from every sin? Is there not any one iniquity, concerning which thy heart says, Let this stay with me? Wilt thou search out thy sins? Wilt thou accomplish a diligent search, sweep every corner, search every chamber of thine heart and life? Wilt thou go down to the bottom of thy great

deep, to find out what lodges there? Wilt thou faithfully endeavour no more to allow thyself in any
known iniquity? Wilt thou use all God's means for
the conquering and casting them out? Wilt thou
forsake the world? Wilt thou cast away thine idols?
shall thy mammon be no more a god, nor a demi-
god to thee? shall it neither carry away thine heart
from him, nor so much as share with him in it?
Wilt thou not bow down to this golden image, nor
serve it? Wilt thou no longer serve thy greedy
appetite? Shall thine heart no longer go after thy
covetousness? wilt thou abandon thine estate, thy
pleasures, thine honours, thy friends and companions,
so far as any of these divide or entice, or steal
away thy heart from thy Lord? Whenever they
say, Come away, wilt thou say, Get you hence?
Wilt thou forsake the devil? wilt thou fear, and fly
from, and no longer hearken to his temptations?
wilt thou no longer regard his promises nor his
threatenings? his flatteries nor his frowns? Coming
off from the tents of all these, wilt thou cleave unto
thy Lord from henceforth, from this day forward,
and not depart from him for ever? Wilt thou hold
on thy course? wilt thou run out thy race? wilt thou
be faithful to the death? wilt thou hope to the end
for the grace that shall be brought unto thee at the
revelation of Jesus Christ?

What sayest thou? If thou sayest No; as the
Lord liveth, thou speakest this word against thine
own life. If thou refusest to enter into this covenant, thou sayest, I will not be the Lord's, I will
none of him, I will not live; let death, and wrath,
and chains, and plagues be my portion for ever. I
will not be the Lord's, I will not leave my sins, and
my pleasures, and my companions for his love;

that is, I will be a fool, and a beast, and a devil; I will die, and will not see life. Mistake not thyself, be not deceived, it is a matter of life and death that is before thee. It is whether heaven or hell, a God or no God, a Christ or no Christ, a soul or a lost soul, everlasting life or everlasting fire shall be thy portion, that stands now to be determined, by thy consent or refusal; look to it, be wise, this once for eternity. Consent, and thou art blessed; consent, and he is thine, and with him the kingdom. Thy Lord hath given his consent already, view the hand-writing, the whole new testament, which is written in blood, and sealed as it is written. There thou hast his " I will," in every line almost, visible before thee, put to thine hand, and it is done. What sayest thou? Dost thou consent? Shall thy heart come in, and put to thy hand, and subscribe for thee—I will? Let that be done, and then say after me:—

A FORM OF WORDS EXPRESSING MAN'S COVENANTING WITH GOD

O most dreadful God, for the passion of thy Son, I beseech thee, accept of thy poor prodigal now prostrating himself at thy door. I have fallen from thee by mine iniquity, and am by nature a son of death, and a thousand-fold more the child of hell by my wicked practice; but of thine infinite grace thou hast promised mercy to me in Christ, if I will but turn to thee with all my heart: therefore upon the call of thy gospel, I am now in; and, throwing down my weapons, submit myself to thy mercy.

The terms of our conversion are either from which, or to which.

And because thou requirest, as the condition of my peace with thee, that I should put away mine idols, and be at defiance with all thine enemies which I acknowledge I have wickedly sided with against thee, I here from the bottom of my heart renounce them all, firmly covenanting with thee, not to allow myself in any known sin, but conscientiously to use all means that I know thou hast prescribed, for the death and utter destruction of all my corruptions. And whereas I have formerly inordinately and idolatrously let out my affections upon the world, I do here resign my heart to thee who madest it, humbly protesting before thy glorious Majesty, that it is the firm resolution of my heart, and that I do unfeignedly desire grace from thee, that when thou shalt call me hereunto, I may practise this my resolution, through thy assistance, to forsake all that is dear unto me in this world, rather than to turn from thee to the ways of sin, and that I will watch against all its temptations, whether of prosperity or adversity, lest they should withdraw my heart from thee, beseeching thee also to help me against the temptations of Satan, to whose wicked suggestions I resolve, by thy grace, never to yield myself a servant. And because my own righteousness is but filthy rags, I renounce all confidence therein, and acknowledge, that I am of myself a hopeless, helpless, undone creature, without righteousness or strength.

The terms from which we must turn, are sin, Satan, the world, and our own righteousness, which must be thus renounced.

And forasmuch as thou hast of thy bottomless mercy offered most graciously to me, wretched sinner, to be again my God through Christ, if I would accept of thee: I call heaven and earth to record this day,

The terms to which we must turn, are either ultimate or mediate.

that I do here solemnly avouch thee for the Lord my God, and with all possible venera-tion, bowing the neck of my soul under the feet of thy most sacred Majesty, I do here take thee the Lord Jehovah, *The ultimate is God, the Father Son, and Holy Ghost, who must be thus accepted.* Father, Son, and Holy Ghost, for my portion and chief good, and do give up myself, body and soul, for thy servant, promising and vowing to serve thee in holiness and righteousness all the days of my life.

And since thou hast appointed the Lord Jesus Christ the only means of coming unto thee, I do here upon the bended knees of my soul accept of him as the only new and living way, by which sinners may have access to thee, and do here *The mediate terms are either principal, or less principal. The principal is Christ the Mediator who must thus be embraced.* solemnly join myself in the marriage-covenant to him.

O blessed Jesus, I come to thee hungry and hardly bestead, poor, and wretched, and miserable, and blind, and naked, a most loathsome, polluted wretch, a guilty, condemned malefactor, unworthy for ever to wash the feet of the servants of my Lord, much more to be solemnly married to the king of glory. But since such is thine unparalleled love, I do here with all my power accept thee, and do take thee for my Head and Husband, for better for worse, for richer for poorer, for all times and conditions, to love, honour, and obey thee before all others, and this to the death. I embrace thee in all thine offices: I renounce mine own unworthiness, and do here avow thee to be the Lord my righteousness. I renounce mine own wisdom, and do here take thee for mine only guide. I renounce mine own will, and take thy will for my law.

And since thou hast told me, that I must suffer if I will reign, I do here covenant with thee to take my lot, as it falls with thee, and by thy grace assisting, to run all hazards with thee, verily supposing, that neither life nor death shall part between thee and me.

And because thou hast been pleased to give me thy holy laws, as the rule of my life, and the way in which I should walk to thy kingdom; I do here willingly put my neck under thy yoke, and set my shoulder to thy burden, and subscribing to all thy laws, as holy, just, and good. I solemnly take them, as the rule of my words, thoughts, and actions; promising that though my flesh contradict and rebel, yet I will endeavour to order and govern my whole life according to thy direction, and will not allow myself in the neglect of anything that I know to be my duty.

The less principals, are the laws of Christ which must be thus accepted.

Only because through the frailty of my flesh, I am subject to many failings; I am bold humbly to protest, that unallowed miscarriages, contrary to the settled bent and resolution of my heart, shall not make void this covenant; for so thou hast said.

Now Almighty God, searcher of hearts, thou knowest that I make this covenant with thee this day, without any known guile or reservation, beseeching thee, that if thou espiest any flaw or falsehood therein, thou wouldst discover it to me, and help me to do it aright.

And now glory be to thee, O God the Father, whom I shall be bold from this day forward to look upon as my God and Father, that ever thou shouldest find out such a way for the recovery of undone sinners. Glory be to thee, O God the Son, who hast loved me, and washed me from my sins in thine own blood, and art now become my Saviour and Redeemer. Glory be to thee, O God the Holy Ghost, who by thine Almighty power hast turned about my heart from sin to God.

O dreadful Jehovah, the Lord God omnipotent, Father, Son, and Holy Ghost; thou art now become my covenant Friend, and I, through thine infinite grace, am become thy covenant servant, Amen. So be it. And the covenant which I have made on earth, let it be ratified in heaven.

CHAPTER XX —*An Exhortation to the Saints*

COME ye people beloved, you that are highly favoured; the Lord is with you. Blessed are you amongst men and women. The lines are fallen to you in a pleasant place, yea, you have a goodly heritage. Come and enter upon your lot; let your hearts be glad, let your glory rejoice, but that your joy may be full, hearken to these following counsels:

I. Make sure your interest in the covenant.

Rejoice not in that which is none of thine. Make sure, all lies upon this: your life, and all the comforts and concerns of it, both your eternal safety hereafter, and your success in all the parts of your christian course here, depend on your interest in the covenant. What have you if Christ be not yours? and what have you in Christ, if you be not in covenant? whence are your hopes, either of mercy at last, or of prospering in any thing at present, but from the covenant of promise? And what have you thence, if your name be not in it? O give not rest to yourselves, till this be put out of doubt;

whatever duties you perform, whatever ease or hope you find hereupon, whatever transport of affection you feel in your hearts, in the midst of all inquire— But am I in covenant? How shall I know that? you will say. Why make a strict and narrow inquiry, whether those special graces already mentioned, be wrought upon you. Common mercies, though even these be covenant mercies to the saints, yet will they not prove themselves so to be; but special graces will be their own evidence. Things outward fall alike to all; " No man knows love or hatred by ought that befalls him," Ecc. ix. 1. Thou mayest be a son or a bastard, notwithstanding all that thou enjoyest or sufferest here; but not one of the fore-mentioned graces, but is a child's portion, God's mark upon the heart, to distinguish children from strangers. Prove that thou truly knowest the Lord, hast one heart, a tender heart, &c. and thou therein provest thyself to be a child of promise. Read over the descriptions that have been given of these graces; observe diligently where the main difference lies betwixt common and special grace; compare thine heart with it, and thereby thou mayest give a judgment of thy state. If it be yet questionable, whether it be found or not, sit not down till thou hast obtained; but having obtained,

II. Keep your evidences clear.

Have you peace? maintain it carefully. The hidden manna will never breed worms by long keeping. Content, not yourselves that you once had peace; it will be but a poor livelihood you will get out of what is wasted and lost. Get you good evidences that God is yours, and keep them by you, till you need them no more. Grace is your best evidence, cherish and preserve it. Get a seeing eye, and keep your eye open; get a single heart, and let it not be again divided; get a tender heart, and keep it tender; let the love and fear of God be acted in holy obedience. An obedient, gracious, watchful, active life, will keep grace in heart; and flourishing grace will speak for itself and you. Look not that the Lord should so far countenance your declinings to a more fleshly careless state, as to smile upon you in such a state; God will not be an abetter to sin. Count upon it, that your grace and peace, your duty and comfort will rise and fall together; suspect those comforts that accompany you into the tents of wickedness, and forsake you not, when you forsake your God. Keep up your spirits, and then lift up your heads, keep heedfully on your way, and your joy shall no man take from you. Particularly,

1. Keep close to God.
2. Keep hold on Christ.
3. Quench not the Spirit.
4. Keep in with conscience.

1. Keep close to God. Keep thyself under his eye and influences. Both thy grace and thy comforts as they had their birth, so must they have their nourishment from Heaven. Lose the sight of the sun, and darkness follows. Let thine eyes be towards the hills. Let divine love be the pleasure of thy life. Let it be thy Lord's cord upon thine heart, let it bind thee to him; he loves captives, let thine ear be bored to the threshold, be familiar in heaven, keep thine acquaintance there, and be at peace; chide back thy gadding heart. Soul, whither art thou going? who hath the words of eternal life? Let the interviews of love betwixt thy Lord and thee, be constant; let them not be only on some few holy days of thy life.

Count not thou hast lived that day, in which thou hast not lived with God.

Keep close to God, by keeping close to duty Keep close to duty, and keep close to God in duty. Call not that a duty, which thou canst not call communion with God. Make not duty to do the work of sin, to take God out of sight. Let not prayer, or hearing, or sacraments, be instead of a God to thee. Such praying and hearing there is amongst many, but know not thou anything for religion, wherein thou meetest not with God.

Behold the face of God, but behold his face in righteousness, Psa. xvii. 15. It is ill-looking on God with a blood-shot eye. Guilt upon the heart, will be a cloud that will make the sun as darkness to thee. Walk in the light of the Lord. Walk in the light, as he is in the light. In thy light (the holiness of thy life) thou shalt see his light. The light of his holiness in thee, will be attended with the light of his countenance upon thee. By the light of his countenance, thou wilt both see thyself in thy way to thy hopes, and learn thy way more perfectly. "Make thy face to shine upon thy servant, and teach me thy statutes," Psa. cxix. 135. God hath many ways of teaching; he teaches by book, he teaches by his finger, he teaches by his rod; but his most comfortable and effectual teaching is by the light of his eye. Send forth thy light and thy truth, let them lead me, let them bring me to thy holy hill.

2. Keep hold on Christ. He is thy peace. Appear not before God, but in the blood of the Lamb let him carry up thy duties, and own not that for a comfort, which is not brought thee by his hand. Let him be thy way to the Father, and thy Father's

way to thee.   Keep fresh upon thine heart the
memory of his death and satisfaction, and let that be
thy life, and thy hope.   Hast thou cast anchor
on this rock? loose not thy hold; hang upon the
horns of the altar.   Thou canst not live, but there ;
if thou must die, say, But I will die here.   Put forth
fresh acts of faith every day and hour.   Believe,
believe, believe, and thou shalt be established.   Fall
not into unbelief, then thou art gone ; thou departest
from the living God, Heb. iii. 12.

3. Quench not the Spirit.   Observe and obey
his motions ; when he excites, get thee on ; when
he checks, get thee back ; know the holy from the
evil spirit, by its according or differing with the
scriptures ; reject that spirit in the heart that is
not the same with the Spirit in the word.   Try the
wind, what and whence it is, by the card and compass ; to the law and to the testimony.   And when
thou perceivest it is from above, hoist up thy sails,
and get thee on.   Quench not the Spirit: grieve
not the Holy Spirit of God, whereby thou art sealed
to the day of redemption.

4. Keep in with conscience.   Make not thy witness thine enemy.   Deal friendly with it ; thou
wilt need its good word, which thou canst not have
if it receive blows from thee ; it will not learn this
lesson, to speak good for evil ; or if thou shouldest
bear it into it, thou art undone ; if an abused conscience speak peace, it becomes thy traitor.

Give due respect to conscience.   Let it abide
with thee, in peace and in power.   Keep up its
authority as God's vicegerent.   Next under God,
commit the keeping of thy soul to conscience ; as the
Lord hath made, so do thou make it superintendent
in thy soul ; the judge and overseer of all thy motions

and actions. Let conscience counsel thee, and tell thee thy way; let conscience quicken thee, and put thee on in thy way; let conscience watch thee, that thou turn not out of thy way; let conscience check thee, and reduce thee into thy way. Wherever thou goest, carry conscience along with thee; carry conscience into thy closet, let it watch thee how thou behavest thyself there; carry conscience into thy shop, let it eye thee what thou dost there; carry conscience into thy fields, into the market, amongst thy friends, amongst thine enemies, let it observe how thou behavest thyself amongst them; carry conscience with thee to thy recreation, to thy bed, to thy table; wherever thou goest, there is like to be but sad work, if conscience be not with thee. Commit the keeping of thy covenant to conscience; let it be the ark in which the tables of the testimony are kept and preserved; let it be the executor of thy testament. Conscience is bound by the covenant, the covenant lays hold on it, let it lay hold on thee. Is thy conscience bound? seek not to be loosed; is thy conscience bound? give it leave to bind thy whole man. Let it bind thy thoughts, and bind thy will, and bind thy affections, and bind thy tongue, and thy whole practice; thou never livest as a man in covenant, longer than thou livest as a man of conscience. What becomes of the covenant, when a breach is made upon conscience? Oh what is there in the world when conscience is not? What faith, or truth, or peace is there left alive? What are vows, and covenants, and promises? What are our duties to the Lord, our dealings with men, when there is no conscience towards God? Keep thy conscience, and thou keepest thy soul; keep thy conscience, and thou keepest thy covenant;

keep thy covenant, and thou keepest thy peace; let that go, and all is lost.

Let conscience govern what God hath put under its power, and let it resist all adverse power. Let it resist temptations. Whenever Satan and thy flesh fall upon thee, and tempt thee, saying, Pity thyself, spare thyself, take thy liberty, take thine ease, take thy pleasure, provide for thy safety; what need is there of so much ado? Why canst thou not take the same liberty, and allow thyself the same latitude as others do? They have souls as well as thou, and they have dangers as well as thou; and they have hopes as well as thou; and they have reasons and understandings to know what they do as well as thou; and why canst thou not be content to do as they? Why, let this be thy answer, But what conscience is there for it? With what conscience can I be idle, when I have said, I will be doing? With what conscience can I take mine ease, when I have said, I will take pains? With what conscience can I serve my flesh, when I have said, I will crucify it? With what conscience can I love this world, when I have said, I will renounce it? With what conscience can I walk at liberty, when I have said, I will walk circumspectly? If all this were more than needs, (far be it from me to have such a thought, till the serving my God, and the saving my soul, be more than needs,) but if it were more than needs, yet is it any more than I am bound to? Are there any such liberties put into my indentures? Was there any exception made of this duty, or that duty? Was there any limitation made to this measure or that measure; hitherto will I go, and no further; this little I will do, and no more? Was there any such proviso put in, I will serve the Lord, provided I

may with ease or with safety? Have I not solemnly
engaged to the Lord, to obey him in all things, to
follow him fully, to love him, and serve him, with all
my heart, with all my soul, with all my strength,
and this to the death? And oh shall I lie unto
God? Is it more than needful to be righteous, and to
keep my faith? Come, O my soul, come on; thou
hast opened thy mouth to the Lord, and thou must
not go back. Be true, be honest; be honest,
though thou must swear for it; be honest, though
thou suffer for it. Remember what thy mouth
hath spoken, and see that thou fulfil it with thy
hand.

Keep conscience pure. It is the book in which
all thy records are written, let no blot be upon thy
book. Beware of sinning against conscience. Every
sin against conscience is a blot upon conscience;
and blots upon conscience are blots upon thy cove-
nant-evidence; thou wilt not be able to read
whether there be anything written there for thee
or not. Ah foolish soul, what art thou doing?
Dashing out all thine hopes with thine own hand.
Beware thou content not thyself with blotted evidences.

Christians, forget not this counsel; keep your
evidences clear. He who hath his whole estate in
bonds or writings, how carefully will he keep them!
If these be torn, or lost, or so blurred, that they
cannot be read, he is undone. Whatever else be
lost, if his money be gone, if his goods be lost, if
house be burnt, yet if his writings be safe, he is
well enough. O take heed, and keep your writings
safe and fair; keep your title to your God clear,
and you can never be poor and miserable. Whatever earth or hell can do against you, till they can

tear the covenant of your God, or make you blot
out your own names, they have left you abundantly
enough, even when they have left you nothing.

Oh how highly are we concerned to be tender of
conscience, and yet how little care is there taken of
it! What is become of the authority of conscience,
when thy thoughts and thy passions, when thine
eyes, and thine ears, and thine appetite, and thy
tongue, are left unbridled and unconquered? When
every servant is set up to be master, and bears rule
in thee, where is thy conscience? what is become
of its authority? When thy soul hath been no better
kept, what poverty and leanness is there grown
upon it, what a starveling is it become both in grace
and peace, eaten out with lust, evaporated into
vanity, sunk into sensuality, thy spirit even transub-
stantiated into flesh, ready to perish, and die away,
for want of good looking to! When thy soul hath
been no better kept, where is thy conscience? when
thy covenant hath been no better kept, when thy
duties thou hast vowed to perform, are so hastily
and heedlessly shuffled over, if not totally thrust
aside; when thy hours of prayer are such short
hours, thy sabbaths such winter days, so short and
so cold too; when thy God is so shamefully neglected, can never hear of thee, but when thou hast
nothing else to do, and, perhaps, not even then;
when thy spare hours are hardly spared for God;
when this earth, thy corn, and thy cattle, and thy
pleasures, and thy friends, which thou hast vowed
to renounce, are let in again upon thy heart, and
have stolen it away from heaven, where is thy conscience? When thou sleepest so, and hast let the
enemy come in and sow his tares in thy field; when
thou art such a busy-body in other men's matters,

and thine own vineyard thou hast not kept, but hast let it lie fallow, like the field of the sluggard, all overgrown with thorns and nettles; when both thy heart and thy house are so much out of order. When thy wife, and thy children, and thy servants are left at random, to do all that is right in their own eyes; when more care is taken for the asses than for thy sons and daughters; when thy house is a very hospital of blind, and lame, and sick souls, ready to die for want of instruction and good discipline, where is thy conscience? and if conscience be not, where is thy covenant? and if thy covenant be not, oh where is thy God and thy peace?

Ah conscience! where art thou? what is become of that good thing committed to thee? yea, what is become of thee?

Ah soul! where is thy peace? how is the keeper of thy peace laid low, and the covenant of thy peace broken! what! peace whilst no conscience, and what hast thou left, whilst no peace? Ah Lord! thy treacherous dealers, how treacherously have they dealt with thee! thy children have forgotten thee, thy servants are runaways from thee; thou art our father, but where is thine honour? thou art our master, but where is thy fear? we are thy servants, but where is our faith? Ah Lord, we have dealt falsely in thy covenant.

Return, O Lord, return; repair thy watches, recover thine honours, reduce thy wanderers, restore conscience, revive our peace, cause us to return, and renew our covenant; and remember, break not thou thy covenant with us.

Christians, let us bewail lost conscience, and let it be recovered; let us weep over our dead, and let their souls return into them. Let those of us that have obtained grace to be faithful, and watchful, and tender, rejoice and take heed: let him that standeth take heed lest he fall. Go on in the name of the Lord: remember his counsels; keep close by God, keep hold on Christ, quench not the Spirit, keep in with conscience; keep thy heart, keep thy garments, keep up thy watch, keep on thy way, finish thy course, keep the faith; and then let the devil do his worst, thy peace shall be extended to thee as a river, and established as a rock; and thou shalt be able to say in the words, and in the faith of the apostle, " Henceforth is laid up for me a crown of righteousness, which God, the righteous Judge, shall give unto me at that day, and not to me only, but to all that love his appearing."

III. Add to your covenant your sacrifice. " Gather my saints together unto me, those that have made a covenant with me by sacrifice," Psa. l. 5. God hath made with you, and he expects that you make covenant with him by sacrifice. Sacrifices were seals of the covenant. As God's part of the covenant, so our part also must be sealed, and sealed with blood; his with the blood of his Son, ours with the blood of our sins.

" I beseech you therefore, brethren, by the mercies of God, that you present your bodies as a living sacrifice, holy, acceptable to God," Rom. xii. 1. The sacrificing of ourselves to the Lord, comprehends in it three things:—1. Alienation ; 2. Dedication.; 3. Oblation.

1. Alienation, or the passing away of ourselves from ourselves. " Ye are not your own, ye are bought with a price." Thus he hath said, and he expects that we should say also, True, Lord, I am not mine own.

2. Dedication, or the passing over ourselves to the Lord. " Ye have consecrated yourselves to the Lord," 2 Chron. xxix. 31. His we are by purchase, but he expects that we be his also by donation : his we are by conquest, but he expects we should be his by consent also. Though he may challenge us as his right, yet the most acceptable claim is, when he hath us by gift. When our hearts say, I am thine, Lord ; then his heart will answer, Soul, thou art mine.

3. Oblation, or the actual surrender or offering up ourselves to him. In the offering this sacrifice is included the immolation, or slaying of it. We must slay ourselves, (in a spiritual sense,) be mortified, be crucified with Christ, and so offered up a sacrifice to him. You will say, How is it then required that we offer up ourselves a living sacrifice ?

Answer. We are never truly alive till we are dead. " Ye are dead, and your life is hid with Christ in God," Col. iii. 3. When our flesh is dead, our spirit is life, Rom. viii. 10. As the apostle, " That which thou sowest," so that which thou sacrificest " is not quickened, except it die," 1 Cor. xv. 36. It is only the mortified christian that is a living sacrifice.

Christians, come and sacrifice yourselves to the Lord, come and slay your sacrifices, and so offer them up. Your sacrifice is then slain (as before it is intimated) when your carnal self, your old man, is crucified with Christ, and the body of sin destroyed, Rom. vi. 6. when the wisdom of the flesh is crucified, and made to vanish before the wisdom of God ; when the will of the flesh is subdued, and swallowed up of the will of God ; when the lusts of the flesh are vanquished, and made captives by the law of God.

Christians, it may be you are willing to make your claim to the covenant of God, but have you made covenant with him? You have entered into covenant with God, but will you confirm your covenant by sacrifice? You will give yourselves a sacrifice to the Lord, but is your sacrifice slain? Is the wisdom of the flesh made foolishness? How is it with your carnal wills? Is the will of the flesh broken, and brought into subjection, yielding itself up to the Lord? O for an emptying of wills into the will of God! What wilt thou do? what wilt thou have? Nothing but what God will. What the Lord will have me do, or avoid, or suffer, I can no longer say him nay. Is this the will of God, my sanctification? so it is mine. Is this the will of God, my humiliation? so it is mine? Is this the will of God, my tribulation? so it is mine. Is God for holiness? through grace so am I. Is God for his own will? so am I. This is all the will I have, that the Lord may have his will of me; may be all to me, have all from me, rule all in me, and dispose of all that concerns me.

How is it with your carnal affections, and fleshly lusts? are these slain? Is your covetousness, your sensuality, your pride and envy; are your carnal joys, and fears, and worldly sorrows, are these destroyed; those wild-fires of passion, and fury, and rage, are these quenched? Come, put the knife to the throat of all these, and then there is a sacrifice for God. Go and offer it up, and let it be, 1. A freewill offering; 2. A thank-offering.

(1.) A freewill offering. Offer yourselves willingly to the Lord. "Thy people shall be willing in the day of thy power," Psa. cx. **3**. O may that glorious day dawn upon us! God loves a cheerful giver; offer up your hearts with all your heart; grudge not what the Lord requires, but bless God that he will accept of an offering; this hath a comfortable signification. If the Lord had meant to destroy us, he would not have accepted an offering at our hands, Judg. xiii. **23**.

(2.) A thank-offering. Offer unto God thanksgiving, and pay thy vows unto the Most High. Offer up yourselves in token of your thankfulness to the Lord. Be ye both the priests and the lambs for the sacrifice. Present yourselves to the Lord as the accomplishments of his covenant, as the fruits of the death of your Redeemer, as the trophies of his victory, as the spoils which he hath recovered from death and hell, making a show of them openly, that it may be seen that the promise of God is not of none effect, and that Christ did not die in vain. Let your Lord Jesus, when he comes down into his garden, where he left his blood, reap his pleasant fruits, and carry up your purified souls, as the signals of his glorious achievement. Offer up your sins to the Lord; these unclean beasts will be an acceptable sacrifice. There is more real honour growing up to the Lord from one mortified saint, than from ten thousand anthems from the most seraphic tongues. Offer up your duties to the Lord; your obedience for a sacrifice. To obey is better than sacrifice , than thousands of rams, and ten thousands of rivers of oil. Let your whole life be this sacrifice. Let every day be a sabbath, every duty an eucharist, every member a cymbal, sounding out the praises of God. Offer up the calves of your lips unto the Lord. O let your souls be filled with wonder, and your mouths

with praise. " Whence is this to me, that the mother of my Lord should come to me ?" Luke i. 43.
Oh whence is this to us, that the Lord our Father
should come, and come so near to us ! Oh whence
is it that the mighty God should indent, and come
into bond with sinful man ! That he who was free
from all men should make himself debtor to any !
That the high and lofty One, that inhabits eternity,
should dwell in houses of clay, and pitch his tabernacle in the dust ! That he who humbleth himself
to behold the heavens should come down into the
earth ; and after what is he come down, but after
so degraded a creature as man ! That he should
make a league with the stones of the ground, with
the beasts of the field, and creeping things ! Should
espouse dust and ashes, and gather up vile worms
into his bosom ! Should set his heart upon shadows, and adopt the refuse of the earth for sons and
daughters to himself ! Should raise the poor out
of the dust, and the beggar from the dunghill !
Should do such great things, and should choose the
foolish, and the weak, and the base, and the contemptible, and bestow on them among all the world
these high honours ! Should make them the head
and the honourable, whom the world hath made the
tail, the filth, and the off-scouring of all things !
Should give himself to be the portion, his Son to
be the ransom, his kingdom to be the heritage of
bankrupts, prisoners, and captives ! Lord, what is
man that thou art thus mindful of him ! Soul, what
is God that thou shouldst be yet unmindful of
him ! How is it that the tongue of the dumb is
not yet loosened, that the feet of the lame do not
leap as an hart ?

Oh what is that love whence this strange thing

hath broken forth? This, this is the womb that bare thee; hence hath thy righteousness sprung forth; hence have thy dignities, thy astonishing hope, and joys arisen to thee; this is it that yearned upon thee in thy misery, that reprieved thee from death, redeemed thee from darkness, rescued thee as a brand out of the burning; that pitied thee in thy blood, washed thee from thy blood, spared thee, pardoned thee, reconciled thee, and brought thee an enemy, a rebel, a traitor, into a covenant of peace with the God of glory. Ah contemptible dust! that ever there should be such compassionate contrivances, and such astonishing condescensions of the eternal Deity, towards so vile a thing! O love the Lord, all ye his saints! O bless the Lord, ye beloved, ye people near unto the Lord. Alas, that our hearts should be so narrow, that the waters should be so shallow with us; where are our eyes if we be not yet filled with wonders ? what hearts have we if we have not yet filled our lips with praise! Open all thy springs, O my soul, let them flow forth in streams of love and joy; let every faculty be tuned and strained to the height; let heart, and hands, and tongue, and eyes lift up their voice; be astonished, O heavens; be moved, ye strong foundations of the earth; fall down, ye elders; strike up, ye heavenly choir; lend, poor mortals, your notes, to sing forth the high praises of God, who rideth on the heavens, and hath caused us to ride on the high places of the earth, and made us sit together in heavenly places, showing forth the exceeding riches of his grace, in his kindness to us in Christ Jesus.

Awake up my glory, awake psaltery and harp, I myself will awake right early; my soul doth magnify the Lord, and my spirit hath rejoiced in God my Saviour; for he that is mighty hath done for me great things, and holy is his name. Blessed be the Lord God of Israel, who hath visited and redeemed his people, who hath raised up an horn of salvation for us in the house of his servant David, who hath laid help on one who is mighty, and exalted one chosen among the people, and hath given him for a covenant to them. Bless the Lord, O my soul, and all that is within me bless his holy name; who hath redeemed thy life from death, and crowned thee with loving kindness and tender mercies. Salvation to our God that sitteth on the throne, and to the Lamb. Let the redeemed of the Lord say so. Worthy is the Lamb that was slain, to receive power, and riches, and wisdom, and strength, and glory, and honour, and blessing; for thou livedst, and wast dead, and art alive for evermore. Thou hast redeemed us to God by thy blood, out of every kindred, and tongue, and people, and nation; and hast made us kings and priests unto our God for ever. Halleluiah, halleluiah.

DIRECTIONS FOR THE RIGHT PERFORMANCE

OF

THE DUTY OF PRAYER:

EXTRACTED FROM VINDICIÆ PIETATIS; OR, A VINDICATION OF
GODLINESS,

BY THE REV. RICHARD ALLEINE

I. Bring yourselves, and hold yourselves to a frequent and constant performance of this duty.

There must be performance, or there cannot be a right performance. As to those that pray not, or but seldom, it is a plain sign that the root of the matter is not in them; they that can live without prayer are dead while they are alive. Prayer is the first fruits of christianity: it was said of Saul, as a token that he was a convert, "Behold he prayeth." The living child comes crying into the world; and as it is a token of life, so it is a means by which this new life is nourished. Prayer is a christian's key to unlock the store-houses and the treasuries of souls: he that can pray, God hath given him a key to all his treasuries. Prayer will not only unlock the clouds, as Elijah's prayer did, and bring down rain to refresh the dry and parched earth, but it will unlock heaven too. It will unlock the ark, and the mercy-seat, and get down spiritual blessings on the soul. Praying is a christian's knocking at the gate of heaven, that knocking to which the promise is made, "Knock and it shall be opened," Matt. vii. 7. The word which the Lord speaks to us is God's knocking at our doors; "Behold, I stand at the door and knock," Rev. iii. 20. And praying is our knocking at the Lord's door, at the gate of heaven, that this may be opened. By the way learn, that if you will not hear God's knock, it is just not to hear yours. If God's voice may not be heard on earth, your voice will not be heard in heaven ; fear not, you shall be heard if you will hear ; hear him that speaks to you from heaven, and your cry shall enter into heaven.

Our souls will never thrive or flourish, unless the rain and the showers of heavenly grace descend and fall upon them : and we cannot look that those showers should come down, unless we look up.

Persons that pray not may be written among the heathen ; " Pour out thy fury upon the heathen, and the families that call not on thy name," Jer. x. 25. and among the profane ones of the earth, who are described by this character ; " They call not upon God ; they are altogether become filthy and abominable, there is none that doeth good, they call not upon God," Psa. xiv. 34.

" Be ye sober and watch unto prayer," 1 Pet. iv. 7. Be ye instant, be constant in prayer ; set up your resolutions and set your time ; set your times, and keep your time ; do not put off this duty by pretending you pray always, every day and every hour ; as the pretence of an every day's sabbath comes just to no sabbath ; so it is usually in the case of prayer ; some carnal wretches' praying always is not praying at all ; " Get thee into thy closet," saith Christ ; get thee a place, set thee a time, wherein thou mayest make it thy business to seek the Lord.

II. Come to pray with an actual and great expectation of obtaining help and grace from God.

Do not barely impose this duty upon you, as

your task, but excite and encourage yourselves to it, by looking for a return: think what it is that you would have, and look to receive it. The reason why we obtain no more in prayer, is, because we expect no more. God usually answers us according to our own hearts: narrow hearts and low expectations have usually as little as they look for or desire: large expectations are ordinarily answered with large returns. Expectation will put life into action: you will then pray with most enlarged hearts, when you are most full of hopes; the reward that is looked for in the evening will much encourage and quicken the labour of the day, fear not to expect too much from Heaven. Be not straitened in your own heart, and you shall not be straitened in the God of compassion: open thy mouth wide, and he will fill it. God will never upbraid his beggars for looking for too great an alms; he hath enough to supply them, and he hath a heart to bestow it. God will never say to you, You are too bold, you ask too much; too much grace, too much holiness, why cannot less content you? God hath given you commission to ask what you will, not to the one half, but the whole of his kingdom; the kingdom you shall have, if no less will serve your turn.

Christians, be thankful for every little you receive, but look for much: be thankful for every little, every little received from God is much: a drop from that fountain is worth the world, yet content not yourselves with some drops, when, if you will, the fountain may be yours. The king of glory loves to give like a king, and will never say, This is too much either for a king to give, or a beggar to receive; since he hath given you leave,

spare not to speak in large your desires.   God hath
promised you, and therefore you may promise yourselves; whatever you ask (that is good for you)
you shall not ask in vain.   Oh, if we had so much
in our eye when we come before the throne of grace,
we should be oftener there, and yet still return with
our load.   Well christians, remember this whenever
you come to beg, look to receive, come not to
prayer as to an empty cistern that will yield no
water.

III. Learn the skill to plead with God in prayer.
Though the Lord be willing to give those that
ask, yet he will have them first prove they are in
earnest.   Store of arguments he hath furnished us
with to press him withal, but he will have us use
them: we must strive with God if we will prevail,
and the best striving is with his own weapons.   The
counsel I give you in this is; Plead hard with God,
but plead with him upon his own arguments: there
are amongst many others these four grounds on
which to found your plea:

1. On God himself.   2. On Christ.   3. On the
promises.   4. On experiences.

1. On God himself.   And there are two special
things, from which you may plead here.

(1.) His gracious nature.   Fetch your arguments
by which you plead with God for mercy thence,
whence he originally fetched his arguments to persuade himself to show mercy; from his own compassion, from his gracious nature, from his natural
goodness and gracious inclination to mercy; "God
so loved the world, that he gave his only Son," &c.
John iii. 16.   "Having predestinated us to the
adoption of children by Jesus Christ to himself,
according to the good pleasure of his will, to the

praise of the glory of his grace, wherein he hath made us accepted in the Beloved; in whom we have redemption through his blood, the forgiveness of sins, according to the riches of his grace; wherein he hath abounded towards us, [in all wisdom and prudence; having made known unto us the mystery of his will, according to his good pleasure which he hath purposed of himself," Eph. i. 5—9. Here we have heaped up, in a few words, the riches of mercy which God hath bestowed on his people. Christ his beloved, redemption through Christ, and the forgiveness of our sins, the adoption of children, acceptance in his sight, the revelation of the mystery of his will, or the discovering or making known these glorious mercies to us. But whence is all this? who is it, or what was it, that persuaded the Lord to this abundant kindness? Why, all this arose from himself. He purposed it in himself. He consulted no other argument, but what he found in his own heart: it was from his love, the good pleasure of his will, his grace, the riches of his grace, wherein he hath abounded towards us, Hos. xi. 8, 9. How shall I give thee up Ephraim? How shall I deliver thee up Israel? I cannot do it, I will not do it. I will not execute the fierceness of mine anger, I will not destroy Ephraim. But why wilt thou be angry, Lord? why wilt thou not destroy Ephraim? Oh, says the Lord, mine heart is turned within me; my heart says, Spare him; my compassion says, Destroy him not. I am God and not man. I love him, and my love is the love of a God. I have compassion on him, and my compassion is the pity of a God: I will bear with him, I am a God of patience: love is my nature; pity, and mercy, and compassion are my nature: I cannot destroy Ephraim, but I must deny mine own nature. Love, and pity, and mercy, and goodness are essential to God. He can as soon cease to be God, as to be gracious, and this is the fountain of all our mercy; hence Christ sprung, hence the gospel came, and all the unsearchable riches of mercy prepared for poor lost and undone creatures.

When you come to pray, fetch your arguments hence. Plead with the Lord upon his own nature, his natural love, grace, and goodness. Thus we find the apostle Peter praying for the christians to whom he wrote, " The God of all grace, make you perfect; stablish, strengthen, settle you," 1 Pet. v. 10. Plead with the Lord in your prayers, as the psalmist pleads with himself in his affliction, " Will the Lord cast off for ever, and will he be favourable no more? Is his mercy clean gone for ever, hath God forgotten to be gracious, hath he in anger shut up his tender mercies? Is his mercy clean gone? Hath God forgotten to be gracious?" Psa. lxxvii. 7—9. That men should be merciless, that men should forget themselves, and their friends, in their low estate, is no such wonder. But hath God, who is all grace, all mercy, all pity, hath God forgotten? Doth mercy cease to be merciful, grace cease to be gracious? do compassions cease to be pitiful? hath God not only forgotten his servant, but forgotten himself? Remember thyself, Lord, thine own heart, thine own soul, and according to it, remember me.

(2.) His glorious name. The Lord's nature is to be gracious, and according to his nature such is his name; " The Lord, the Lord God, merciful and gracious, long-suffering, and abundant in goodness and truth," Exod. xxxiv. 6. This is an argument which the Lord puts into the mouths of his people, telling them, " I had pity for my holy name; this I do, not for your sakes, but for my holy name's sake," Ezek. xxxvi. 21, 22. And upon this we find them frequently pleading with him; "For thy name's sake, lead me, and guide me," Psa. xxxi. 3. " Do not abhor us for thy name's sake; do not disgrace the throne of thy glory; remember, break not thy covenant with us," Jer. xiv. 21. Go you and do likewise.

2. On Christ. And there are four things from which you may plead with God upon this account.

(1.) The Lord's giving of Christ to you as your Lord and your Saviour. Upon which gift, you may call him your own.

(2.) The purchase of Christ; who hath bought from the hands of the Father, all that you stand in need of: he hath bought your lives; " Ye are bought with a price," 1 Cor. vi. 20. He hath bought you a livelihood, hath purchased an inheritance and possession for you, 1 Pet. i.

(3.) The interest that Christ hath in the Father; being the Son of God, the Son of his love, the Servant of God, in whom his soul delights; "Behold my servant whom I have chosen, mine elect, in whom my soul delighteth," Isa. xlii. 1. whose name is so precious, and powerful with the Father, that it will carry any suit, obtain any request; "Whatever you ask the Father in my name, he will give it you," John xvi. 23.

(4.) The interest that you have in Christ. As he is precious to his Father, so you are precious to him; as the Father can deny him nothing, so he can deny his nothing; " Whatsoever you shall ask the Father in my name, I will do it," John xiv. 13. He gives you commission to put his name upon all your requests, and whatsoever prayer comes up with this name upon it, he will procure it an answer

Now when you are praying for any mercy, especially for any soul-mercy, make use of all these arguments ; Lord, hast thou given Christ unto me, and wilt thou not with him give me all things I stand in need of ? Hast thou given me the fountain, and wilt thou deny me the stream ? When I beg pardon of sin, when I beg power against sin, when I beg holiness, &c. is not all this granted me, in thy gift of Christ to me ? Is Christ mine, and is not his blood mine, to procure my pardon ? his Spirit mine to subdue my iniquities ? Are these mine, and wilt thou withhold them from me ? Oh, shall this guilt lie upon me, these sins live in me, these lusts rule over me, when by giving me in hand that whereof thou hast already given me a grant, all this would be removed from me ? look upon Christ, Lord ; thou hast said to me, Look unto Jesus, and give thy servant leave to say the same to thee, Look thou upon Jesus, and give out to me, what thou hast given me, in giving him to me. Look upon the purchase of Christ ; do I want any thing, or desire anything but what my Lord hath bought and paid for, and thou hast accepted of the price ? Look upon the name of Christ, which thou mayest behold written upon every prayer I make ; though thou mayest say, For thy own sake thou shalt have nothing, not a drop, not a crumb, yet wilt thou say, Nor for his name's sake neither ? Is not that name still a mighty name, a precious name before the Lord ? &c. By these hints you may learn how to plead with God from any other arguments drawn from his promises, your experience, &c.

Question. These arguments the saints may use in

prayer: but is there no plea for poor natural men, that are yet in their sins, to make use of? what may they say for themselves, when they come before the Lord? Have you never a word to put in their mouths? they have more need of arguments than any? What shall they say?

Answer 1. I shall premise, that it is the duty of mere natural men to pray; For, 1. Prayer is a part of God's natural worship. If there were no positive law requiring it, yet the law of nature enjoins it, and no man is exempted from the obligation of the law of nature. 2. Otherwise it were none of their sin to neglect and restrain prayer; where no law is, there is no transgression. Now we find in scripture, that neglect of prayer is reckoned up amongst wicked men's sins, " They are altogether become filthy, &c. they call not upon God," Psa. xiv. 3, 4. Sin, though it doth disable, yet it doth not disoblige to duty.

When a sinner, being struck with a sense of his sin, and of his necessity of changing his way, and of his utter inability to turn of himself, under the fears and troubles of his heart, goes to God and cries out, Lord, what shall I do; I see I am in an evil case, my soul is running on in sin, and thy curse and wrath I behold running on upon me; Lord, save me; Lord, help me; Lord, pardon, Lord convert me, break me off from my sins, break me off from my sinful companions; I cannot get loose, my heart is too hard, my lusts are too strong, my temptations are too many for me to overcome of myself; Lord help me; turn me and I shall be turned, pluck my foot out of the snare, that I be not utterly destroyed; forgive mine iniquity, make me a clean heart, make me thy child, make me thy servant;

that I may never again yield up myself a servant to sin : such a prayer as this, if it be hearty and in earnest, if there be no promise of audience, yet at least there is a half promise; who can tell? it may be the Lord will hear.

Consider that sinners, if they have but a heart to it, have also a price in their hands ; God hath put arguments into their mouths also, to plead with him for mercy, as,

1. The grace of God or his gracious nature ; his readiness to show mercy; this even strangers may lay hold upon.

2. God's call or gracious invitation, " Ho, every one that thirsteth, come to the waters, and he that hath no money ; come ye, buy and eat ; buy wine and milk, without money and without price," Isa. lv. 1. " Look unto me, and be ye saved, all the ends of the earth." " Come unto me all that are weary and heavy laden, and I will give you rest." Rise sinner, he calleth thee : go to the Lord, and when thou goest, tell him, Lord, thou hast bid me come, and behold here I am ; I come, Lord, at thy word, I come for a little water, I come for thy wine and thy milk; I have brought no price in my hand, but thou hast bid me come, and buy without money and without price. Though I have no grace, yet behold at thy word I come for grace ; though I have no Christ, yet I come for Christ ; though I cannot call thee Father, yet being called, I come to thee as fatherless ; " With thee the fatherless shall find mercy." If I am not thy child, may I not be made thy child? Hast thou not a child's blessing left yet to bestow upon me ? Thou hast bid me come, come for a blessing, bless me, even me also, O Lord. Wherefore hast thou sent for me ? Shall I be sent

away as I came; I come at thy word, do not say again, Begone, begone out of my sight; I cannot go at thy word; I will not go; for, "whither shall I go from thee? thou hast the words of eternal life." Since thou wilt have me speak, Lord answer; though I dare not say, Be just to me a saint, yet I do say, I will say, I must say, "Lord, be merciful to me a sinner."

3. *Christ.* And there are two things in Christ, upon which sinners may plead with God.

(1.) His sufficiency. There is enough in Christ, in his obedience and death, to save the worst of sinners, to save the whole world of sinners. There is a fulness in Christ, "It pleased the Father, that in him should all fulness dwell," Col. i. 19. There is a fulness of merit to obtain pardon, to make reconciliation for whoever comes; a fulness of the Spirit to sanctify, and cleanse them from their sins. "He is able to save unto the uttermost, all those that come unto God by him." From this, sinners may reason thus with the Lord. O Lord, I do not come to beg that of thee, which cannot be had; thou hast enough by thee; Look upon Jesus that sits at thy right hand: is there not righteousness enough in him to answer for all my unrighteousness? Are there not riches enough in him to supply my poverty? Hear, Lord, send me not away without an alms, when thou hast it by thee.

(2.) His office: which is to bring sinners to God, to make reconciliation for sinners, to make intercession for transgressors, Isa. liii. 12. "Thou hast received gifts for men, yea even for the rebellious also," Psa. lxviii. 18. What a strange and mighty plea is here for poor sinners! Oh, it is true, Lord, I am a transgressor, and have been from the womb: I have played the traitor, and been a rebel against thee all my days ; but is there none in heaven that will intercede for a transgressor ? Hath the Lord Jesus received no gift for this poor rebel, that falls down before thee ? though I am a rebel, Lord, yet I am a returning rebel : though I am a rebel, yet let me receive a rebel's gift, not a rebel's reward, (Lord, that would be dreadful,) but some of those gifts which Christ received for the rebellious.   Doth Christ make intercession for transgressors, and shall not he be heard ? If thou wilt not hear me who am a sinner, yet wilt thou not hear Him that speaks for sinners, whose blood speaks, whose mercy speaks, whose Spirit speaks? Doth he speak for sinners, and yet not for me ?

4. Their own necessity.   Sinners are necessitous creatures, they have nothing of value left them ; in the fulness of their sufficiency they are in straits. As a sinner of a hundred years is but a child, so a sinner of thousands by the year is but a beggar ; poor, miserable, blind, and naked : he can want nothing, and yet doth want every thing that is good. Sin hath stripped him to the skin ; stubbed him to the heart, the iron hath entered into his soul, it hath left him nothing but wounds, and bruises, and putrefying sores : it is thy case, sinner, and hast thou nothing to say ? Spread thy wants and necessities before the Lord, and let these speak for thee.

Open thy wounds and thy sores, tell him how desperately sad thy case is, tell him of the guilt that is upon thy head, the curse that is on thy back, the plague that is in thy heart : God of compassion look hither, behold what a poor, blind, dead, hardened, unclean, guilty creature, what a naked, empty, helpless creature I am : look upon my sin and my misery, and let thine eye affect thine heart: "One deep calls to another," a deep of misery cries out to a deep of mercy. Oh my very sins, which cry so loud against me, speak also for me. My misery speaks, my curses, the woe and the wrath that lies upon me ; my bones speak, my perishing soul speaks, and all cry in thine ears, Help, Lord, God of pity, help, help and heal me, help and save me: come unto me, for I am a sinful man, O Lord: I dare not say as once it was said, Depart from me, for I am a sinful man : come, Lord, for I am a sinful man. Thou couldst never come where is more need : who have need of the physician but the sick ? Come, Lord ; I have too often said, Depart from me, but if thou wilt not say, Depart, to me, I hope I shall never again say, Depart, to thee. My misery saith, Come; my wants say, Come ; my guilt and my sins say, Come ; and my soul saith, Come. Come and pardon, come and convert, come and teach, come and sanctify, come and save me ; even so come Lord Jesus.

Thus you have the sinner's plea. Poor sinner, art thou willing to return from thy sins, fear not to go to thy God. Go, and the Lord help thee, give thee thy heart's desire, and fulfil all thy mind, and for thy encouragement take along with thee this scripture; "Seek ye the Lord while he may be found, call ye upon him while he is near : let the wicked forsake his way, and the unrighteous man his thoughts: and let him return unto the Lord, and he will have mercy upon him ; and to our God, for he will abundantly pardon," Isa. lv. 6, 7.

London : J. Hill, Printer, Black Horse Court, Fleet Street.